Second Workshop on Scholarly Document Processing (SDP 2021)

Online
10 June 2021

ISBN: 978-1-7138-3027-6

Printed from e-media with permission by:

Curran Associates, Inc.
57 Morehouse Lane
Red Hook, NY 12571

Some format issues inherent in the e-media version may also appear in this print version.

Association for Computational Linguistics
209 N. Eighth Street
Stroudsburg, Pennsylvania 18360

Phone: 1-570-476-8006
Fax: 1-570-476-0860

acl@aclweb.org

Additional copies of this publication are available from:

Curran Associates, Inc.
57 Morehouse Lane
Red Hook, NY 12571 USA
Phone: 845-758-0400
Fax: 845-758-2633
Email: curran@proceedings.com
Web: www.proceedings.com

NAACL 2021

Second Workshop on Scholarly Document Processing

Proceedings of the Workshop

June 10, 2021
Online

Message from the Program Chairs

Welcome to the Second Workshop on Scholarly Document Processing (SDP) at NAACL 2021.

Next to keeping up with the growing literature in their own and related fields, scholars increasingly also need to rebut pseudo-science and disinformation. To address this challenge, computational work on enhancing search, summarization, and analysis of scholarly documents has flourished. However, the various strands of research on scholarly document processing remain fragmented. To reach to the broader NLP and AI/ML community, pool distributed efforts and enable shared access to published research, we held the 2nd Workshop on Scholarly Document Processing at NAACL 2021. The SDP workshop consisted of a research track and three Shared Tasks, geared towards easier access to scientific methods and results. https://sdproc.org/2021/

Organizing Committee

Iz Beltagy, Allen Institute for Artificial Intelligence, USA
Arman Cohan, Allen Institute for Artificial Intelligence, USA
Guy Feigenblat, IBM Research AI, Haifa Research Lab, Israel
Dayne Freitag, SRI International, San Diego, USA
Tirthankar Ghosal, Institute of Formal and Applied Linguistics, Charles University, Czech Republic
Keith Hall, Google AI, USA
Drahomira Herrmannova, Oak Ridge National Laboratory, USA
Petr Knoth, Open University, UK
Kyle Lo, Allen Institute for Artificial Intelligence, USA
Philipp Mayr, GESIS – Leibniz Institute for the Social Sciences, Germany
Robert Patton, Oak Ridge National Laboratory, USA
Michal Shmueli-Scheuer, IBM Research AI, Haifa Research Lab, Israel
Anita de Waard, Elsevier, USA
Kuansan Wang, Microsoft Research, USA
Lucy Lu Wang, Allen Institute for Artificial Intelligence, USA

Table of Contents

Conference Program

Keynote Paper

Determining the Credibility of Science Communication
Isabelle Augenstein

Research Track: Long Papers

Unsupervised Document Expansion for Information Retrieval with Stochastic Text Generation
Soyeong Jeong, Jinheon Baek, ChaeHun Park and Jong Park

Task Definition and Integration For Scientific-Document Writing Support
Hiromi Narimatsu, Kohei Koyama, Kohji Dohsaka, Ryuichiro Higashinaka, Yasuhiro Minami and Hirotoshi Taira

Detecting Anatomical and Functional Connectivity Relations in Biomedical Literature via Language Representation Models
Ibrahim Burak Ozyurt, Joseph Menke, Anita Bandrowski and Maryann Martone

The Biomaterials Annotator: a system for ontology-based concept annotation of biomaterials text
Javier Corvi, Carla Fuenteslópez, José Fernández, Josep Gelpi, Maria-Pau Ginebra, Salvador Capella-Guitierrez and Osnat Hakimi

Research Track: Short Papers

Keyphrase Extraction from Scientific Articles via Extractive Summarization
Chrysovalantis Giorgos Kontoulis, Eirini Papagiannopoulou and Grigorios Tsoumakas

Argument Mining for Scholarly Document Processing: Taking Stock and Looking Ahead
Khalid Al Khatib, Tirthankar Ghosal, Yufang Hou, Anita de Waard and Dayne Freitag

Bootstrapping Multilingual Metadata Extraction: A Showcase in Cyrillic
Johan Krause, Igor Shapiro, Tarek Saier and Michael Färber

The Effect of Pretraining on Extractive Summarization for Scientific Documents
Yash Gupta, Pawan Sasanka Ammanamanchi, Shikha Bordia, Arjun Manoharan, Deepak Mittal, Ramakanth Pasunuru, Manish Shrivastava, Maneesh Singh, Mohit Bansal and Preethi Jyothi

No Day Set (continued)

Finding Pragmatic Differences Between Disciplines
Lee Kezar and Jay Pujara

Extractive Research Slide Generation Using Windowed Labeling Ranking
Athar Sefid, Prasenjit Mitra, Jian Wu and C Lee Giles

Shared Task: LongSumm

LongSumm 2021: Session based automatic summarization model for scientific document
senci ying, Zheng Yan Zhao and wuhe zou

CNLP-NITS @ LongSumm 2021: TextRank Variant for Generating Long Summaries
Darsh Kaushik, Abdullah Faiz Ur Rahman Khilji, Utkarsh Sinha and Partha Pakray

Unsupervised document summarization using pre-trained sentence embeddings and graph centrality
Juan Ramirez-Orta and Evangelos Milios

Shared Task: SCIVER

QMUL-SDS at SCIVER: Step-by-Step Binary Classification for Scientific Claim Verification
Xia Zeng and Arkaitz Zubiaga

Determining the Credibility of Science Communication

Isabelle Augenstein
Dpt. of Computer Science
University of Copenhagen
augenstein@di.ku.dk

Abstract

Most work on scholarly document processing assumes that the information processed is trustworthy and factually correct. However, this is not always the case. There are two core challenges, which should be addressed: 1) ensuring that scientific publications are credible – e.g. that claims are not made without supporting evidence, and that all relevant supporting evidence is provided; and 2) that scientific findings are not misrepresented, distorted or outright misreported when communicated by journalists or the general public. I will present some first steps towards addressing these problems and outline remaining challenges.

1 The Life Cycle of Scientific Research

Scientific research is highly diverse not just when it comes to the topic of study, but also how studies are conducted, how the resulting research is described and when and where it is published. However, what different fields still have in common is a certain life cycle, starting with planning a study and ending with promoting the research post-publication, in the hopes of the article finding readership and having an impact.

Scholary document processing aims to support researchers throughout this life cycle of scientific research, by offering various tools to automate otherwise manual processes. Most research within scholarly document processing has focused on supporting information discovery for finding related work. Most prominently, research has focused on methods to condense scientific documents, using entity extraction and linking, keyphrase or relation extraction (Augenstein et al., 2017; Augenstein and Søgaard, 2017; Wright et al., 2019; Gábor et al., 2018; Ammar et al., 2018) or automatic summarisation (Collins et al., 2017; Yasunaga et al., 2019).

Once papers are written and submitted for peer review, it is pertinent to evaluate them fairly and objectively. This process is far from straightforward, as, among others, reviewers have certain biases, including against truly novel research (Rogers and Augenstein, 2020; Bhattacharya and Packalen, 2020). Research has thus focused on automatically generating peer reviews from paper content (Wang et al., 2020), as well as on studying how well review scores can be predicted from review texts (Kang et al., 2018; Plank and van Dalen, 2019).

Finally, post-publication, the impact of scientific work can be tracked, using citations and citation counts as a proxy for this. It is again worth noting that there are significant biases in this – e.g. author information is among the, if not the most salient feature for predicting citation counts (Yan et al., 2011; Holm et al., 2020). Looking further into what papers are cited and why, Mohammad (2020b,a) find that there are significant topical as well as gender biases when it comes to who is cited and by whom.

2 Credibility and Veracity of Science Communication

While all of the work referenced above is important in supporting researchers, it neglects one crucial aspect, namely that it assumes the resulting scientific documents and broader communication about them are credible and supported by the underlying evidence. Though it is the task of peer reviewers to spot issues regarding credibility, and the task of journalists to check their sources when they report on scientific studies, distortions, exaggerations and outright misrepresentations can still happen.

The ongoing COVID-19 pandemic has highlighted the disastrous and direct consequences misreporting of scientific findings can have on our everyday lives, yet, there is still relatively little work on detecting issues in the credibility of scientific writing. This especially holds for detecting smaller nuances of untrustworthy scientific writing, whereas there is comparatively more work on de-

Proceedings of the Second Workshop on Scholarly Document Processing, pages 1–6
June 10, 2021. ©2021 Association for Computational Linguistics

Biology
Wood Frogs (Rana sylvatica) are a charismatic species of frog common in much of North America. They breed in explosive choruses over a few nights in late winter to early spring. *The incidence in Wood Frogs was associated with a die-off of frogs during the breeding chorus in the Sylamore District of the Ozark National Forest in Arkansas*~~(Trauth et al., 2000)~~.

Computer Science
Land use or cover change is a direct reflection of human activity, such as land use, urban expansion, and architectural planning, on the earth's surface caused by urbanization~~[1]~~. Remote sensing images are important data sources that can efficiently detect land changes. *Meanwhile, remote sensing image-based change detection is the change identification of surficial objects or geographic phenomena through the remote observation of two or more different phases*~~[2]~~.

Table 1: Excerpts from training samples in CITEWORTH (Wright and Augenstein, 2021) from the Biology and Computer Science fields. Green sentences are cite-worthy sentences, from which citation markers are removed during dataset construction.

tecting outright scientific misinformation (Vijjali et al., 2020; Lima et al., 2021).

Here, we highlight two important and so far understudied tasks to address issues with such smaller nuances of untrustworthy scientific writing, which can come into play at different stages of the life cycle of scientific research. The first one is *cite-worthiness detection*, which is about detecting whether or not a sentence ought to contain a citation to prior work. This task could help to ensure that claims are not made without supporting evidence, i.e. support researchers in writing more trustworthy scientific publications.

The second task is *exaggeration detection*, which is to determine whether a statement describing the findings of a scientific study exaggerates them, e.g. by claiming that two variables are strongly correlated when in reality they only co-occur. We argue that this task could be useful to verify if popular science reporting faithfully describes scientific research, or also to determine whether citation sentences (sentences which contain a citation; also called *citances*) faithfully describe the research documented in the cited papers.

2.1 Cite-Worthiness Detection

The CITEWORTH Dataset To study cite-worthiness detection, we first introduce a new rigorously curated dataset, CITEWORTH (Wright and Augenstein, 2021), for cite-worthiness detection from scientific articles. It is created from S2ORC, the Semantic Scholar Open Research Corpus (Lo et al., 2020). CITEWORTH consists of 1.2M sentences, balanced across 10 diverse scientific fields. While others have studied this task for few and/or narrow domains (Sugiyama et al., 2010; Färber et al., 2018), and have also studied very related tasks, such as claim check-worthiness detection (Wright and Augenstein, 2020a) or citation recommendation (Jürgens et al., 2018), this is the largest and most diverse dataset for this task to date.

An excerpt of our introduced dataset, CITEWORTH can be found in Table 1. The dataset curation process involves: 1) data filtering, to identify credible papers with relevant metadata such as venue information; 2) citation span identification and masking, of which we only keep papers with citation spans at the end of sentences to avoid rendering sentences ungrammatical; 3) discarding paragraphs without citations, or where not all sentences have citation spans in accordance with our heuristics; 4) evenly sampling paragraphs, such that the resulting dataset is equally balanced for the domains of Biology, Medicine, Engineering, Chemistry, Psychology, Computer Science, Materials Science, Economics, Mathematics, and Physics.

Given this dataset, we then study: how cite-worthy sentences can be detected automatically; to what degree there are domain shifts between how different fields use citations; and if cite-worthiness data can be used to perform transfer learning to downstream scientific text tasks.

Methods for Cite-Worthiness Detection We find that the best performance can be achieved by a Longformer-based model (Beltagy et al., 2020), which encodes entire paragraphs in papers and jointly predicts cite-worthiness labels for each of the sentences contained in the paragraph. Additional gains in recall can be achieved by using positive unlabelled learning, as documented in Wright and Augenstein (2020a) for the related task

Exaggerated Claims
Press Release: Players of the game rock paper scissors subconsciously copy each other's hand shapes, significantly increasing the chance of the game ending in a draw, according to new research.
Abstract: Specifically, the execution of either a rock or scissors gesture by the blind player was predictive of an imitative response by the sighted player.

Exaggerated Advice
Press Release: Parents should dilute fruit juice with water or opt for unsweetened juices, and only allow these drinks during meals.
Abstract: Manufacturers must stop adding unnecessary sugars and calories to their FJJDS.

Table 2: Examples of exaggerated claims and exaggerated advice given in press releases about scientific papers.

of claim check-worthiness detection. Our best-performing model outperforms baselines such as a carefully fine-tuned SciBERT (Beltagy et al., 2019) by over 5 points in F1.

Domain Differences To study domain effects, we perform a cross-evaluation, where we hold out one domain for testing and evaluate model performance on that, and compare this against an in-domain evaluation setting, where all domains observed at test time are also observed at training time. We find that there is a high variance in the maximum performance for each field ($\sigma = 3.32$), and between different fields on the same test data, despite large pretrained Transformer models being relatively invariant across domains (Wright and Augenstein, 2020b). This suggests stark differences in how different fields employ citations.

Downstream Applicability We evaluate our models on downstream scientific document processing tasks from Beltagy et al. (2019), which can be grouped into: named entity recognition tasks; relation extraction tasks; and text classification tasks. Specifically, we use our best-performing model, pre-trained for cite-worthiness detection and masked language modelling, and fine-tune them for 10 different downstream tasks. We find that improvements over the state of the art can be achieved for two citation intent classification tasks.

2.2 Exaggeration Detection

We frame exaggeration detection in the context of popular science communication. Specifically, we ask the question: how can one automatically detect if popular science articles overstate the claims made in scientific articles?

Prior work has shown that exaggeration of findings of scientific articles is highly prevalent (Sumner et al., 2014; Bratton et al., 2019; Woloshin et al., 2009; Woloshin and Schwartz, 2002). Exaggeration can mean a sensationalised take-away of the applicability of the work in terms, i.e. giving advice for which there is no scientific basis. Moreover, the strength of the main causal claims and conclusions of a paper can be exaggerated. Table 2 shows examples of those two types of claims from the datasets curated by Sumner et al. (2014) and Bratton et al. (2019), which we use in our work.

Prior work (Yu et al., 2019, 2020; Li et al., 2017) uses datasets based on PubMed abstracts and paired press releases from EurekAlert.[1] Their core limitations of is that they are limited to only observational studies from PubMed, which have structured abstracts, which strongly simplifies the task of identifying the main claims of a paper. This also holds for the test settings they consider, meaning that the proposed models have a limited applicability.

By contrast, we study how to best identify exaggerated claims in popular science communication in the wild, without highly curated data with annotations about core claims. This represents a more realistic experimental setup, which is more suited to supporting downstream use cases such as flagging exaggerated popular news articles as well as exaggerated summaries of scientific papers as referenced in other scientific papers.

Our method is a semi-supervised approach, which first identifies sentences containing claims in both scientific articles and popular science communication within the medical domain, then identifies the main conclusion of both articles, and lastly predicts to what degree popular science articles exaggerate those findings. We further analyse to what degree exaggeration of findings is correlated

[1] https://www.eurekalert.org/

with the perceived media bias of popular science communication outlets.

3 Conclusion

This paper discusses research avenues for automatically determining the credibility of science communication, both in terms of scientific papers and popular science communication. These avenues are put in the context of scholarly data processing more broadly, and how different tasks can be used to assist the life cycle of scientific research. While existing research has focused on developing models for assisting with information discovery, peer review and citation tracking, comparatively little work has been done on identifying non-credible claims and assisting authors in making sure their research is backed up by sufficient evidence where needed. The suggestion is therefore to focus on two tasks: cite-worthiness detection, to identify sentences requiring citations; and exaggeration detection, to identify cases in which scientific findings have been overstated. A core problem for both tasks is the lack of appropriate training data, which we address by introducing a new dataset, and a semi-supervised learning method, respectively. We hope our research will inspire future work on developing tools to assist authors and journalists in ensuring that research is described in a credible and evidence-based way.

Acknowledgements

The research documented in this paper has received funding from the European Union's Horizon 2020 research and innovation programme under the Marie Skłodowska-Curie grant agreement No 801199.

Thank you to Dustin Wright for the fruitful discussions and feedback on this extended abstract.

References

Waleed Ammar, Dirk Groeneveld, Chandra Bhagavatula, Iz Beltagy, Miles Crawford, Doug Downey, Jason Dunkelberger, Ahmed Elgohary, Sergey Feldman, Vu Ha, Rodney Kinney, Sebastian Kohlmeier, Kyle Lo, Tyler Murray, Hsu-Han Ooi, Matthew Peters, Joanna Power, Sam Skjonsberg, Lucy Wang, Chris Wilhelm, Zheng Yuan, Madeleine van Zuylen, and Oren Etzioni. 2018. Construction of the Literature Graph in Semantic Scholar. In *Proceedings of the 2018 Conference of the North American Chapter of the Association for Computational Linguistics: Human Language Technologies, Volume 3 (Industry Papers)*, pages 84–91, New Orleans - Louisiana. Association for Computational Linguistics.

Isabelle Augenstein, Mrinal Das, Sebastian Riedel, Lakshmi Vikraman, and Andrew McCallum. 2017. SemEval 2017 task 10: ScienceIE - extracting keyphrases and relations from scientific publications. In *Proceedings of the 11th International Workshop on Semantic Evaluation (SemEval-2017)*, pages 546–555, Vancouver, Canada. Association for Computational Linguistics.

Isabelle Augenstein and Anders Søgaard. 2017. Multi-task learning of keyphrase boundary classification. In *Proceedings of the 55th Annual Meeting of the Association for Computational Linguistics (Volume 2: Short Papers)*, pages 341–346, Vancouver, Canada. Association for Computational Linguistics.

Iz Beltagy, Kyle Lo, and Arman Cohan. 2019. SciBERT: A Pretrained Language Model for Scientific Text. In *Proceedings of the 2019 Conference on Empirical Methods in Natural Language Processing and the 9th International Joint Conference on Natural Language Processing (EMNLP-IJCNLP)*, pages 3606–3611.

Iz Beltagy, Matthew E. Peters, and Arman Cohan. 2020. Longformer: The Long-Document Transformer. *CoRR*, abs/2004.05150.

Jay Bhattacharya and Mikko Packalen. 2020. Stagnation and scientific incentives. Technical report, National Bureau of Economic Research.

Luke Bratton, Rachel C Adams, Aimée Challenger, Jacky Boivin, Lewis Bott, Christopher D Chambers, and Petroc Sumner. 2019. The Association Between Exaggeration in Health-Related Science News and Academic Press Releases: A Replication Study. *Welcome open research*, 4.

Ed Collins, Isabelle Augenstein, and Sebastian Riedel. 2017. A supervised approach to extractive summarisation of scientific papers. In *Proceedings of the 21st Conference on Computational Natural Language Learning (CoNLL 2017)*, pages 195–205, Vancouver, Canada. Association for Computational Linguistics.

Michael Färber, Alexander Thiemann, and Adam Jatowt. 2018. To Cite, or Not to Cite? Detecting Citation Contexts in Text. In *European Conference on Information Retrieval*, pages 598–603. Springer.

Kata Gábor, Davide Buscaldi, Anne-Kathrin Schumann, Behrang QasemiZadeh, Haifa Zargayouna, and Thierry Charnois. 2018. Semeval-2018 task 7: Semantic relation extraction and classification in scientific papers. In *Proceedings of The 12th International Workshop on Semantic Evaluation*, pages 679–688.

Andreas Nugaard Holm, Barbara Plank, Dustin Wright, and Isabelle Augenstein. 2020. Longitudinal citation prediction using temporal graph neural networks. *arXiv preprint arXiv:2012.05742*.

David Jürgens, Srijan Kumar, Raine Hoover, Dan McFarland, and Dan Jurafsky. 2018. Measuring the Evolution of a Scientific Field through Citation Frames. *Transactions of the Association for Computational Linguistics*, 6:391–406.

Dongyeop Kang, Waleed Ammar, Bhavana Dalvi, Madeleine van Zuylen, Sebastian Kohlmeier, Eduard Hovy, and Roy Schwartz. 2018. A dataset of peer reviews (PeerRead): Collection, insights and NLP applications. In *Proceedings of the 2018 Conference of the North American Chapter of the Association for Computational Linguistics: Human Language Technologies, Volume 1 (Long Papers)*, pages 1647–1661, New Orleans, Louisiana. Association for Computational Linguistics.

Yingya Li, Jieke Zhang, and Bei Yu. 2017. An nlp analysis of exaggerated claims in science news. In *Proceedings of the 2017 EMNLP Workshop: Natural Language Processing meets Journalism*, pages 106–111.

Lucas Chaves Lima, Dustin Brandon Wright, Isabelle Augenstein, and Maria Maistro. 2021. University of copenhagen participation in trec health misinformation track 2020. *arXiv preprint arXiv:2103.02462*.

Kyle Lo, Lucy Lu Wang, Mark Neumann, Rodney Kinney, and Daniel S Weld. 2020. S2ORC: The Semantic Scholar Open Research Corpus. In *Proceedings of the 58th Annual Meeting of the Association for Computational Linguistics*, pages 4969–4983.

Saif M. Mohammad. 2020a. Examining citations of natural language processing literature. In *Proceedings of the 58th Annual Meeting of the Association for Computational Linguistics*, pages 5199–5209, Online. Association for Computational Linguistics.

Saif M. Mohammad. 2020b. Gender gap in natural language processing research: Disparities in authorship and citations. In *Proceedings of the 58th Annual Meeting of the Association for Computational Linguistics*, pages 7860–7870, Online. Association for Computational Linguistics.

Barbara Plank and Reinard van Dalen. 2019. CiteTracked: A Longitudinal Dataset of Peer Reviews and Citations. In *BIRNDL@ SIGIR*, pages 116–122.

Anna Rogers and Isabelle Augenstein. 2020. What can we do to improve peer review in NLP? In *Findings of the Association for Computational Linguistics: EMNLP 2020*, pages 1256–1262, Online. Association for Computational Linguistics.

Kazunari Sugiyama, Tarun Kumar, Min-Yen Kan, and Ramesh C Tripathi. 2010. Identifying Citing Sentences in Research Papers Using Supervised Learning. In *2010 International Conference on Information Retrieval & Knowledge Management (CAMP)*, pages 67–72. IEEE.

Petroc Sumner, Solveiga Vivian-Griffiths, Jacky Boivin, Andy Williams, Christos A Venetis, Aimée Davies, Jack Ogden, Leanne Whelan, Bethan Hughes, Bethan Dalton, et al. 2014. The Association Between Exaggeration in Health Related Science News and Academic Press Releases: Retrospective Observational Study. *BMJ*, 349.

Rutvik Vijjali, Prathyush Potluri, Siddharth Kumar, and Sundeep Teki. 2020. Two stage transformer model for COVID-19 fake news detection and fact checking. In *Proceedings of the 3rd NLP4IF Workshop on NLP for Internet Freedom: Censorship, Disinformation, and Propaganda*, pages 1–10, Barcelona, Spain (Online). International Committee on Computational Linguistics (ICCL).

Qingyun Wang, Qi Zeng, Lifu Huang, Kevin Knight, Heng Ji, and Nazneen Fatema Rajani. 2020. ReviewRobot: Explainable paper review generation based on knowledge synthesis. In *Proceedings of the 13th International Conference on Natural Language Generation*, pages 384–397, Dublin, Ireland. Association for Computational Linguistics.

Steven Woloshin and Lisa M Schwartz. 2002. Press Releases: Translating Research Into News. *Jama*, 287(21):2856–2858.

Steven Woloshin, Lisa M Schwartz, Samuel L Casella, Abigail T Kennedy, and Robin J Larson. 2009. Press Releases by Academic Medical Centers: Not So Academic? *Annals of Internal Medicine*, 150(9):613–618.

Dustin Wright and Isabelle Augenstein. 2020a. Claim Check-Worthiness Detection as Positive Unlabelled Learning. In *Findings of the Association for Computational Linguistics: EMNLP 2020*, pages 476–488, Online. Association for Computational Linguistics.

Dustin Wright and Isabelle Augenstein. 2020b. Transformer Based Multi-Source Domain Adaptation. In *Proceedings of the 2020 Conference on Empirical Methods in Natural Language Processing (EMNLP)*, pages 7963–7974, Online. Association for Computational Linguistics.

Dustin Wright and Isabelle Augenstein. 2021. CiteWorth: Cite-Worthiness Detection for Improved Scientific Document Understanding. In *Findings of the Association for Computational Linguistics: ACL 2021*, Online. Association for Computational Linguistics.

Dustin Wright, Yannis Katsis, Raghav Mehta, and Chun-Nan Hsu. 2019. Normco: Deep disease normalization for biomedical knowledge base construction. In *AKBC*.

Rui Yan, Jie Tang, Xiaobing Liu, Dongdong Shan, and Xiaoming Li. 2011. Citation count prediction: learning to estimate future citations for literature. In *Proceedings of the 20th ACM International Conference on Information and Knowledge Management*, pages 1247–1252.

Michihiro Yasunaga, Jungo Kasai, Rui Zhang, Alexander R Fabbri, Irene Li, Dan Friedman, and Dragomir R Radev. 2019. Scisummnet: A large annotated corpus and content-impact models for scientific paper summarization with citation networks. In *Proceedings of the AAAI Conference on Artificial Intelligence*, volume 33, pages 7386–7393.

Bei Yu, Yingya Li, and Jun Wang. 2019. Detecting Causal Language Use in Science Findings. In *EMNLP*, pages 4656–4666.

Bei Yu, Jun Wang, Lu Guo, and Yingya Li. 2020. Measuring Correlation-to-Causation Exaggeration in Press Releases. In *Proceedings of the 28th International Conference on Computational Linguistics*, pages 4860–4872.

Unsupervised Document Expansion for Information Retrieval with Stochastic Text Generation

Soyeong Jeong[1] **Jinheon Baek**[2] **ChaeHun Park**[1] **Jong C. Park**[1*]
School of Computing[1] Graduate School of AI[2]
Korea Advanced Institute of Science and Technology[1,2]
{syjeong,ddehun,park}@nlp.kaist.ac.kr
jinheon.baek@kaist.ac.kr

Abstract

One of the challenges in information retrieval (IR) is the *vocabulary mismatch* problem, which happens when the terms between queries and documents are lexically different but semantically similar. While recent work has proposed to expand the queries or documents by enriching their representations with additional relevant terms to address this challenge, they usually require a large volume of query-document pairs to train an expansion model. In this paper, we propose an **U**nsupervised **D**ocument **E**xpansion with **G**eneration (UDEG) framework with a pretrained language model, which generates diverse supplementary sentences for the original document without using labels on query-document pairs for training. For generating sentences, we further stochastically perturb their embeddings to generate more diverse sentences for document expansion. We validate our framework on two standard IR benchmark datasets. The results show that our framework significantly outperforms relevant expansion baselines for IR.

1 Introduction

Information retrieval (IR) is the task of retrieving the most relevant documents, including scientific ones (Boudin et al., 2020; Noh and Kavuluru, 2020), for a given query. IR systems have received considerable attention as they are not only required to search documents for information, but are also used as a core component in various downstream language understanding tasks such as open-domain question answering (Seo et al., 2019; Qu et al., 2020), fact verification (Thorne et al., 2018; Li et al., 2020) and information extraction (Narasimhan et al., 2016; Das et al., 2020).

As the simplest approach to IR tasks, classical term-based ranking models, such as BM25 (Robertson et al., 1994) and Query Likelihood (QL) models (Zhai and Lafferty, 2017), have been widely used. These term-based ranking models measure the lexical overlaps between query and document pairs using a sparse representation of words, to match the relevant documents for the given query. Notwithstanding their simplicity, they achieve decent performances, even compared to the recent dense representation models (Lin, 2019; Xiong et al., 2020), which require a large number of paired query-document samples. However, these term-based sparse models are intrinsically vulnerable to the *vocabulary mismatch* problem, which happens when a query and its relevant document are lexically divergent.

Thus, we should address the limitations of both sparse and dense models, about the vocabulary mismatch problem and the need for a large amount of training data, respectively. Along this line, there are methods that expand queries and documents with their relevant terms. They include document expansion methods (Nogueira et al., 2019; Boudin et al., 2020) that introduce additional context-related terms to given documents and query expansion methods (Mao et al., 2020; Claveau, 2020) that augment given queries with additional terms. By doing so, we can explicitly generate lexically richer documents or queries.

Compared with query expansion, document expansion has two strengths. First, a document expansion model can generate much more relevant terms for the given document, since documents are generally much longer than queries. Also, documents can be expanded during indexing time so that the responding process for the user's query is not delayed, in contrast to queries that must be expanded during retrieval time. Thus, document expansion is more appropriate for a real-time system, together with making available more context-related words from the given information (Nogueira et al., 2019).

In this work, we focus on document expansion, and propose to abstractly generate the key infor-

* Corresponding author

Proceedings of the Second Workshop on Scholarly Document Processing, pages 7–17
June 10, 2021. ©2021 Association for Computational Linguistics

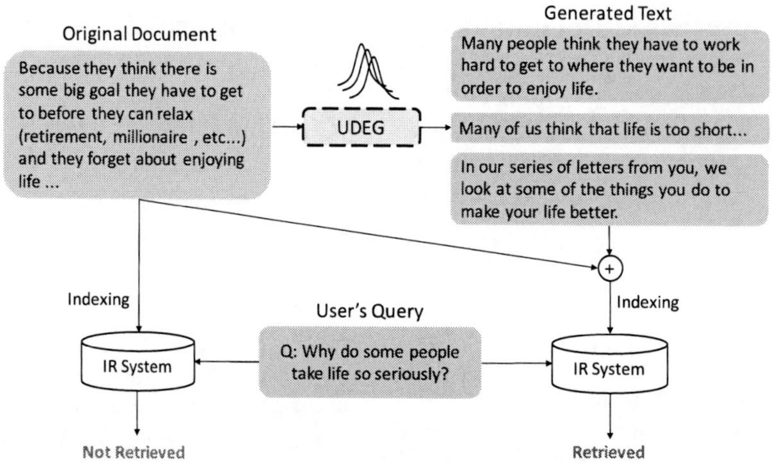

Figure 1: The overall framework of our Unsupervised Document Expansion with Generation (UDEG), where the example is generated from our framework. Given an original document (green box), our UDEG framework stochastically generates several sentences (orange box) relevant to the given document, and augments the generated sentences to the input document to improve its expressiveness. After every document in the corpus is expanded, documents are indexed in the IR system, and searched in response to the given query.

mation corresponding to the given document in an unsupervised manner, henceforth referred to as *Unsupervised Document Expansion with Generation* (UDEG). We first generate document-related sentences using a pre-trained language model, and then stack up the newly generated sentences on the original documents to enrich the expressiveness of document representation. Specifically, in order to generate sentences containing particular information for the documents, we use a language model that is already trained for summarizing sentences from a sufficient amount of texts. However, such a scheme generates only one static sentence at a time, so we further propose to stochastically generate multiple relevant sentences for the given document. This helps the proposed UDEG framework to minimize the vocabulary mismatch cases by generating many relevant words, which reflect diverse points of view for the given document. The overall UDEG framework is illustrated in Figure 1.

We experimentally validate the proposed UDEG framework on standard benchmark datasets for IR tasks, ANTIQUE (Hashemi et al., 2020) and MS MARCO (Nguyen et al., 2016), with five different evaluation metrics. The experimental results show that our framework outperforms all baselines on all evaluation metrics by a large margin. Also, a detailed analysis of UDEG shows that its stochastic generation significantly improves the IR performances, and that our UDEG framework does not depend on specific language models for generation.

Our contributions in this work are threefold:

- To mitigate the vocabulary mismatch problem, we present a novel document expansion framework that augments the document with abstractly generated sentences without using paired query-document data for training.
- Under an unsupervised document expansion framework, we generate document-related sentences with a pre-trained language model, and further stochastically perturb the embeddings for more diverse sentences.
- We show that our framework achieves outstanding performances on benchmark datasets for IR tasks with various evaluation metrics.

2 Related work

Information Retrieval A two-stage pipeline is the most prominent approach for IR. This pipeline first retrieves query-relevant documents with their sparse representations, and then re-ranks them by using neural networks (Mitra and Craswell, 2018; Nogueira et al., 2019, 2020). In this two-stage pipeline, the overall performance is critically dependent on the first retrieval stage, since the failure of the retrieval stage would highly affect the second re-ranking stage. Therefore, this bottleneck on the first stage has to be addressed for performance enhancement (Karpukhin et al., 2020). BM25 and query likelihood (QL) are the most popular *ad-hoc* retrieval models for the first stage (Nogueira et al., 2019; Boudin et al., 2020; Tang and Arnold, 2020). More recently, instead of using sparse models, methods of using dense representations have been proposed (Karpukhin et al., 2020; Xiong et al., 2020; Qu et al., 2020), which can help alleviate the vocabulary mismatch problem through a dense representation space. However, recent work has revealed the limitations on their performance and efficiency (Lin, 2019; Xiong et al., 2020; Luan et al., 2020). Furthermore, these dense representation methods are based on supervised learning, where pairs of query and related-document are usually required to ensure reasonable performance.

Query / Document Expansion Query and document expansions have been widely used in IR systems. In terms of query expansion, Jaleel et al. (2004) proposed pseudo relevance feedback (RM3), which is revisited in more recent work (Dibia, 2020; Mao et al., 2020) for its strength. There are also methods that expand queries using generation schemes (Mao et al., 2020; Claveau, 2020). However, query expansion suffers from its intrinsic drawbacks, as queries need to be manipulated during the retrieval phase and have relatively less information than documents (Nogueira et al., 2019). Thus, we take the alternative route: expanding documents. Nogueira et al. (2019) and Tang and Arnold (2020) proposed to expand documents with generated text using a supervised model trained on query-document pairs. In contrast, our framework generates document-related sentences regardless of the existence of the corresponding query. Boudin et al. (2020) proposed to expand documents with sequence-to-sequence models which output keyphrases; however, their models have to be trained from scratch on a specific domain.

Document-relevant Text Generation In order to enrich the given document efficiently with the document-relevant text, such text should contain the document's key context which can appear in the summarized sentence. Earlier, Erkan and Radev (2004) and Mihalcea and Tarau (2004) proposed unsupervised models of extracting key sentences, which are adopted in various recent work for their robustness (Nikolov and Hahnloser, 2020a; Zhang et al., 2020b; Kazemi et al., 2020). In contrast, an abstractive approach aims at generating summarized sentences containing novel terms that might not exist in the given document (Zhang et al., 2020a; Yang et al., 2020). Nikolov and Hahnloser (2020b) proposed to first extract the key sentences and then paraphrase them with back-translation. Recent work has reported that the improved performance of text summarization approaches is attributed to the pre-trained language models (Zhang et al., 2020a; Lewis et al., 2020; Xu et al., 2020). In this work, we aim at abstractly generating a document-related sentence with a pre-trained language model and further propose to diversely generate sentences with stochastic perturbation, not just using a single summarized sentence.

3 Method

Our goal is to expand the document for IR tasks by generating document-related text, which contains novel but semantically similar terms for the given document without using query-document pairs. In this section, we describe formal description of the IR task.

3.1 Preliminaries

We begin with a formal description of the IR task, and then introduce a document expansion scheme.

Information Retrieval The objective of an IR task is to retrieve the most relevant document $\boldsymbol{d} \in \mathcal{D}$ for the given query $\boldsymbol{q} \in \mathcal{Q}$, where $\mathcal{Q}$ and $\mathcal{D}$ indicate query and document set, respectively. Note that the query and document pair can be represented as either sparse (Robertson et al., 1994; Zhai and Lafferty, 2017) or dense (Lin, 2019; Xiong et al., 2020), which gives rise to different implementation details.

Suppose that we are given a query-document pair $(\boldsymbol{q}, \boldsymbol{d})$ in the correct query-document set τ: $(\boldsymbol{q}, \boldsymbol{d}) \in \tau$, where $\tau \subset \mathcal{Q} \times \mathcal{D}$. Then, the system should retrieve the most relevant document $\boldsymbol{d}$ for the given query $\boldsymbol{q}$ in the correct query-document set τ, denoted as follows:

$$\max \sum_{(\boldsymbol{q},\boldsymbol{d}) \in \tau} f(\boldsymbol{q}, \boldsymbol{d}), \quad (1)$$

where $f : \mathcal{Q} \times \mathcal{D} \rightarrow \mathcal{R}$ is a score function that measures the similarity of the correct query-document pairs, to retrieve the most relevant document for the given but unseen query at test time.

Document Expansion While an IR system can work alone as in Equation 1 by using either sparse or dense representations for queries and documents,

Document (Input): Because they think there is some big goal they have to get to before they can relax (retirement, millionaire, etc...) and they forget about enjoying life ...
Ext (Output): relax (retirement, millionaire , etc...)
Abs (Output): Many people think they have to work hard to get to where they want to be in order to enjoy life.
Abs + S (Output): 1) Many people think they have to work hard to get to where they want to be in order to enjoy life. **2)** Many of us think that life is too short... **3)** In our series of letters from you, we look at some of the things you do to make your life better.

Table 1: Examples of the generated text from different text-generation schemes. Generated terms are appended to the input document before indexing them for the IR system. Ext and Abs denote the extractive and abstractive generation, respectively. Also, + S symbol denotes the stochastic generation.

we need to deal with the vocabulary mismatch problem, which happens when the terms between queries and documents are lexically different but semantically related. To address this problem, we focus on the document expansion scheme, which augments the document with relevant terms to make a richer document.

Formally, the goal of document expansion is to generate semantically relevant terms $\boldsymbol{t} = [t_i]_{i=1}^K$ for the given document $\boldsymbol{d} \in \mathcal{D}$, denoted as follows:

$$[t_i]_{i=1}^K = g(\boldsymbol{d}; \boldsymbol{\theta}), \tag{2}$$

where K is the number of terms associated with each document $\boldsymbol{d}$ and g is the document expansion model parameterized by $\boldsymbol{\theta}$. After generating relevant terms $\boldsymbol{t} = [t_i]_{i=1}^K$ for the document, we concatenate them with the original document $\boldsymbol{d}$ to construct the more meaningful document-representation $\bar{\boldsymbol{d}}$, denoted as follows:

$$\bar{\boldsymbol{d}} = [\boldsymbol{t} \oplus \boldsymbol{d}], \tag{3}$$

where $\oplus$ is the concatenation operation.

By expanding relevant terms to the given document with the generation model g, the similarity between the query $\boldsymbol{q}$ and expanded document $\bar{\boldsymbol{d}}$ becomes stronger than the similarity between query $\boldsymbol{q}$ and original document $\boldsymbol{d}$, as follows: $f(\boldsymbol{q}, \boldsymbol{d}) \leq f(\boldsymbol{q}, \bar{\boldsymbol{d}})$. In order to maximize the similarity score between $\boldsymbol{q}$ and $\bar{\boldsymbol{d}}$, we need the model g that generates document-related terms without using labels of query-document pairs τ for training, which we describe in the next subsection.

3.2 Unsupervised Text Generation for Document Expansion

We now describe our *Unsupervised Document Expansion with Generation* (UDEG) framework, which generates relevant terms for the given document $\boldsymbol{d}$ without using labels on query-document pairs $(\boldsymbol{q}, \boldsymbol{d}) \in \tau$. We first introduce the extractive and abstractive text generation schemes, which are two representative methods for unsupervised text generation, and then propose a stochastic generation scheme for a richer vocabulary.

Extractive Text Generation Extractive text generation is to select the representative words or sentences on the given document. Formally, an extractive text generation scheme is defined as follows:

$$\begin{aligned} \boldsymbol{t}_{ext} = [(t_{ext})_i]_{i=1}^K = g_{ext}(\boldsymbol{d}; \boldsymbol{\theta}_{ext}), \\ [(t_{ext})_i]_{i=1}^K \subset \boldsymbol{d}, \end{aligned} \tag{4}$$

where g_{ext} is an extractive text generation model parameterized by $\boldsymbol{\theta}_{ext}$. After extracting terms $\boldsymbol{t}_{ext} = [(t_{ext})_i]$, they are used to expand the document as in Equation 3 (i.e., $\bar{\boldsymbol{d}} = [\boldsymbol{t}_{ext} \oplus \boldsymbol{d}]$), which can enrich the representation of the given document by counting important terms multiple times (See Table 1 for examples of extractive generation).

Abstractive Text Generation While the previously described extractive text generation model aims at enriching the given document with key terms extracted from it, the expressiveness of this extractive scheme is highly restricted since novel but semantically similar terms cannot be generated as in Equation 4: $[(t_{ext})_i]_{i=1}^K \subset \boldsymbol{d}$. To overcome this limitation, one should further consider generating related-terms that are not contained in the original document. To this end, we propose an abstractive text generation model to obtain the relevant but novel terms for the given document $\boldsymbol{d}$.

Formally, novel terms for the original document are denoted as $[(t'_{abs})_l]_{l=1}^N \not\subset \boldsymbol{d}$, whereas existing terms on the document are denoted as $[(t_{abs})_j]_{j=1}^{K-N} \subset \boldsymbol{d}$. N is the number of newly generated document-related terms. Then, an abstractive generation model is defined as follows:

$$\begin{aligned} \boldsymbol{t}_{abs} &= \left[[(t'_{abs})_l]_{l=1}^N \oplus [(t_{abs})_j]_{j=1}^{K-N} \right] \\ &= g_{abs}(\boldsymbol{d}; \boldsymbol{\theta}_{abs}), \end{aligned} \tag{5}$$

where g_{abs} is the abstractive generation model parameterized by $\boldsymbol{\theta}_{abs}$. We provide concrete examples of abstractive generation in Table 1.

Specific details of unsupervised text generation models, which do not use labels for query-document pairs, are described in § 4.3.

Stochastic Generation While a naïve abstractive generation scheme can generate novel terms that are not included in the original document, a major drawback of this scheme is that they cannot generate a high volume of different terms for the given document. In other words, this scheme is suboptimal since it only generates a single sequence, though the terms within the document can have many synonymous expressions. To overcome this limitation, we stochastically generate terms for the given document by perturbing its embeddings for text generation via applying Monte Carlo (MC) dropout (Gal and Ghahramani, 2016). Compared to the abstractive generation scheme in Equation 5, which only produces one typical sequence of terms $\boldsymbol{t}_{abs}$, we obtain S different sequences $\boldsymbol{T}_{abs}$ from the stochastic generation scheme, as follows:

$$\begin{aligned} \boldsymbol{T}_{abs} &= \left[\boldsymbol{t}^i_{abs}\right]^S_{i=1} \\ \boldsymbol{t}^i_{abs} &= g'_{abs}(\boldsymbol{d}; \boldsymbol{\theta}_{abs}), \end{aligned} \tag{6}$$

where g'_{abs} randomly masks weights on the model even at test time. We provide examples of stochastic generation with $S = 3$ in Table 1. As shown in Table 1, examples of stochastic generation are more relevant to the document and more diverse.

4 Experimental Setups

Here, we describe datasets, models, evaluation metrics, and implementation details for experiments.

4.1 Datasts

We use two benchmark datasets for IR to evaluate our UDEG framework as follows:

ANTIQUE: This is a dataset with 403,666 documents from Yahoo! Answer, including open-domain non-factoid questions (Hashemi et al., 2020). The test set consists of 200 queries and 6,589 query-document pairs.

MS MARCO: This is a collection of 8,841,823 passages from Bing search engine (Nguyen et al., 2016). Since the test set is not publicly available, we use the development set containing 6,980 queries and 59,273 query-document pairs. We randomly sample 1,000,000 passages, while using the same development set for queries and query-document pairs, due to the limitation of computational resources on expanding 8,841,823 passages.

4.2 Retrieval Models

In this subsection, we describe two retrieval models that are widely used for IR systems.

BM25: This is one of the standard *ad-hoc* retrieval models based on Term Frequency-Inverse Document Frequency (TF-IDF), which measures overlapping terms between query and document (Robertson et al., 1994).

QL: This is also one of the standard *ad-hoc* retrieval models. Specifically, QL returns a ranked list of documents sorted by the probability of $P(d|q)$, where q is a query and d is a document (Zhai and Lafferty, 2017).

4.3 Expansion Models

We compare our UDEG framework against the following baselines:

No Expansion (No Expan.): This is a naïve model of retrieving the original documents without query or document expansion.

RM3: This is a query expansion model that uses a pseudo-relevance feedback scheme (RM3) (Jaleel et al., 2004). Note that this can be simultaneously used with document expansion models.

MP-rank: This is an extractive document expansion model, which extracts keyphrases based on a multipartite graph, where the nodes are keyphrase candidates and an edge connects nodes having different topics (Boudin, 2018).

LexRank: This is an extractive document expansion model that extracts the key sentence with PageRank algorithm (Page et al., 1998), which constructs vertices as sentences and edges as TF-IDF weights (Erkan and Radev, 2004).

PEGASUS$_{ext}$: This is an extractive document expansion model (Zhang et al., 2020a), which extracts sentences using pre-trained knowledge for generating masked sentences on the CNN/DailyMail dataset (Nallapati et al., 2016).

LexRank + paraphrase (Lex. + Para.): This is an abstractive document expansion model, which first extracts key sentences with LexRank, and then paraphrases them with an unsupervised model (Liu et al., 2020) based on simulated annealing.

UDEG: Our framework of expanding documents with abstractly generated sentences from a pre-trained language model. Diverse sentences are generated with stochastic perturbation by MC dropout.

		No Expan.	MP-rank	LexRank	Lex.+Para.	PEGASUS$_{ext}$	UDEG (Ours)
MRR	BM25	0.595	0.584	0.571	0.561	0.585	**0.645**
	BM25+RM3	0.558	0.579	0.542	0.567	0.555	**0.616**
	QL	0.499	0.534	0.567	0.518	0.562	**0.650**
	QL+RM3	0.396	0.447	0.456	0.432	0.504	**0.583**
R@10	BM25	0.218	0.220	0.208	0.209	0.207	**0.237**
	BM25+RM3	0.217	0.221	0.208	0.204	0.213	**0.226**
	QL	0.189	0.199	0.203	0.196	0.205	**0.232**
	QL+RM3	0.159	0.179	0.182	0.162	0.191	**0.211**
P@3	BM25	0.378	0.381	0.346	0.351	0.356	**0.431**
	BM25+RM3	0.361	0.355	0.360	0.373	0.366	**0.433**
	QL	0.301	0.333	0.340	0.315	0.358	**0.418**
	QL+RM3	0.240	0.281	0.275	0.271	0.301	**0.386**
MAP	BM25	0.211	0.212	0.199	0.202	0.201	**0.238**
	BM25+RM3	0.212	0.213	0.203	0.203	0.207	**0.234**
	QL	0.172	0.191	0.192	0.181	0.199	**0.230**
	QL+RM3	0.150	0.168	0.170	0.158	0.180	**0.212**
NDCG@3	BM25	0.437	0.442	0.417	0.425	0.419	**0.478**
	BM25+RM3	0.424	0.434	0.423	0.433	0.426	**0.470**
	QL	0.356	0.389	0.400	0.375	0.413	**0.471**
	QL+RM3	0.277	0.324	0.319	0.306	0.350	**0.424**

Table 2: Retrieval results on the ANTIQUE dataset. We use five evaluation metrics: MRR, R@10, P@3, MAP, and NDCG@3. Also, the best performance is marked in **bold**.

4.4 Metrics

We evaluate the models with five metrics, ranging from precision- to recall-oriented, as follows:

Mean Reciprocal Rank (MRR): MRR measures the location of the first relevant document for the given query in a binary sense.

Recall (R@K): R@K measures the recall up to K recommended documents.

Precision (P@K): P@K measures the precision up to K recommended documents.

Mean Average Precision (MAP): Similar to P@K, MAP evaluates all related documents with an ordered list of them.

Normalized Discounted Cumulative Gain (NDCG@K): Compared to the MAP that uses binary relevance metrics, this further manipulates the recommended list by using the fact that some documents are more relevant than others.

4.5 Implementation Details

All of the retrieval models are implemented using Anserini open-source IR toolkit (Yang et al., 2018) with the default hyperparameter values. The PEGASUS-large model, already fine-tuned on the XSUM dataset (Narayan et al., 2018), is used as a pre-trained language model in UDEG for abstractive text generation. For the decoding algorithm, we use a beam search algorithm and set the beam size as 8. Also, we set the number S of stochastic generation for document expansion as 4.

		No Expan.	LexRank	UDEG (Ours)
MRR	BM25	0.427	0.441	**0.463**
	BM25+RM3	0.366	0.385	**0.415**
	QL	0.402	0.420	**0.454**
	QL+RM3	0.319	0.337	**0.382**
R@10	BM25	0.636	0.646	**0.679**
	BM25+RM3	0.600	0.617	**0.651**
	QL	0.611	0.633	**0.671**
	QL+RM3	0.552	0.579	**0.629**
P@1	BM25	0.311	0.324	**0.344**
	BM25+RM3	0.248	0.265	**0.291**
	QL	0.289	0.302	**0.334**
	QL+RM3	0.202	0.215	**0.255**
MAP	BM25	0.422	0.435	**0.457**
	BM25+RM3	0.361	0.380	**0.409**
	QL	0.398	0.414	**0.448**
	QL+RM3	0.315	0.333	**0.377**

Table 3: Retrieval results on MS MARCO dataset. We use following evaluation metrics: MRR, R@10, P@1 and MAP. The best performance is marked in **bold**.

5 Results and Discussion

In this section, we show the overall performance of our UDEG, and then analyze the results in detail.

5.1 Overall Results

Results on the ANTIQUE dataset and sampled MS MARCO dataset are shown in Table 2 and Table 3, respectively. Our UDEG framework significantly outperforms all baselines in all evaluation metrics. Interestingly, the retrieval performance of QL is

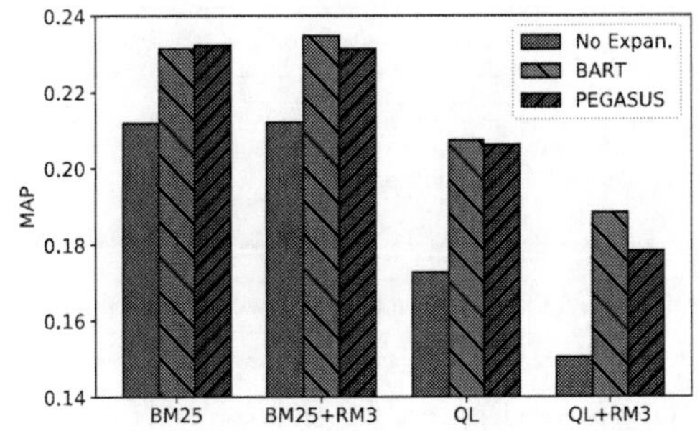

Figure 2: Comparison of BART and PEGASUS language models. The numbers of generated sentences for expansion are both set to one.

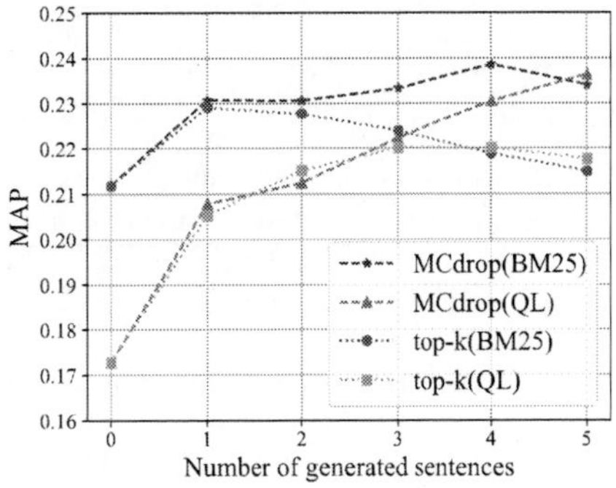

Figure 3: MAP scores of two different stochastic generation strategies (MC dropout vs. top-k sampling) with a varying number of generated sentences. When the number of generated sentences is 0, it refers to the naïve model without expansion.

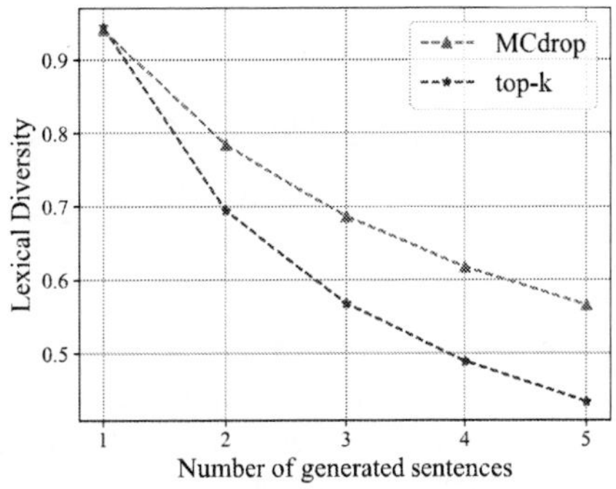

Figure 4: Lexical diversity of two different stochastic generation strategies (MC dropout vs. top-k sampling) with a varying number of expanded sentences.

impressively enhanced when using our framework. Note that the retrieval performance of QL without expansion is much lower than BM25; however, QL shows comparable and even outstanding performance with our expansion framework.

Effectiveness of Abstractive Generation Compared to the extractive and the paraphrasing baselines, our proposed abstractive framework outperforms them in all metrics. Notably, even though PEGASUS$_{ext}$ is pre-trained on the same PEGASUS pipeline with the UDEG framework, the expansion model with the extractive generation scheme is ineffective, since it cannot solve the vocabulary mismatch problem. However, the proposed UDEG framework can solve it by generating novel words, which demonstrates the effectiveness of the abstractive generation scheme.

Effectiveness of Query Expansion When RM3 is applied, the performance is negatively affected in most cases. As Nogueira et al. (2019) reported, we can also interpret the obtained results as evidence that document expansion is more effective than query expansion since a document often contains more signals than a query with its longer length.

5.2 Ablation and Discussion

Which attributes contribute how much to the performance improvement? To see this, we further perform an ablation study, as follows.

Robustness on Different Language Models To validate the robustness of our framework on different language models, we compare the performances of PEGASUS and BART (Lewis et al., 2020), both of which are trained on the XSUM dataset. As shown in Figure 2, the UDEG framework with PEGASUS shows performance similar to the one with BART, both of which consistently outperform the naïve baseline, which neither expands the query nor the document. Thus, the results show that the UDEG framework does not depend on a specific language model, but robustly improves the overall retrieval performance.

Comparison of Stochastic Generation Strategy We compare two stochastic generation strategies, MC dropout and top-k sampling. The top-k sampling is designed to generate diverse outputs by sampling the next word from the k most likely candidates, instead of deterministically selecting the next word (Fan et al., 2018). As shown in Figure 3, even though both strategies aim at generating diverse sentences stochastically, the MC dropout strategy outperforms the top-k sampling strategy. Where does this performance difference come from? The hypothesis is that MC dropout makes more diverse terms across sentences than top-k sampling. Specifically, we often obtain the same starting words from top-k sampling, which leads to generate a number of sentences that might share same starting words. On the other hand, MC

Query	How is the chemistry is a basic of science?
Relevant Document	Chemistry is a basic because all matter can be broken down into elements (i.e., hydrogen, oxygen, nitrogen, etc.); without matter, nothing could be studied.
Generated Sentences	**1)** Chemistry is the study of atoms and molecules. **2)** Chemistry is the study of matter and how it is made. **3)** Chemistry is the study of matter. **4)** Chemistry is a basic **science**.
	Original Document Rank: 104 Expanded Document Rank: 5
Query	How is the library consider as a heart of university?
Relevant Document	Whatever you are studying has to be found somewhere for you to learn it. That's where the library comes into focus.
Generated Sentences	**1)** If you're studying at **university**, you'll need a library. **2)** A library is a place where you can find out more about the subject you are studying. **3)** If you're studying, you'll be studying. **4)** There are many different ways you can study.
	Original Document Rank: 636 Expanded Document Rank: 32
Query	What do doctors do when a patient has a Do Not Resuscitate Order?
Relevant Document	All healthcare professionals involved in the care of that patient will not do anything to prolong the patient's life if in case patient deteriorates/dies. DNR orders may be modified, some may choose mechanical ventilation, or drugs. Usually when a pt is DNR, comfort measures is provided only.
Generated Sentences	**1)** DNR is not life-support. **2)** When a patient is in a "do not resuscitated" (DNR) state, that patient's life will not be saved. **3)** A DNR is a decision made by the patient's family or health care provider to prolong the life of the patient. **4)** A "do not resuscitate"(DNR) order does not mean that a patient should be put on life support.
	Original Document Rank: 40 Expanded Document Rank: 1

Table 4: Examples of generated sentences by the UDEG framework on the ANTIQUE dataset. Note that the first example contains scientific information. The generated terms are highlighted in red if the terms are novel but relevant to the document, and further highlighted in **bold** if the novel terms appear in the query.

dropout randomly perturbs the embeddings at the beginning of generating each sentence, which leads to a diversity of terms even at the starting point. To verify this hypothesis, we compare the lexical diversity of MC dropout and top-k sampling strategies with a varying number of generated sentences. The lexical diversity is calculated by averaging the proportion of the unique unigrams in generated sentences for each document. As Figure 4 shows, the lexical diversities of the generated sentences by top-k sampling are consistently lower and drop more rapidly than that by MC-dropout.

Varying the Number of Expanded Sentences To understand how stochastically generated sentences with MC dropout improves the retrieval performance, we experiment our UDEG with a varying number of generated sentences on two retrieval models, BM25 and QL. Figure 3 shows that the performances of both models tend to improve with increasing numbers of expanded sentences. Interestingly, QL is largely improved as stochastically generated sentences are stacked up to the original document. Meanwhile, the performance is slightly dropped when expanding five sentences for BM25. These results indicate that setting an appropriate number of generated sentences is important for optimal results, since too much information may degrade the context of the original document.

5.3 Case Study

For a qualitative analysis, we conduct a case study to explore the strengths of the UDEG framework. Table 4 shows examples of successfully retrieved expanded-documents with the UDEG framework compared to the original documents without expansion. Note that the original documents are retrieved with lower ranks, but get higher ranks after applying the UDEG framework. We note that the generated sentences contain novel words, while they sometimes contain copied terms. This tendency of copying increases the importance of the keyphrases which contributes to the effective term re-weighting. At the same time, newly generated terms are found to resolve the vocabulary mismatch problem by introducing synonyms or semantically related terms. These findings advocate for the importance of using abstractly generated sentences for document expansion in *ad-hoc* retrieval systems, which can help term re-weighting and alleviate the vocabulary mismatch problem at the same time.

6 Conclusion

We presented a novel framework, which we refer to as **U**nsupervised **D**ocument **E**xpansion with **G**eneration (UDEG), that generates diverse terms with stochastic perturbation over pre-trained language models, and efficiently enriches the document representation, without using any query information for training. Remarkably, UDEG employed in a retrieval system shows significant performance improvements on two standard benchmark datasets. Also, a detailed analysis shows that an abstractive generation framework with stochastic perturbation positively contributes to the retrieval performance. Not only synonymy, but also other problems of the IR system such as polysemy could be addressed using our UDEG framework, to be left for the future work. We believe that the benefits of using diversely generated document-relevant sentences would allow further improvements on any IR system, targeting at scholarly and scientific information.

Acknowledgements

This work was supported by Institute for Information and communications Technology Promotion (IITP) grant funded by the Korea government MSIT) (No. 2018-0-00582, Prediction and augmentation of the credibility distribution via linguistic analysis and automated evidence document collection).

References

Florian Boudin. 2018. Unsupervised keyphrase extraction with multipartite graphs. In *Proceedings of the 2018 Conference of the North American Chapter of the Association for Computational Linguistics: Human Language Technologies, NAACL-HLT, New Orleans, Louisiana, USA, June 1-6, 2018, Volume 2 (Short Papers)*, pages 667–672. Association for Computational Linguistics.

Florian Boudin, Ygor Gallina, and Akiko Aizawa. 2020. Keyphrase generation for scientific document retrieval. In *Proceedings of the 58th Annual Meeting of the Association for Computational Linguistics, ACL 2020, Online, July 5-10, 2020*, pages 1118–1126. Association for Computational Linguistics.

Vincent Claveau. 2020. Query expansion with artificially generated texts. *arXiv preprint arXiv:2012.08787*.

Debasmita Das, Yatin Katyal, Janu Verma, Shashank Dubey, AakashDeep Singh, Kushagra Agarwal, Sourojit Bhaduri, and RajeshKumar Ranjan. 2020. Information retrieval and extraction on COVID-19 clinical articles using graph community detection and Bio-BERT embeddings. In *Proceedings of the 1st Workshop on NLP for COVID-19 at ACL 2020*, Online. Association for Computational Linguistics.

Victor Dibia. 2020. Neuralqa: A usable library for question answering (contextual query expansion + BERT) on large datasets. In *Proceedings of the 2020 Conference on Empirical Methods in Natural Language Processing: System Demonstrations, EMNLP 2020 - Demos, Online, November 16-20, 2020*, pages 15–22. Association for Computational Linguistics.

Günes Erkan and Dragomir R. Radev. 2004. Lexrank: Graph-based lexical centrality as salience in text summarization. *J. Artif. Intell. Res.*, 22:457–479.

Angela Fan, Mike Lewis, and Yann N. Dauphin. 2018. Hierarchical neural story generation. In *Proceedings of the 56th Annual Meeting of the Association for Computational Linguistics, ACL 2018, Melbourne, Australia, July 15-20, 2018, Volume 1: Long Papers*, pages 889–898. Association for Computational Linguistics.

Yarin Gal and Zoubin Ghahramani. 2016. Dropout as a bayesian approximation: Representing model uncertainty in deep learning. In *Proceedings of the 33nd International Conference on Machine Learning, ICML 2016, New York City, NY, USA, June 19-24, 2016*, volume 48 of *JMLR Workshop and Conference Proceedings*, pages 1050–1059. JMLR.org.

Helia Hashemi, Mohammad Aliannejadi, Hamed Zamani, and W. Bruce Croft. 2020. Antique: A non-factoid question answering benchmark. In *Advances in Information Retrieval - 42nd European Conference on IR Research, ECIR 2020, Lisbon, Portugal, April 14-17, 2020, Proceedings, Part II*, volume 12036 of *Lecture Notes in Computer Science*, pages 166–173. Springer.

Nasreen Abdul Jaleel, James Allan, W. Bruce Croft, Fernando Diaz, Leah S. Larkey, Xiaoyan Li, Mark D. Smucker, and Courtney Wade. 2004. Umass at TREC 2004: Novelty and HARD. In *Proceedings of the Thirteenth Text REtrieval Conference, TREC 2004, Gaithersburg, Maryland, USA, November 16-19, 2004*, volume 500-261 of *NIST Special Publication*. National Institute of Standards and Technology (NIST).

Vladimir Karpukhin, Barlas Oguz, Sewon Min, Patrick S. H. Lewis, Ledell Wu, Sergey Edunov, Danqi Chen, and Wen-tau Yih. 2020. Dense passage retrieval for open-domain question answering. In *Proceedings of the 2020 Conference on Empirical Methods in Natural Language Processing, EMNLP 2020, Online, November 16-20, 2020*, pages 6769–6781. Association for Computational Linguistics.

Ashkan Kazemi, Verónica Pérez-Rosas, and Rada Mihalcea. 2020. Biased TextRank: Unsupervised graph-based content extraction. In *Proceedings of the 28th International Conference on Computational Linguistics*, pages 1642–1652, Barcelona, Spain (Online). International Committee on Computational Linguistics.

Mike Lewis, Yinhan Liu, Naman Goyal, Marjan Ghazvininejad, Abdelrahman Mohamed, Omer Levy, Veselin Stoyanov, and Luke Zettlemoyer.

2020. BART: denoising sequence-to-sequence pre-training for natural language generation, translation, and comprehension. In *Proceedings of the 58th Annual Meeting of the Association for Computational Linguistics, ACL 2020, Online, July 5-10, 2020*, pages 7871–7880. Association for Computational Linguistics.

Xiangci Li, Gully A. Burns, and Nanyun Peng. 2020. A paragraph-level multi-task learning model for scientific fact-verification. *arXiv preprint arXiv:2012.14500*.

Jimmy Lin. 2019. The neural hype and comparisons against weak baselines. *SIGIR Forum*, 52(2):40–51.

Xianggen Liu, Lili Mou, Fandong Meng, Hao Zhou, Jie Zhou, and Sen Song. 2020. Unsupervised paraphrasing by simulated annealing. In *Proceedings of the 58th Annual Meeting of the Association for Computational Linguistics, ACL 2020, Online, July 5-10, 2020*, pages 302–312. Association for Computational Linguistics.

Yi Luan, Jacob Eisenstein, Kristina Toutanova, and Michael Collins. 2020. Sparse, dense, and attentional representations for text retrieval. *arXiv preprint arXiv:2005.00181*.

Yuning Mao, Pengcheng He, Xiaodong Liu, Yelong Shen, Jianfeng Gao, Jiawei Han, and Weizhu Chen. 2020. Generation-augmented retrieval for open-domain question answering.

Rada Mihalcea and Paul Tarau. 2004. TextRank: Bringing order into text. In *Proceedings of the 2004 Conference on Empirical Methods in Natural Language Processing*, pages 404–411, Barcelona, Spain. Association for Computational Linguistics.

Bhaskar Mitra and Nick Craswell. 2018. An introduction to neural information retrieval. *Found. Trends Inf. Retr.*, 13(1):1–126.

Ramesh Nallapati, Bowen Zhou, Cicero dos Santos, Çağlar Gulçehre, and Bing Xiang. 2016. Abstractive text summarization using sequence-to-sequence rnns and beyond. In *Proceedings of The 20th SIGNLL Conference on Computational Natural Language Learning*, pages 280–290, Berlin, Germany. Association for Computational Linguistics.

Karthik Narasimhan, Adam Yala, and Regina Barzilay. 2016. Improving information extraction by acquiring external evidence with reinforcement learning. In *Proceedings of the 2016 Conference on Empirical Methods in Natural Language Processing, EMNLP 2016, Austin, Texas, USA, November 1-4, 2016*, pages 2355–2365. The Association for Computational Linguistics.

Shashi Narayan, Shay B. Cohen, and Mirella Lapata. 2018. Don't give me the details, just the summary! Topic-aware convolutional neural networks for extreme summarization. In *Proceedings of the 2018 Conference on Empirical Methods in Natural Language Processing*, Brussels, Belgium.

Tri Nguyen, Mir Rosenberg, Xia Song, Jianfeng Gao, Saurabh Tiwary, Rangan Majumder, and Li Deng. 2016. Ms marco: A human generated machine reading comprehension dataset. In *Proceedings of the Workshop on Cognitive Computation: Integrating neural and symbolic approaches 2016 co-located with the 30th Annual Conference on Neural Information Processing Systems (NIPS 2016), Barcelona, Spain, December 9, 2016*, volume 1773 of *CEUR Workshop Proceedings*. CEUR-WS.org.

Nikola I. Nikolov and Richard H. R. Hahnloser. 2020a. Abstractive document summarization without parallel data. In *Proceedings of The 12th Language Resources and Evaluation Conference, LREC 2020, Marseille, France, May 11-16, 2020*, pages 6638–6644. European Language Resources Association.

Nikola I. Nikolov and Richard H. R. Hahnloser. 2020b. Abstractive document summarization without parallel data. In *Proceedings of The 12th Language Resources and Evaluation Conference, LREC 2020, Marseille, France, May 11-16, 2020*, pages 6638–6644. European Language Resources Association.

Rodrigo Nogueira, Zhiying Jiang, Ronak Pradeep, and Jimmy Lin. 2020. Document ranking with a pretrained sequence-to-sequence model. In *Proceedings of the 2020 Conference on Empirical Methods in Natural Language Processing: Findings, EMNLP 2020, Online Event, 16-20 November 2020*, pages 708–718. Association for Computational Linguistics.

Rodrigo Nogueira, Wei Yang, Jimmy Lin, and Kyunghyun Cho. 2019. Document expansion by query prediction. *arXiv preprint arXiv:1904.08375*.

Jiho Noh and Ramakanth Kavuluru. 2020. Literature retrieval for precision medicine with neural matching and faceted summarization. *Findings of the Association for Computational Linguistics: EMNLP 2020*.

L. Page, S. Brin, R. Motwani, and T. Winograd. 1998. The pagerank citation ranking: Bringing order to the web. In *Proceedings of the 7th International World Wide Web Conference*, pages 161–172, Brisbane, Australia.

Yingqi Qu, Yuchen Ding, Jing Liu, Kai Liu, Ruiyang Ren, Xin Zhao, Daxiang Dong, Hua Wu, and Haifeng Wang. 2020. Rocketqa: An optimized training approach to dense passage retrieval for open-domain question answering. *arXiv preprint arXiv:2010.08191*.

Stephen E. Robertson, Steve Walker, Susan Jones, Micheline Hancock-Beaulieu, and Mike Gatford. 1994. Okapi at TREC-3. In *Proceedings of The Third Text REtrieval Conference, TREC 1994, Gaithersburg, Maryland, USA, November 2-4, 1994*, volume 500-225 of *NIST Special Publication*, pages 109–126. National Institute of Standards and Technology (NIST).

Min Joon Seo, Jinhyuk Lee, Tom Kwiatkowski, Ankur P. Parikh, Ali Farhadi, and Hannaneh Hajishirzi. 2019. Real-time open-domain question answering with dense-sparse phrase index. In *Proceedings of the 57th Conference of the Association for Computational Linguistics, ACL 2019, Florence, Italy, July 28- August 2, 2019, Volume 1: Long Papers*, pages 4430–4441. Association for Computational Linguistics.

Cheng Tang and Andrew Arnold. 2020. Neural document expansion for ad-hoc information retrieval. *arXiv preprint arXiv:2012.14005*.

James Thorne, Andreas Vlachos, Oana Cocarascu, Christos Christodoulopoulos, and Arpit Mittal. 2018. The fact extraction and VERification (FEVER) shared task. In *Proceedings of the First Workshop on Fact Extraction and VERification (FEVER)*, pages 1–9, Brussels, Belgium. Association for Computational Linguistics.

Lee Xiong, Chenyan Xiong, Ye Li, Kwok-Fung Tang, Jialin Liu, Paul Bennett, Junaid Ahmed, and Arnold Overwijk. 2020. Approximate nearest neighbor negative contrastive learning for dense text retrieval.

Jiacheng Xu, Shrey Desai, and Greg Durrett. 2020. Understanding neural abstractive summarization models via uncertainty. In *Proceedings of the 2020 Conference on Empirical Methods in Natural Language Processing, EMNLP 2020, Online, November 16-20, 2020*, pages 6275–6281. Association for Computational Linguistics.

Peilin Yang, Hui Fang, and Jimmy Lin. 2018. Anserini: Reproducible ranking baselines using lucene. *ACM J. Data Inf. Qual.*, 10(4):16:1–16:20.

Ziyi Yang, Chenguang Zhu, Robert Gmyr, Michael Zeng, Xuedong Huang, and Eric Darve. 2020. TED: A pretrained unsupervised summarization model with theme modeling and denoising. In *Proceedings of the 2020 Conference on Empirical Methods in Natural Language Processing: Findings, EMNLP 2020, Online Event, 16-20 November 2020*, pages 1865–1874. Association for Computational Linguistics.

Chengxiang Zhai and John D. Lafferty. 2017. A study of smoothing methods for language models applied to ad hoc information retrieval. *SIGIR Forum*, 51(2):268–276.

Jingqing Zhang, Yao Zhao, Mohammad Saleh, and Peter J. Liu. 2020a. PEGASUS: pre-training with extracted gap-sentences for abstractive summarization. In *Proceedings of the 37th International Conference on Machine Learning, ICML 2020, 13-18 July 2020, Virtual Event*, volume 119 of *Proceedings of Machine Learning Research*, pages 11328–11339. PMLR.

Yong Zhang, Fen Chen, Wufeng Zhang, Haoyang Zuo, and Fangyuan Yu. 2020b. Keywords extraction based on word2vec and textrank. In *ICBDE '20: The 3rd International Conference on Big Data and Education, London, UK, April 1-3, 2020*, pages 37–42. ACM.

Task Definition and Integration for Scientific-Document Writing Support

Hiromi Narimatsu[1], **Kohei Koyama**[2], **Kohji Dohsaka**[3], **Ryuichiro Higashinaka**[1]
Yasuhiro Minami[2], **Hirotoshi Taira**[4]
[1]NTT Communication Science Laboratories
[2]The University of Electro-Communication
[3]Akita Prefectural University, [4]Osaka Institute of Technology
{hiromi.narimatsu.eg, ryuichiro.higashinaka.tp}@hco.ntt.co.jp
k1710245@edu.cc.uec.ac.jp, dohsaka@akita-pu.ac.jp
minami.yasuhiro@is.uec.ac.jp, hirotoshi.taira@oit.ac.jp

Abstract

With the increase in the number of published academic papers, growing expectations have been placed on research related to supporting the writing process of scientific papers. Recently, research has been conducted on various tasks such as citation worthiness (judging whether a sentence requires citation), citation recommendation, and citation-text generation. However, since each task has been studied and evaluated using data that has been independently developed, it is currently impossible to verify whether such tasks can be successfully pipelined to effective use in scientific-document writing. In this paper, we first define a series of tasks related to scientific-document writing that can be pipelined. Then, we create a dataset of academic papers that can be used for the evaluation of each task as well as a series of these tasks. Finally, using the dataset, we evaluate the tasks of citation worthiness and citation recommendation as well as both of these tasks integrated. The results of our evaluations show that the proposed approach is promising.

1 Introduction

When writing a scientific paper, it is important to search for relevant papers and cite them appropriately. However, despite the importance of this requirement, the recent sharp increase in published scientific papers is making it difficult for researchers to comprehensively carry out this process. Consequently, much work has been devoted to developing systems that support the writing of scientific papers.

For example, some studies have attempted to summarize papers on a particular subject (Teufel and Moens, 2002; Qazvinian and Radev, 2008; Bai et al., 2019). The creation of knowledge graphs of scientific papers has also been proposed (Dessì et al., 2020), and Gábor et al. (2018) proposed an automatic content-analysis method by extracting the semantic relations of entities in abstracts.

Other studies have focused on citation recommendation (Huang et al., 2014; He et al., 2010) and generation of citation text (Xing et al., 2020; Luu et al., 2020). Using the database of PubMed[1] papers, Bhagavatula et al. (2018) proposed recommending citations on the basis of keywords as well as the contents of a paper. Mohammad et al. (2009) proposed the generation of citation text, and Färber et al. (2018) proposed a classification model for the task of judging whether a sentence requires citation (citation worthiness).

Although many reports have been presented and an abundance of effort has been expended on data creation (Färber and Jatowt, 2020; Kardas et al., 2020; Saier and Färber, 2020), each previous study has focused on a particular problem in scientific-writing support and has been performed independently using its own specific dataset. Therefore, we do not yet know whether these investigations can be successfully pipelined nor how to ascertain the overall performance of a system that can comprehensively recommend citations. Consequently, it is currently impossible to verify that the technologies centered around scientific-paper writing are actually helpful in comprehensively supporting real-world scientific-paper writing.

In this paper, we first define a series of tasks related to scientific-paper writing that can be pipelined. Then, we create a dataset [2] of academic papers that can be used for the evaluation of each task in scientific-paper writing as well as a series of these tasks. Finally, using the dataset, we evalu-

[1]https://pubmed.ncbi.nlm.nih.gov/

[2]Our dataset is available at https://github.com/citation-minami-lab/citation-dataset.

Proceedings of the Second Workshop on Scholarly Document Processing, pages 18–26
June 10, 2021. ©2021 Association for Computational Linguistics

ate the individual tasks of citation worthiness and citation recommendation as well as the integrated task composed of these two individual tasks. Experimental results show that our task setting and the dataset can be successfully used for scientific-paper writing support.

2 Handling "Related Work" Section

In a scientific paper, the section generally called "Related Work" is important for situating one's research in the field and clarifying the new contribution of the proposed work. However, the task of writing the Related Work section is time-consuming because one needs to read through many papers in related areas and carefully cite them. Due to this cost, much work has been directed to improving the efficiency of this process.

At the beginning stages of this line of research, we saw many studies aimed at helping authors understand the gist of a paper, that is, preparing a summary of the paper highlighting important points such as objective, problem, and methods (Teufel and Moens, 2002). There have also been studies that consider how a paper is cited in summarizing the paper in question (Qazvinian and Radev, 2008). The summarization of scientific papers continues to be an important research focus (Yasunaga et al., 2019). However, capturing the summarization of a particular paper in isolation would obviously not produce a universal solution when facing the abundance of papers that are available to readers.

Recent years have seen an increase in work related to citation recommendation, and this work has been greatly aided by the availability of large-scale article data in electronic form. Such studies have mainly focused on the papers that one should cite due to their authority and relevance based on keywords (Ren et al., 2014). Recently, some studies have focused on recommending papers that might be overlooked by limiting the scope to authority and relevance. Such methods utilize a citation network and more fine-grained content similarity, making it possible to identify specific papers that should be cited (Chakraborty et al., 2015; Bhagavatula et al., 2018). Moreover, Ali et al. (2020) proposed a method for citation recommendation by categorizing relevant papers on the basis of their data, methods, and problems. In our approach, we list tasks related to scientific-paper writing and include the task of citation recommendation. We show how this task can be combined with other tasks as well as how individual problems in citation recommendation can be combined.

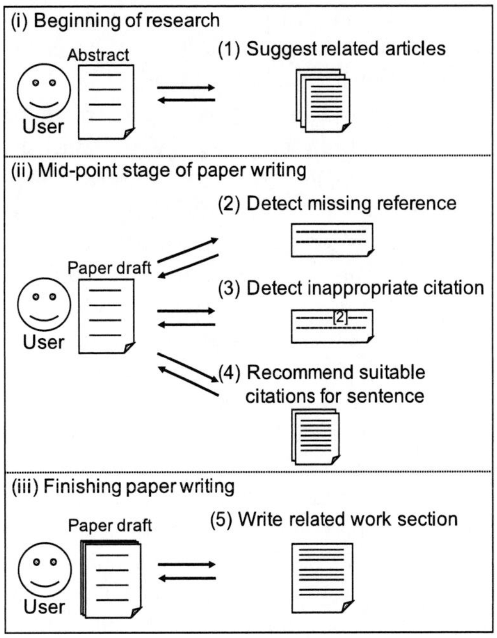

Figure 1: Scientific-paper writing support for each phase of research

In order to facilitate paper writing and peer review, the task of citation worthiness, that is, detecting whether a sentence requires citation, has been carried out (Färber et al., 2018). Färber et al. also released a dataset of scientific papers for this particular task. Other studies have generated citation texts given a portion of a Related Work section. Mohammad et al. (2009) used a rule-based technique to generate citation texts using, as templates, the sentences of the same author and the generic sentences that can be used for citation.

We believe today's high research activity related to handling citation has the potential to create technologies that can actually be useful for human support; however, we also believe that these studies need to be combined appropriately for them to be useful. This has motivated us to list up tasks related to citation and to create a dataset that enables us to evaluate combined tasks as well as individual ones.

3 Listing of tasks

We listed tasks related to citation that can cover the main phases in scientific-paper writing: (i) when we conceive an idea, (ii) when we obtain research results and are ready to situate the work, and (iii) when we finalize the Related Work section.

Figure 1 shows how scientific-paper writing can be supported in each phase. At (i), which happens at the beginning of research, one is apprehensive that the conceived idea may not be original and thus feels the need to perform a survey of related work. In this situation, it is desired that the scientific-paper writing support system recommends relevant papers (Fig. 1 (1)) using as input the research problem and its approach, which are typically written in the paper's abstract. At (ii), which is done in the mid-point stage of paper writing, there may be cases when citations are not appropriate or missing. Therefore, it is necessary to provide support for the detection of missing references (Fig. 1 (2)), the detection of inappropriate citations (Fig. 1 (3)), and the recommendation of suitable citations (Fig. 1 (4)). At (iii), which is when the author applies finishing touches to the paper, support for tailoring the Related Work section would be appropriate (Fig. 1 (5)), such as how the references should be categorized and how they should be presented.

Tasks (1)–(5) in the figure can be broken down into more fine-grained tasks as follows:

(1)-1: Citation extraction Given an abstract, the task of citation extraction retrieves relevant papers from a large database of scientific documents.

(1)-2: Citation recommendation for draft paper Given a draft paper comprising an abstract plus some body text, this task presents the list of relevant papers retrieved from a large database of scientific documents.

(2): Citation worthiness Given a sentence in the Related Work section of a draft, this task detects whether the sentence needs citations.

(3)-1: Citation allocation Given sentences in the Related Work section of a draft and the body of relevant papers, this task allocates appropriate papers to the sentences.

(3)-2: Sentence-citation pair classification Given a sentence and its possible citation, this task classifies whether the allocation of the citation is appropriate for that paper. This is a sub-task of (3)-1.

(4): Citation recommendation for sentence In (2) and (3), there may be sentences with missing citations, that is, when the sentence requires citation but the allocation of citations has failed. In such a case, a citation needs to be retrieved from a large body of scientific papers. This task performs citation recommendation for a citation-missing sentence. Note that this task focuses only on the sentences suggested as citation-worthy by the citation worthiness task because these tasks form a pipeline.

(5)-1: Citation categorization Given sentences with citations, this task categorizes them based on their underlying themes so that the citations can be more appropriately organized.

(5)-2: Citation sentence generation Given sentences with citations, this task suggests alternative citation text for the sentences to achieve better clarity and fluency.

(5)-3: Citation text generation Given Related Work text, which includes multiple sentences with citations, this task suggests alternative citation text for the content. This task is different from (5)-2 in that the text of the entire Related Work section is generated instead of simply generating a sentence for a citation.

As can be seen in the above listing, the tasks follow the chronological order of how a paper is written in its research phases. They can be pipelined. These tasks have mostly been identified and tackled in previous studies, but they have been researched separately. The list of tasks includes (3)-2, which we newly conceived in this work; in pipelining the paper-writing process, we considered this a useful sub-task for citation allocation.

4 Data Creation

After having defined the tasks, we created a dataset for the evaluation of the individual tasks and, moreover, the integrated (pipelined) tasks. For this purpose, we use the same data as source.

4.1 Procedure

The process of data creation is depicted in Figure 2. We first extract key materials from a *target paper* in an archive of published papers. The target

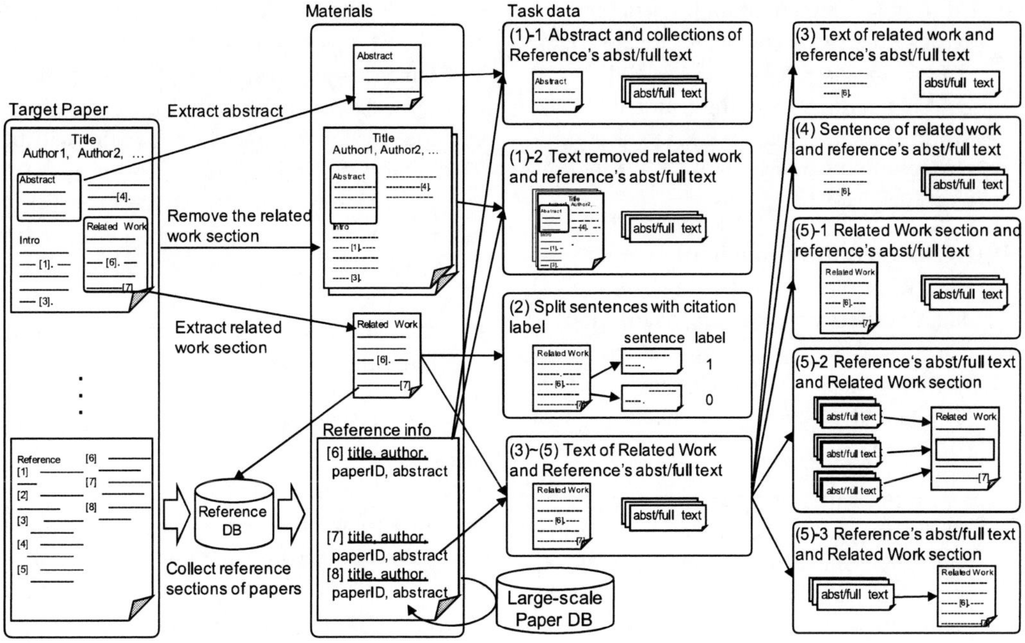

Figure 2: Data-creation process

paper, which is an arbitrary paper in the archive, is the starting point for creating the dataset. We extract elements from the target paper or remove certain elements from it so that we can simulate the incomplete versions of the paper as they appear during the research phases. First, from the target paper, we extract four key elements: abstract, paper without Related Work, Related Work, and references. These can be created directly by extracting certain parts of the target paper. As for the references, we refer to a large-scale reference database to extract their paper IDs (e.g., arXiv paper ID), abstracts, and full text (if retrievable) by using the title and author names. On the basis of these key materials, we create task data for the tasks listed in the previous section. In the following, we describe the detailed process for creating the task data for tasks (1)–(5).

(1)-1: Citation extraction We use the abstract and the list of references for the target paper. Since this is the initial phase of research, we remove from the abstract those sentences related to experiments and results with a rule-based extractor, using the resulting text as the input for this task. The references become the gold data to be retrieved from a large-scale paper database.

(1)-2: Citation recommendation for draft paper We use the paper without the Related Work section as input and use the references as gold output.

(2): Citation worthiness We use the sentences in the Related Work section as task data. We create task data by coupling each sentence with a label indicating whether that sentence has a citation.

(3)-1: Citation allocation We use the text of related work and the references' abstracts and full text (if available) for this task data. We extract sentences from the text of related work and retain only those sentences with citations. Then, we couple these sentences with their citations to create the task data. Although it is not done in this paper, surrounding sentences can also be included in the task data because such sentences may contain helpful information and can serve as context.

(3)-2: Sentence-citation pair classification For the sentences with citations, we create pairs of a sentence with the gold citation and also a pair containing a sentence with an incorrect citation taken from the references of the target paper.

(4): Citation recommendation for sentence We use the sentences of the Related Work section and its references as task data. As gold citations, we use those in the Related Work section. The task is to accurately retrieve the references from the large-scale paper database.

(5)-1: Citation categorization We use the Related Work section and the references as task data. We first extract paragraphs from the text and identify the clusters of citations by extracting citations from each paragraph. The task is to correctly allocate citations to each paragraph.

(5)-2: Citation sentence generation We use the references cited in the Related Work section and the sentences in the Related Work section. For each sentence with a citation, the task is to generate a sentence from the cited reference with its abstract/full text.

(5)-3: Citation text generation We use the references with abstract/full text and the entire text of Related Work. The task is to generate a complete Related Work section using the reference information.

4.2 Created dataset

In this work, we created the task data for (2), (3)-1 and (3)-2. We created a dataset for these tasks because we wanted to verify our approach within a minimal setting; these tasks can be tackled with only the related work sections and the abstracts of the papers cited in them, without requiring the large-scale paper DB or the papers' full texts. Using data covering multiple tasks, we can at least verify whether it is possible to evaluate the performance of individual tasks as well as the integrated task. Although we created the data for the subset of the listed tasks, as can be seen, the procedure for creating task data is mostly straightforward. Once we have verified our approach, as we do in this paper, we will be able to construct data covering all tasks.

To create the data, we first collected target papers from the AxCell dataset (Kardas et al., 2020), which has been made public for the purpose of leaderboard generation. AxCell contains approximately 100K papers.

Since we need papers having a Related Work section, we extracted papers with section titles such as "Related work" and "Related studies." As a result, we successfully obtained 34,416 papers. The sentences included in the Related Work sections of these papers become the task data for (2) Citation worthiness. Table 1 shows the statistics. The numbers of total, positive, and negative examples of the task data for (2) are shown in the first row. We first randomly split the papers into three sets having 22,416, 6,000, and 6,000 target papers. Then we made train/dev/test sets by extracting sentences from these sets. The test data are used for testing throughout the following tasks in order to guarantee a fair evaluation. The inclusion relationship among datasets is shown in Figure 3.

Next, from the target papers used for the task data of (2), we created the task data for (3)-2 Sentence-citation pair classification. Using the citations in the Related Work sections and matching them with the references in the paper in the bbl files, we obtained titles and authors. Then, we used the titles and authors to retrieve their paper IDs and abstracts through the arXiv API [3]. We also retrieved full text when available as tex source or a PDF file. We obtained 7,946 target papers that contain Related Work sections having citations with retrieved abstracts. The number has been reduced greatly due to the fact that many abstracts could not be retrieved via the arXiv API. These examples were split into three sets having 6,946, 500, and 500 target papers, maintaining the inclusion relationship shown in Figure 3. Then we made train/dev/test sets by extracting sentences with citations as positive examples and creating the same number of negative examples by randomly assigning a different citation. For the total number of examples in the task data of (3)-2, see the third row in Table 1.

From the target papers in the test data of (3)-2, we first extracted those that have Related Work sections with three or more citations. We found 600 such sentences. Then, from these, we extracted sentences with only one citation in order to create the task data for (3)-1 Citation allocation. We found 586 such sentences (see second row in Table 1). These sentences are used as test data for (3)-1. Note that, since citation allocation is performed by using the trained model of (3)-2, we have only test data for this task, although the model for this task can also be trained by creating

[3] https://arxiv.org/help/api/

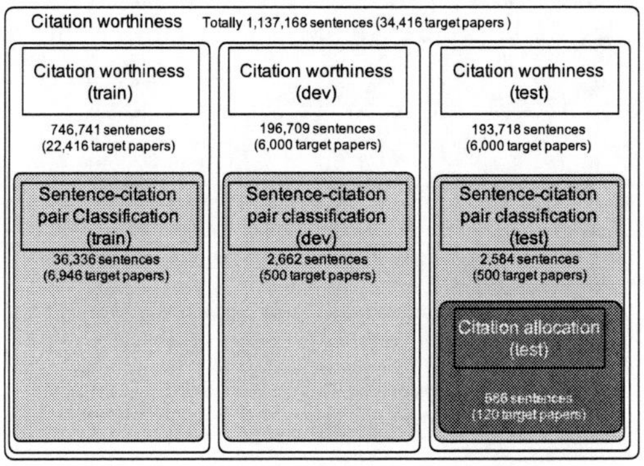

Figure 3: Inclusion relationship among datasets

its individual train/dev data.

5 Experiment

Using the task data, we evaluated baseline performance for these tasks. The aim of the experiment is to show the feasibility of our approach, that is, to test the performance of individual tasks and the integrated task using the same dataset. If this were successful, it would mean that our approach is effective for supporting various phases in scientific-paper writing.

5.1 Citation worthiness

Using the dataset for (2), we trained a BERT-based classifier (Devlin et al., 2019). We used `BertForSequenceClassification` from huggingface[4]. We used the bert-base-uncased model. For training, we used the train/dev data for this task as described in the previous section. The input format used for the classifier was "[CLS] sentence [SEP]." We used the Adam optimizer at a learning rate of $1.0e^{-5}$. We trained for 50 epochs and chose the model that achieved the highest accuracy for the development set. As evaluation metrics, in addition to accuracy, we used precision, recall, and F1 of positive labels (i.e., needs citation). Table 2 shows the results. As can be seen, the accuracy as well as F1 is quite high, much higher than previously reported (Bonab et al., 2018; Färber et al., 2018), which is probably due to the use of BERT.

5.2 Sentence-citation pair classification

Before citation allocation, we first describe the results of sentence-citation pair classification because it is a sub-task. This task determines whether a pair of a sentence and the abstract of its citation form a valid pair. Using the dataset for (3)-2, we trained a BERT-based classifier. In addition to a random baseline, we also prepared two other classifiers: a Doc2Vec-based classifier and an XLNet-based classifier. The methods used for comparison in this experiment are summarized below.

Random Randomly determines whether the citation is appropriate.

Doc2Vec This method utilizes Doc2Vec (Lau and Baldwin, 2016) to vectorize sentences and abstracts for similarity calculation. The Doc2Vec model was trained with the training data of this task. For all sentences with citations, we first concatenated a sentence and the abstract of the cited paper, then a Doc2Vec model was trained using the gensim[5] library. The trained model was used to convert a sentence and an abstract into vectors in order to calculate their cosine similarity. When the similarity increases above a predefined threshold (empirically set to 0.02 using the dev set), it is deemed appropriate.

BERT For training, each of the sentences and each abstract text in the references are paired to create training data while regarding the correct pair as a positive example or otherwise as a negative example. Then, the data are used for training a BERT-based classifier. Here, the input format is "[CLS] sentence [SEP] abstract text [SEP]." In the test phase, a pair consisting of a sentence and an abstract is fed to the trained classifier. We use the probability threshold of 0.5 to determine whether the pair is valid.

XLNet Instead of the BERT model, this method uses the XLNet (Yang et al., 2019) model (XLNet-base-model) for classification. This can be easily done using the huggingface library. The input format is the same as that for BERT.

For BERT and XLNet, we used the train/dev data for this task for fine-tuning. The training setting was the same as that used for citation worthiness.

[4]https://huggingface.co/

[5]https://radimrehurek.com/gensim/

Task	# Examples	# Positive examples	# Negative examples
(2) Citation worthiness	1,137,168	461,882	675,286
(3)-1 Citation allocation	586	N/A	N/A
(3)-2 Sentence-citation pair classification	41,582	20,791	20,791

Table 1: Statistics of task data

	Accuracy	P	R	F1
Random	0.499	0.408	0.500	0.449
BERT	0.911	0.925	0.852	0.887

Table 2: Accuracy for (2) Citation worthiness

	Accuracy	P	R	F1
Random	0.488	0.489	0.492	0.490
Doc2Vec	0.558	0.541	0.763	0.633
BERT	0.816	0.822	0.806	0.814
XLNet	0.844	0.846	0.841	0.843

Table 3: Accuracy for (3)-2 Sentence-citation pair classification

	Accuracy
Random	0.280
Doc2Vec	0.349
BERT	0.747
XLNet	0.795

Table 4: Accuracy for (3)-1 Citation allocation

	Accuracy
BERT	0.623

Table 5: Accuracy of integrated task composed of (2) Citation worthiness and (3)-1 Citation allocation, which includes (3)-2 Sentence-citation pair classification.

Table 3 shows the results for sentence-citation pair classification. As can be seen, the random baseline performs rather poorly, with an accuracy below 0.5. This is surpassed by the Doc2Vec method, which performed at an accuracy of 0.558. However, the two other models based on BERT and XLNet overwhelmed these with over 0.8 accuracy and F1. In this experiment, we can see that XLNet performs better than BERT.

5.3 Citation allocation

Using the dataset for (3)-1, we compared the four methods used in (3)-2, as shown below.

Random This method randomly chooses a citation from a list of possible references.

Doc2Vec This method uses the results of cosine similarity for sentence-citation pairs and chooses the highest-ranking one when it surpasses a predefined threshold of 0.02.

BERT This method uses the output of the BERT-based classifier for sentence-citation pairs. The highest-ranking pair is chosen as its citation when the output probability surpasses 0.5.

XLNet In place of the BERT model, this method uses the XLNet model for sentence-citation pairs.

The evaluation was carried out using test data containing 586 sentences.

Table 4 shows the results. The results clearly follow those of (3)-2, but accuracy is visibly lower. This is reasonable, since the results build on the sub-task. Reflecting the results obtained for sentence-citation pair classification, XLNet achieved the best performance at 0.795.

5.4 Integration of citation worthiness and citation allocation

We performed another experiment that spans two tasks: (2) Citation worthiness and (3)-1 Citation allocation. Note that task (3)-2 is included in (3)-1. Here, the input is a sentence that is first checked for citation worthiness. When it is determined that a citation is needed, the sentence is coupled with the abstracts of possible citations to check whether the pair is appropriate according to the sentence-citation pair classifier. Finally, the citation with the highest probability is chosen when it surpasses a predefined threshold. In this experiment, we used BERT-based methods for all tasks.

Table 5 shows the result of 0.623 for accuracy, indicating that cascading the tasks worsens performance in comparison with the individual tasks. Although a reasonable accuracy can be achieved for a single task, this result shows that when they are combined, the performance may not be comparably high. The results would likely be even lower when more tasks are combined, which can give us clues on to how to improve overall performance and how to jointly train models. Using our design, it would thus be possible to evaluate the performance of a method to support scientific-paper writing at the various phases of research.

6 Summary and future work

In this paper, to achieve better support of scientific-paper writing, we first defined a series of tasks that can be pipelined. Then, focusing on the tasks of citation worthiness, citation allocation, and sentence-citation pair classification, we created a dataset of academic papers that could be used for the evaluation of each task as well as an integrated series of the tasks. We showed experimental results for citation worthiness, citation allocation, and sentence-citation pair classification for individual tasks as well as the case when these tasks are combined. Our series of experimental results shows the feasibility of our approach. We also showed the current performance using the same dataset.

Future work includes creating data for other tasks and performing experiments with them as well as their combinations in pipelined tasks. We will also consider the use of domain-specific pretrained language models, such as SciBERT (Beltagy et al., 2019), in order to improve performance. Furthermore, we plan to perform a human-in-the-loop evaluation in which a system supports researchers in their various writing phases. Finally, it would also be useful to improve the accuracy of the tasks we tackled in this paper.

Acknowledgments

We thank Hiroaki Sugiyama of NTT Communication Science Laboratories, Junji Yamato of Kogakuin University, and Genichiro Kikui of the National Agricultural Research Organization for their helpful comments and suggestions.

References

Zafar Ali, Guilin Qi, Pavlos Kefalas, Waheed Ahmad Abro, and Bahadar Ali. 2020. A graph-based taxonomy of citation recommendation models. *Artificial Intelligence Review*, 53(7):1573–7462.

Xiaomei Bai, Mengyang Wang, Ivan Lee, Zhuo Yang, Xiangjie Kong, and Feng Xia. 2019. Scientific paper recommendation: A survey. *IEEE Access*, 7:9324–9339.

Iz Beltagy, Kyle Lo, and Arman Cohan. 2019. SciBERT: A pretrained language model for scientific text. In *Proceedings of the 2019 Conference on Empirical Methods in Natural Language Processing and the 9th International Joint Conference on Natural Language Processing*, pages 3615–3620".

Chandra Bhagavatula, Sergey Feldman, Russell Power, and Waleed Ammar. 2018. Content-based citation recommendation. In *Proceedings of the 2018 Conference of the North American Chapter of the Association for Computational Linguistics: Human Language Technologies, Volume 1 (Long Papers)*, pages 238–251.

Hamed Bonab, Hamed Zamani, Erik Learned-Miller, and James Allan. 2018. Citation worthiness of sentences in scientific reports. In *Proceedings of the 41st International ACM SIGIR Conference on Research Development in Information Retrieval*, page 1061–1064.

Tanmoy Chakraborty, Natwar Modani, Ramasuri Narayanam, and Seema Nagar. 2015. DiSCern: A diversified citation recommendation system for scientific queries. In *Proceedings of the 2015 IEEE 31st International Conference on Data Engineering*, pages 555–566.

Danilo Dessì, Francesco Osborne, Diego Reforgiato Recupero, Davide Buscaldi, Enrico Motta, and Harald Sack. 2020. AI-KG: An automatically generated knowledge graph of artificial intelligence. In *Proceedings of International Semantic Web Conference*, pages 127–143. Springer.

Jacob Devlin, Ming-Wei Chang, Kenton Lee, and Kristina Toutanova. 2019. BERT: Pre-training of deep bidirectional transformers for language understanding. In *Proceedings of the 2019 Conference of the North American Chapter of the Association for Computational Linguistics: Human Language Technologies, Volume 1 (Long and Short Papers)*, pages 4171–4186.

Michael Färber and Adam Jatowt. 2020. Citation recommendation: approaches and datasets. *International Journal on Digital Libraries*, 21(4):375–405.

Michael Färber, Alexander Thiemann, and Adam Jatowt. 2018. To cite, or not to cite? Detecting citation contexts in text. In *Advances in Information Retrieval*, pages 598–603, Cham. Springer International Publishing.

Kata Gábor, Davide Buscaldi, Anne-Kathrin Schumann, Behrang QasemiZadeh, Haifa Zargayouna, and Thierry Charnois. 2018. SemEval-2018 task

7: Semantic relation extraction and classification in scientific papers. In *Proceedings of the 12th International Workshop on Semantic Evaluation*, pages 679–688.

Qi He, Jian Pei, Daniel Kifer, Prasenjit Mitra, and Lee Giles. 2010. Context-aware citation recommendation. In *Proceedings of the 19th International Conference on World Wide Web*, WWW '10, page 421–430.

Wenyi Huang, Zhaohui Wu, Prasenjit Mitra, and C. Lee Giles. 2014. Refseer: A citation recommendation system. In *IEEE/ACM Joint Conference on Digital Libraries*, pages 371–374.

Marcin Kardas, Piotr Czapla, Pontus Stenetorp, Sebastian Ruder, Sebastian Riedel, Ross Taylor, and Robert Stojnic. 2020. Axcell: Automatic extraction of results from machine learning papers. In *Proceedings of the 2020 Conference on Empirical Methods in Natural Language Processing*, pages 8580–8594.

Jey Han Lau and Timothy Baldwin. 2016. An empirical evaluation of doc2vec with practical insights into document embedding generation. In *Proceedings of the 1st Workshop on Representation Learning for NLP*, pages 78–86, Berlin, Germany. Association for Computational Linguistics.

Kelvin Luu, Rik Koncel-Kedziorski, Kyle Lo, Isabel Cachola, and Noah A. Smith. 2020. Citation text generation. *ArXiv*, abs/2002.00317.

Saif Mohammad, Bonnie Dorr, Melissa Egan, Ahmed Hassan, Pradeep Muthukrishan, Vahed Qazvinian, Dragomir Radev, and David Zajic. 2009. Using citations to generate surveys of scientific paradigms. In *Proceedings of Human Language Technologies: The 2009 Annual Conference of the North American Chapter of the Association for Computational Linguistics*, pages 584–592.

Vahed Qazvinian and Dragomir R. Radev. 2008. Scientific paper summarization using citation summary networks. In *Proceedings of the 22nd International Conference on Computational Linguistics (Coling 2008)*, pages 689–696.

Xiang Ren, Jialu Liu, Xiao Yu, Urvashi Khandelwal, Quanquan Gu, Lidan Wang, and Jiawei Han. 2014. Cluscite: Effective citation recommendation by information network-based clustering. In *Proceedings of the 20th ACM SIGKDD international conference on Knowledge discovery and data mining*, pages 821–830.

Tarek Saier and Michael Färber. 2020. unarxive: a large scholarly data set with publications' full-text, annotated in-text citations, and links to metadata. *aScientometrics*, 125(3):3085–3108.

Simone Teufel and Marc Moens. 2002. Summarizing scientific articles: Experiments with relevance and rhetorical status. *Computational linguistics*, 28(4):409–445.

Xinyu Xing, Xiaosheng Fan, and Xiaojun Wan. 2020. Automatic generation of citation texts in scholarly papers: A pilot study. In *Proceedings of the 58th Annual Meeting of the Association for Computational Linguistics*, pages 6181–6190.

Zhilin Yang, Zihang Dai, Yiming Yang, Jaime Carbonell, Russ R Salakhutdinov, and Quoc V Le. 2019. XLNet: Generalized autoregressive pretraining for language understanding. In *Proceedings of Advances in Neural Information Processing Systems 32*, pages 5753–5763.

Michihiro Yasunaga, Jungo Kasai, Rui Zhang, Alexander R Fabbri, Irene Li, Dan Friedman, and Dragomir R Radev. 2019. ScisummNet: A large annotated corpus and content-impact models for scientific paper summarization with citation networks. In *Proceedings of the AAAI Conference on Artificial Intelligence*, volume 33, pages 7386–7393.

Detecting Anatomical and Functional Connectivity Relations in Biomedical Literature via Language Representation Models

Ibrahim Burak Ozyurt
FDI Lab Dept. of Neuroscience
UCSD La Jolla, USA
iozyurt@ucsd.edu

Joseph Menke
Scicrunch.com
San Diego, USA
joe@scicrunch.com

Anita Bandrowski
FDI Lab Dept. of Neuroscience
UCSD La Jolla, USA
abandrowski@ucsd.edu

Maryann E. Martone
FDI Lab Dept. of Neuroscience
UCSD La Jolla, USA
maryann@ncmir.ucsd.edu

Abstract

Understanding of nerve-organ interactions is crucial to facilitate the development of effective bioelectronic treatments. Towards the end of developing a systematized and computable wiring diagram of the autonomic nervous system (ANS), we introduce a curated ANS connectivity corpus together with several neural language representation model based connectivity relation extraction systems. We also show that active learning guided curation for labeled corpus expansion significantly outperforms randomly selecting connectivity relation candidates minimizing curation effort. Our final relation extraction system achieves F_1 = 72.8% on anatomical connectivity and F_1 = 74.6% on functional connectivity relation extraction.

1 Introduction

The NIH Common Fund's Stimulating Peripheral Activity to Relieve Conditions (SPARC) program aims to transform our understanding of nerve-organ interactions to help spur the development of effective bioelectronic treatments. Bioelectronic medicine represents the convergence of molecular medicine, neuroscience, engineering and computing to develop devices to diagnose and treat diseases (Olofsson and Tracey, 2017). One of the projects within this large consortium is to create a systematized and computable wiring diagram of the autonomic nervous system, a part of the "wiring system" that travels throughout the body transmitting messages between the peripheral organs and the brain or spinal cord. While diagrams of nerves are currently available in medical texts (Standring and Gray, 2008), the SPARC program seeks to map these connections at higher levels of detail and with greater accuracy. Additionally, the diagrams in these medical texts are not generally queryable, nor are they sufficiently detailed to include the granular paths that these nerves travel. Such information would be needed, for example, to understand where reliable access points to a particular nerve might be so that stimulation only affects the most relevant nerve or to understand the mechanisms behind stimulation applied at particular locations. Many scientific studies contain information about individual nerves and at times the paths they traverse, but to our knowledge, no systematic approach has been attempted to bring these large quantities of information together into a computationally accessible format.

The SPARC project is building a cross-species connectivity knowledge base that contains detailed information about individual nerves, their pathways, cells of origin and synaptic targets. To date, this knowledge base has been populated through the development of detailed models of circuitry by experts funded through the SPARC project using the ApiNATOMY platform (Kokash and de Bono, 2021). ApiNATOMY provides a modeling language for representing the complexity of functional and anatomical circuitry in a standardized form. The circuitry contained in these models represent expert knowledge derived from the synthesis of the expert's own work and the synthesis of, in some cases , hundreds of scientific publications. However, to ensure that information in the SPARC knowledge base is comprehensive and up to date, i.e., it represents the current state of knowledge about autonomic nervous system (ANS) connectivity, we sought to augment the expert-based model approach with experimental information derived from the primary scientific literature. As there are thousands of papers and additional sources like text books, we utilized natural language processing to identify sentences that contained information on neuronal connectivity in the ANS.

Proceedings of the Second Workshop on Scholarly Document Processing, pages 27–35
June 10, 2021.

The task was approached by first gathering the relevant scientific literature by matching bodily structures at a variety of anatomical levels (i.e. gasserian ganglion, vagus nerve, brainstem, etc.) from a constructed set of vocabulary at sentence level. Then, annotators classified each structure to structure relationship using only the information provided within the sentence based on the connectivity types defined in our annotation guideline. This structured data were then used to train our connectivity relations models. Data from two curators was used to assess the inter-curator agreement to determine if the annotation guidelines are sufficient to "teach" the task to humans. We assessed connectivity statements into several types including, anatomical connectivity, functional connectivity, structural connectivity, topological connectivity and general connectivity as well as no connectivity. The general connectivity and no connectivity categories can be thought of as statements that are too vague to be of much direct use for our use case. The most important statements are anatomical connectivity, elucidating which parts are connected physically and functional connectivity, elucidating which parts are connected functionally. A definition and an example for each connectivity type used for annotation is shown in Table 1. Of course with single sentences, it is difficult to define a direct functional relationship, which typically rests on the latency with which a signal is detected between two elements (Bennett, 2001). However, statements about latency are very rare in the subset of the peripheral nervous system literature, whereas somewhat more general statements about functional relationships that, for example, describe damage to one area and altered functioning in another, are more abundant. We hypothesize that when such statements are reasonably abundant, a detection classifier will be easier to train.

In relation extraction, long-range relations are usually handled using dependency parse tree information. In traditional feature-based models, paths in the dependency parse tree between entities are used used as features (Kambhatla, 2004) which suffered from the sparsity of the feature patterns. More recently, neural models are increasingly employed for relation extraction instead of feature engineering using vectorized word embeddings. The dependency information is represented as computation graphs along the parse tree (Zhang et al., 2018). Sequence models, on the other hand, work at the surface level and represent long distance relationships via either convolutional or recurrent neural networks and an attention mechanism (Zhang et al., 2017).

In biomedical domain, relation extraction work is traditionally focused on protein-protein, gene-disease or protein-chemical interactions. Several labeled datasets, such as GAD (Bravo et al., 2015) (a gene-disease relation dataset) and CHEMPROT (Krallinger et al., 2017) (a protein-chemical multi-relation dataset) are publicly available. Neural sequence models have also been applied to protein-chemical relation extraction task (Lim and Kang, 2018).

Recently, sentence level transformer based language representation models such as BERT (Devlin et al., 2019) have shown superior downstream performance on many NLP tasks. A biomedical domain adapted version of BERT called BioBERT (Lee et al., 2019) has been shown state of the art performance on several biomedical relation extraction tasks.

While most of the transformer based language representation models are pretrained on sentences where a predefined percentage of the tokens are masked and the model learns to predict the masked tokens, a recently introduced language representation model, ELECTRA (Clark et al., 2020) learns to discriminate if a token in the original input is replaced by a language generator model or not. The generator model is a BERT like generative model that is co-trained with the discriminative model.

While there are efforts to extract brain connectivity information from neuroscience literature (Richardet et al., 2015), their focus is in the cognitive parts of the brain instead of ANS. In this paper, we introduce a labeled ANS connectivity corpus, together with four biomedical domain adapted ELECTRA models, that we have used to develop an anatomical and functional connectivity relation extraction system that outperforms BioBERT.

2 Methods

2.1 Vocabulary

In order to better structure information from papers, anatomical structure labels were drawn from a set of relevant ontologies, also approved for use by the SPARC project. These ontology terms include primarily FMA (RRID:SCR_003379), UBERON (RRID:SCR_010668), and NIFSTD (RRID:SCR_005414) terms, and they are listed

Relation	Definition	Example
functional	a relationship was determined to exist between two structures using physiological techniques	The HB reflex is a reflex initiated by **lung** inflation, which excited the myelinated fibers of **vagus nerve**, pulmonary stretch receptors [11,19].
anatomical	a physical synaptic relationship was observed between two structures using anatomical techniques such as tract tracing	Only the most prominent nervous connections, such as the **penis nerve cord** (pnc, Fig. 8a), connecting the **ventral ganglion** to the penis ganglion can be detected.
structural	a relationship that reflected continuity between segments of nerves	The term vocal fold paralysis (VFP) refers to the reduced or absent function of the **vagus nerve** or its distal branch, the **recurrent laryngeal nerve** (RLN) [1-3].
topological	a relationship that reflected the course of a nerve	**Oculomotor nerve** (III) exited from the middle tectum nearby ventro-medial **midbrain** and was observed on 6-day-old fish.
general	a statement that contained general information about connectivity but did not specify the technique used or otherwise failed to elucidate the exact type of connectivity discussed	Moreover, an interoceptive circuit connecting the **gut** to the **nucleus tractus solitarius (NTS)** via the vagus nerve has been demonstrated to convey the state of the gut to the limbic system (Figure 9; Maniscalco and Rinaman, 2018).

Table 1: Connectivity relation types

on the SPARC anatomy working group web pages, which include term lists. In order to provide a more targeted set of sentences for training, we selected a set of terms that was specifically associated with the ANS. These terms included sympathetic and parasympathetic nerves and ganglia from the FMA and UBERON. Terms were selected by the SPARC Anatomical Working Group, a group of anatomical experts who provide expertise to the SPARC knowledge engineers.

2.2 Corpus Generation

The sentences of interest for connectivity relation extraction were detected by longest phrase match from the target vocabulary of anatomical terms. We have used four million full-length PMC open access papers downloaded on November 2020 to search for sentences of interest. All the sentences mentioning at least two distinct anatomical structures from our vocabulary are selected. To focus our curation effort to a manageable portion of the vocabulary, a smaller vocabulary consisting of only ANS nerve and ganglion terms were selected to further filter the candidate sentence set where only sentences having at least one structure from the focused vocabulary set is selected. Since the resulting candidate set was still too large for curation, up to three examples from each unique focused vocabulary term encountered is randomly sampled to create our base corpus of 808 sentences to be curated.

2.2.1 Annotation of the Corpus and Inter-annotator Agreement

Three curators/domain experts were involved in the connectivity corpus labeling process. Our main curator (J.M.) is a full-time curator with several years of experience with biomedical named entity recognition, relation extraction and text classification curation tasks. Dr. A.B. is a neurophysiologist by training with expertise in microcircuitry. Dr. M.M. is a trained anatomist with expertise in microcircuitry and a professor of neuroscience. All curators annotated training sets using the relation annotator tool developed in-house. The tool allows the curators both to edit entities (if automatically detected anatomical structure boundaries are not correct) and to label automatically generated binary relation combinations arising from the two or more anatomical structures detected in the curated sentence.

To start, A.B. and J.M. completed 30 sentences together to gauge the difficulty of the task and train J.M. on the differences between anatomical and functional connectivity. Then, M.M. and J.M. independently annotated 102 relation labels. In this first iteration, connectivity between structures could only be classified as anatomical connectivity, functional connectivity, or no relation. The initial inter-annotator agreement was 66.7%; Cohen's kappa was 0.25. Even when simply comparing binary connectivity vs. no relation, there was only an inter-annotator agreement of 72%; Cohen's kappa was 0.34. After discussing disagreements, additional connectivity types were added to the relation annotator tool. After expansion, connectivity could be classified as structural, topological, or general in addition to the previous versions labels: anatomical, functional, and no relation. This was done to make each connectivity type more explicit with less potential overlap, especially between our main connectivity types of interest (anatomical vs. functional).

In our second iteration, M.M. and J.M. independently annotated another 170 relation labels across 100 sentences. This time, the inter-annotator agreement was 73.5%; Cohen's kappa was 0.25. Annotation differences though were primarily found to be between our general connectivity and no relation tags. If we consider general connectivity to be the same as no relation (collapsing them together), then our inter-annotator agreement jumps to 91.2%; likewise, Cohen's kappa also increases to 0.55. Because our primary disagreements were between two tags of less interest (general connectivity vs. no-relation), we believe our inter-annotator agreement is acceptable for this high difficulty task.

2.3 Models

2.3.1 ELECTRA based language representation models for Biomedical Domain

Domain specific language representation models result in performance improvements on downstream NLP tasks as demonstrated by BioBERT (Lee et al., 2019). Similarly, we have pretrained four ELECTRA (Clark et al., 2020) based models on biomedical corpus.

For pretraining corpus we have used both PubMed abstracts and PubMed Central (PMC) open access full-length papers. 21.2 million PubMed abstracts from the January 2021 baseline distribution are used to build our main pretraining corpus. Sentences extracted from the paper title and abstract text resulted in a corpus of 3.6 billion words. For the PMC open access papers, sentences extracted from all sections except the references section of the full-length papers are used to build a 12.3 billion words corpus. A domain specific word piece vocabulary is generated using SentencePiece byte-pair-encoding (BPE) model (Sennrich et al., 2016) from PubMed abstract texts. The models are pretrained for one million steps on the PubMed abstracts corpus followed by 200,000 steps training on the PMC open access papers corpus.

During training, ELECTRA uses a small transformers based encoder model using masked language objective like in BERT to generate possible replacements for the larger discriminative model which is also based on transformers architecture. Both models are trained jointly. During fine-tuning, only the discriminative model parameters are used. The discriminative model has essentially the same architecture as BERT but trained in a discriminative manner using a different objective. We have trained three different model sizes; a base model with embedding and hidden size of 768, 12 attention heads and 12 transformer layers; a mid sized model with embedding size of 384, hidden size of 512, 8 attention heads and 12 transformer layers; a mid sizes tall model having same parameters as the mid sized model but with 24 transformer layers. We have also trained another mid sized model with the combined PubMed abstract and PMC open access full paper corpus instead of the two corpus cascaded training approach used for the other three Bio-ELECTRA models. For all models, the maximum allowed input sequence length was set to 512. For all models besides the mid-tall model, the batch size was set to 256. The mid-tall model had a batch size of 128 because of the memory limitations of a single tensor processing unit (TPU). The model architectures, sizes and training times are summarized in Table 2. All the models are trained on a single 8 core version 3 TPU with 128 GB RAM.

While, we have used our Bio-ELECTRA models for connectivity relation extraction only, the models like BioBERT are applicable to many downstream biomedical NLP tasks.

3 Experiments

We conducted our experiments in two phases. In the first phase, all the binary connectivity relation candidates in the 805 sentences extracted from the open access subset of PubMed Central is annotated by a curator. The curated base set is then randomly split into 80/20% train/test set. Afterwards, ten randomly initialized models are trained. The reported results are average of 10 runs together with

Model	Params	Architecture	Steps	Train Time/Hardware
Mid	50M	hidden:512, layers:12	1.2M	6.5d on 8 TPUv3s
Base	110M	hidden:768, layers:12	1.2M	12.5d on 8 TPUv3s
Mid-tall	88M	hidden:512, layers:24, batch:128	1M	5.5d on 8 TPUv3s
Mid Combined	50M	hidden:512, layers:12	1.2M	6.5d on 8 TPUv3s

Table 2: ELECTRA Models for Biomedical Domain

standard deviation. In the second phase, the base set is enhanced via active learning.

As our baseline model, we have used a graph convolution over dependency parse tree neural model (Zhang et al., 2018) where the dependency graph structure is represented by an adjacency matrix over which convolution operations are performed. The model uses word embedding vectors for input encoding and stacked layers of graph convolution network (GCN) layers to encode relations. The input encodings can be further contexualized via a bi-directional long-short-term memory (LSTM) layer, which we have used in our experiments. For word embeddings we have used 300 dimensional Common Crawl (840B tokens) trained GloVe (Pennington et al., 2014) vectors. The dependency parse trees for the input sentences were generated via Stanford CoreNLP (Manning et al., 2014) package.

All the other models are fine-tuned from pretrained transformers based language representation models. We have downloaded Bio-ELECTRA++ from Zenodo[1]. Besides our four biomedical corpus pretrained ELECTRA models, we have used BioBERT (Lee et al., 2019) version 1.1 and ELECTRA Base models. The binary anatomical structure entities are masked in candidate sentences as in (Zhang et al., 2018; Lee et al., 2019). Besides that, no further preprocessing is done. All the models are trained for three epochs, using the the default learning rate and maximum allowed batch size for our 8GB Nvidia RTX 2070 GPU.

The test performance of models tested are summarized in Table 3. Even after the benefit of dependency parses, contextualized graph convolution networks were at the bottom of the performance rank tying with the smallest language representation model. Two Bio-ELECTRA models, namely Bio-ELECTRA Base and Bio-ELECTRA Mid outperformed BioBERT. Given that the Bio-ELECTRA Mid has less than half the parameters of Bio-BERT, its performance is especially impressive. We chose the best performing Bio-ELECTRA Base model for the second stage.

3.1 Extending Curation Set via Active Learning

Since labeled data set generation is costly and time consuming, we have tried to leverage active learning to minimize curation effort while trying to maximize prediction performance. To this end, 250 randomly selected candidate sentences from the nerve-ganglia PMC data set, are interactively curated by our curator in ten iterations. Each iteration has consisted of 25 candidate sentences selected by the binary relation extraction classifier trained on all the the curated sentences from the previous iterations plus the base training set. In the first iteration, the classifier is trained on the base training set only. For the control set, we have randomly selected 250 candidate sentences from the nerve-ganglia PMC data set, which are annotated separately by our curator. We have used uncertainty sampling as our oracle query strategy where the 25 unlabeled sentences that are closest to the decision boundary (probability estimate of 0.5) are selected for curation at each iteration. After each iteration, the extended training set is used to train ten randomly initialized models which are tested on the testing set. The precision and F_1 performance scores over the active learning set is shown in Figure 1.

The testing performance of active learning based vs random selection based training set expansion is shown in Table 4. Active learning strategy was significantly better than random selection based on two-tailed t test.

3.2 Effect of Hyperparameter Optimization

The additional 500 curated sentences (250 from active learning, 250 from random control set) are combined with the base training set. To maximize relation extraction performance, we used hyperparameter tuning on the 80%/20% training/dev set split of the combined training set. Using hyper-

[1] https://doi.org/10.5281/zenodo.3971235

Model	Parameters	Precision	Recall	F_1
Contextualized-GCN		71.05 (4.36)	54.23 (4.20)	61.36 (3.01)
ELECTRA Base	110M	69.35 (4.23)	70.85 (5.43)	70.03 (4.39)
BioBERT	110M	67.82 (4.71)	72.34 (2.18)	69.89 (2.40)
Bio-ELECTRA++	11M	54.41 (2.11)	70.32 (3.38)	61.26 (1.33)
Bio-ELECTRA Mid	50M	69.16 (3.53)	73.83 (2.24)	71.36 (2.16)
Bio-ELECTRA Base	110M	**69.93 (2.91)**	74.26 (3.55)	**71.99 (2.76)**
Bio-ELECTRA Mid Combined	50M	67.66 (2.38)	**74.36 (5.80)**	70.70 (2.78)
Bio-ELECTRA Mid-tall	88M	63.89 (4.51)	65.96 (3.81)	64.78 (2.98)

Table 3: Binary connectivity/no-connectivity relation extraction on base set

Data Set	Precision	Recall	F_1
Random	70.29 (1.69)	74.04 (3.27)	72.06 (1.68)
Active learning	**75.88 (2.70)**	**75.11 (2.39)**	**75.47 (2.30)**

Table 4: Test performance effect for active learning vs random selection based labeled set expansion

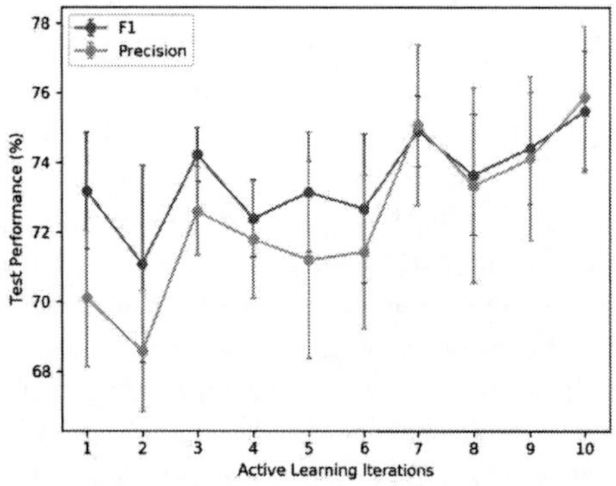

Figure 1: Average test performance over active learning iterations

opt (Bergstra et al., 2013) Python package, we searched for the optimum F_1 value for the following hyperparameters; the learning rate among the values 1e-5, 5e-5, 1e-4 and 5e-4, number of epochs among the values 3, 5, 10. We have used the maximum possible batch size of 16 for our 8GB RAM GPU. The best performing hyperparameter combination was then used to train ten randomly initialized Bio-ELECTRA Base based connectivity relation extraction classifiers. The results together with ten runs using default learning parameters are shown in Table 5. Hyperparameter optimization performance was significantly better than default learning parameter performance as determined by two-tailed t test (p = 0.014)

To detect anatomical and functional connectivity relations among candidate structure binary relation sentences, we have introduced a three class classifier based on the same Bio-ELECTRA Base language representation model as the connectivity/no-connectivity classifier. Ten randomly initialized classifiers are trained using optimized hyperparameters. The test performance is shown in Table 6.

4 Discussion

Connectivity relations constituted only about 12% of the connectivity relationship candidates in our corpus. Taking this into account, the anatomical and functional connectivity detection performance of our final classifier is good enough to be used for ANS connectivity knowledge base construction with drastically reduced domain expert curation.

When looking at our model's performance, we considered errors at the level of individual connectivity relations labels, meaning we could (and did) have some sentences with multiple errors. We defined errors as cases where relation labels tagged by the model and the annotator did not agree. We performed our error analysis in two phases. In phase 1, our analysis was performed using only binary connectivity data (i.e. did annotators mark a relationship using any type of connectivity or as no relation) from 40 connectivity errors: 19 false positives and 21 false negatives. False positives were defined as instances when the model predicted connectivity when there was actually no relationship (as defined by the annotator). Inversely, false negatives were cases when the model predicted structures to have no relationship when there was actually some type of connectivity. In phase 2, our

Model	Precision	Recall	F_1
Bio-ELECTRA Base (default)	76.97 (2.72)	74.68 (2.32)	75.77 (1.99)
Bio-ELECTRA Base (opt)	77.32 (2.39)	77.98 (1.65)	77.62 (1.33)

Table 5: Connectivity/No-Relation test performance on the extended training set

Relation	Precision	Recall	F_1
Anatomical connectivity	68.93 (2.94)	77.12 (1.37)	72.77 (1.99)
Functional connectivity	82.79 (2.39)	68.00 (2.80)	74.61 (2.35)

Table 6: Anatomical/functional connectivity test performance on the extended training set

analysis was performed on anatomical connectivity errors (18 false positives; 15 false negatives) and functional connectivity errors (5 false positives; 11 false negatives). With both phases, we noticed patterns emerging among the errors, although in most cases, these errors were present across all connectivity types. In other words, there was very little difference between the errors seen in phase 1 vs. the errors seen in phase 2.

The first identified error pattern was mislabeled data due to human error. We noticed 4 instances where the data was mislabeled. The second type of error occurred because a solid line of demarcation between connectivity types was difficult to establish due to ambiguities in our curation guidelines and the overall difficulty of the task. When we began annotating, connectivity between structures could only be defined as anatomical, functional or having no relation. After discussing the differences in our annotations though, it became apparent we needed to add additional connectivity types to clarify the lines of demarcation between each. As a result, we added structural, topological, and general connectivities, and while we did see improved classifier performance after adding these, it appears we weren't entirely successful in our attempts to explicate our connectivity types. In the example,

> "The central amygdaloid nucleus (CeA) and the **bed nucleus of the stria terminalis** (BNST), which is considered to be a component of the "**extended amygdala**", establish important connections with the hypothalamus and other brain areas controlling visceral and sensory information."

BNST and the extended amygdala were incorrectly identified as having anatomical connectivity. This "part of the whole" pattern was seen multiple times in our errors (binary, anatomical and functional), primarily as a false positive. In future works, it might benefit curation efforts to add additional connectivity type(s), e.g. fractional connectivity for this "part of the whole" pattern, in order to further elucidate lines of demarcation. Additionally, because connections between structures are not always obvious, even to human curators (i.e. if A is connected to B and B is connected to C, is A always connected to C?), the lines of demarcation separating connectivity types may always remain somewhat hazy.

We were able to identify a few additional patterns by comparing the syntax and vocabulary of sentences with errors to that of sentences without errors. In general though, sentences with errors tended to have far more complex sentence structure than sentences without. More specifically, error prone sentences generally contained far more prepositional phrases and compound subject and verb phrases. For example, we saw multiple errors within the following sentence:

> "**Chemoreceptors** in the **carotid body** or **aortic body** in the walls of the **internal carotid artery** or the **aorta** sense the level of oxygen or carbon dioxide in the blood and convey these signals via the **glossopharyngeal** and **vagus nerves** to the **nucleus of the tractus solitarius**."

Just from a cursory glance, it becomes obvious that this sentence is complicated; it contains multiple subject and verb phrases clouded by prepositional phrases. Unfortunately, the convoluted nature of the sentence hurts readability for both humans and machines. Because humans also tend to have issues understanding these highly complex sentences, we feel the best solution is for authors to limit the complexity of their sentences to reasonable levels when possible. If a sentence is too complex for a human to understand, it will most likely be too complex for a computer. Additionally, we noticed persistent issues when subjects were not explicit. Unresolved pronouns (e.g. pronouns whose antecedents are unknown) and ambiguous body structures (i.e. fibers) tended to cause errors wherein the model would correctly identify that the sentence contained connectivity but would incorrectly identify which structures are connected. With regards to verb usage, our model seemed to perform better when the connectivity between structures was described in active voice rather than passive. One potential explanation is that sentences using active voice tend to be more clear and simple than sentences using passive voice. Lastly, our model seemed to perform worse the further apart the two connecting structures were within the sentence.

5 Conclusions

In this paper, we introduced a labeled corpus for ANS connectivity relations which is further expanded via active learning. The labeled ANS connectivity relation corpus is used to develop relation extraction systems mostly based on language representation neural models. We have introduced four biomedical domain pretrained ELECTRA (Clark et al., 2020) based discriminative language representation models, two of which have outperformed BioBERT (Lee et al., 2019) on the ANS connectivity relation extraction task. Using active learning guided curation, the labeled corpus is expanded minimizing the curation effort while significantly improving ANS connectivity relation extraction performance.

Based on the observed benefits of the active learning, we are planning to use our Bio-ELECTRA based relation extraction system in a web based tool for ANS connectivity knowledge base construction with active learning based continuous learning ability.

Software and Data Availability

All pretrained Bio-ELECTRA models are available on Zenodo (`https://doi.org/10.5281/zenodo.4699034`). The labeled connectivity corpus and codebase including the connectivity relation annotation tool are available on Github (`https://github.com/SciCrunch/connectivity-re`).

Acknowledgements

This work was conducted under the auspices of the Stimulating Peripheral Activity to Relieve Conditions (SPARC) program (RRID:SCR_017041) supported by the NIH Common fund award numbers 1OT3OD025349 and K-CORE 1OT2OD030541. The content is solely the responsibility of the authors and does not necessarily represent the official views of the National Institutes of Health. We would also like to thank Google TensorFlow Research Cloud (TFRC) program for providing us with free TPUs which allowed us to pretrain our ELECTRA models.

Conflicts of interest

AB, MM, and IBO are co-founders of SciCrunch Inc, a company devoted to improving scholarly communication.

References

M. R. Bennett. 2001. *History of the Synapse*. CRC Press.

J. Bergstra, D. Yamins, and D. D. Cox. 2013. Making a science of model search: Hyperparameter optimization in hundreds of dimensions for vision architectures. In *Proceedings of the 30th International Conference on International Conference on Machine Learning - Volume 28*, ICML'13, page I–115–I–123. JMLR.org.

Àlex Bravo, Janet Piñero, Núria Queralt-Rosinach, Michael Rautschka, and Laura I Furlong. 2015. Extraction of relations between genes and diseases from text and large-scale data analysis: implications for translational research. *BMC bioinformatics*, 16(1):55.

Kevin Clark, Minh-Thang Luong, Quoc V. Le, and Christopher D. Manning. 2020. Electra: Pretraining text encoders as discriminators rather than generators.

Jacob Devlin, Ming-Wei Chang, Kenton Lee, and Kristina Toutanova. 2019. BERT: Pre-training of deep bidirectional transformers for language understanding. In *Proceedings of the 2019 Conference of the North American Chapter of the Association for Computational Linguistics: Human Language Technologies, Volume 1 (Long and Short Papers)*, pages 4171–4186, Minneapolis, Minnesota. Association for Computational Linguistics.

Nanda Kambhatla. 2004. Combining lexical, syntactic, and semantic features with maximum entropy models for information extraction. In *Proceedings of the ACL Interactive Poster and Demonstration Sessions*, pages 178–181, Barcelona, Spain. Association for Computational Linguistics.

N. Kokash and B. de Bono. 2021. Knowledge representation for multi-scale physiology route modeling. *Frontiers in Neuroinformatics*, 15(560050).

Martin Krallinger et al. 2017. Overview of the BioCreative VI chemical-protein interaction track. In *Proceedings of the BioCreative VI Workshop*, pages 141–146, Bethesda, MD.

Jinhyuk Lee, Wonjin Yoon, Sungdong Kim, Donghyeon Kim, Sunkyu Kim, Chan Ho So, and Jaewoo Kang. 2019. BioBERT: a pre-trained biomedical language representation model for biomedical text mining. *Bioinformatics*, 36(4):1234–1240.

Sangrak Lim and Jaewoo Kang. 2018. Chemical-gene relation extraction using recursive neural network. *Database*, 2018. Bay060.

Christopher D. Manning, Mihai Surdeanu, John Bauer, Jenny Finkel, Steven J. Bethard, and David McClosky. 2014. The Stanford CoreNLP natural language processing toolkit. In *Association for Computational Linguistics (ACL) System Demonstrations*, pages 55–60.

P. S. Olofsson and K. J. Tracey. 2017. Bioelectronic medicine: technology targeting molecular mechanisms for therapy. *Journal of internal medicine*, 282(1).

Jeffrey Pennington, Richard Socher, and Christopher Manning. 2014. GloVe: Global vectors for word representation. In *Proceedings of the 2014 Conference on Empirical Methods in Natural Language Processing (EMNLP)*, pages 1532–1543, Doha, Qatar. Association for Computational Linguistics.

Renaud Richardet, Jean-Cédric Chappelier, Martin Telefont, and Sean Hill. 2015. Large-scale extraction of brain connectivity from the neuroscientific literature. *Bioinformatics*, 31(10):1640–1647.

Rico Sennrich, Barry Haddow, and Alexandra Birch. 2016. Neural machine translation of rare words with subword units. In *Proceedings of the 54th Annual Meeting of the Association for Computational Linguistics (Volume 1: Long Papers)*, pages 1715–1725, Berlin, Germany. Association for Computational Linguistics.

S. Standring and H. Gray. 2008. *Gray's anatomy: The anatomical basis of clinical practice.* Churchill Livingstone/Elsevier, Edinburgh.

Yuhao Zhang, Peng Qi, and Christopher D. Manning. 2018. Graph convolution over pruned dependency trees improves relation extraction. In *Proceedings of the 2018 Conference on Empirical Methods in Natural Language Processing*, pages 2205–2215, Brussels, Belgium. Association for Computational Linguistics.

Yuhao Zhang, Victor Zhong, Danqi Chen, Gabor Angeli, and Christopher D. Manning. 2017. Position-aware attention and supervised data improve slot filling. In *Proceedings of the 2017 Conference on Empirical Methods in Natural Language Processing*, pages 35–45, Copenhagen, Denmark. Association for Computational Linguistics.

The Biomaterials Annotator: a system for ontology-based concept annotation of biomaterials text

Javier Corvi[1], Carla V. Fuenteslópez[2], José M. Fernández[1], Josep Lluis Gelpí[1,3], Maria Pau Ginebra[4], Salvador Capella-Gutierrez[1] and Osnat Hakimi[1,5]

[1]Barcelona Supercomputing Center (BSC), Barcelona, Spain

[2]Institute of Biomedical Engineering, Botnar Research Centre, University of Oxford, UK

[3]Dept. of Biochemistry and Molecular Biology, University of Barcelona, Spain

[4]Dept. of Material Science and Engineering, Universitat Politècnica de Catalunya, Spain

[5]Faculty of Medicine and Health Sciences, Universitat Internacional de Catalunya, Spain

javier.corvi@bsc.es

osnat.hakimi@gmail.com

Abstract

Biomaterials are synthetic or natural materials used for constructing artificial organs, fabricating prostheses, or replacing tissues. The last century saw the development of thousands of novel biomaterials and, as a result, an exponential increase in scientific publications in the field. Large-scale analysis of biomaterials and their performance could enable data-driven material selection and implant design. However, such analysis requires identification and organization of concepts, such as materials and structures, from published texts. To facilitate future information extraction and the application of machine-learning techniques, we developed a semantic annotator specifically tailored for the biomaterials literature. The Biomaterials Annotator has been implemented following a modular organization using software containers for the different components and orchestrated using Nextflow as workflow manager. Natural language processing (NLP) components are mainly developed in Java. This set-up has allowed named entity recognition of seventeen classes relevant to the biomaterials domain. Here we detail the development, evaluation and performance of the system, as well as the release of the first collection of annotated biomaterials abstracts. We make both the corpus and system available to the community to promote future efforts in the field and contribute towards its sustainability.

1 Introduction

The last two decades saw the field of biomaterials and tissue engineering grow from a small niche of biomedical research to an extensive domain, covering topics such as functional materials, cell-material interaction, nanomaterials and medical devices. The expanding scientific data generated by the field is primarily available in text documents, such as peer-reviewed research papers, patents and conference abstracts. This ever-growing knowledge is increasingly harder for researchers to efficiently discover, organize and use. For example, systematically reviewing the applications and scaffolds made of a commonly used polymer such as poly-lactic-glycolic-acid (PLGA), requires skimming through >12,000+ abstracts (MEDLINE search on October 2020). Among the different alternatives for the automated processing of available texts, Natural Language Processing (NLP) workflows for information retrieval and indexing offer a much needed automated solution. Such computational workflows facilitate information discovery, information extraction and organization, saving researchers time and minimizing manual tasks.

Central to information retrieval and indexing is the extraction of concepts of interest, also known as Named Entity Recognition (NER). NER is an integral part of NLP workflows as it allows the automated identification of concepts in unstructured text and its assignment to a pre-defined category or class. For example, in the field of biomaterials, categories may include 'Biomaterials' ('PLGA'), 'Structures' (such as 'fibre' or 'sponge') and 'Tissues' (such as 'tendon' or 'bone'). The use of NER to automatically recognize entities enables several downstream applications, including machine translation, information retrieval and indexing as well as automated question-answering mechanisms.

The recognition of concepts in the biomaterials domain is complicated by language and terminology originating from multiple scientific disciplines (chemistry, engineering, biology, medicine). A significant challenge lies in identifying and combining

Proceedings of the Second Workshop on Scholarly Document Processing, pages 36–48
June 10, 2021.

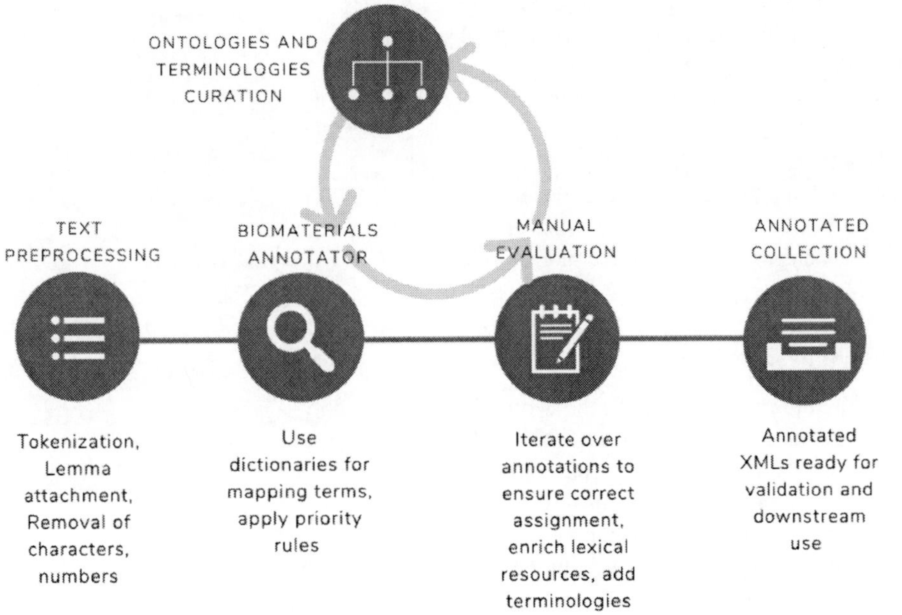

Figure 1: Overview of the workflow used in the development and validation of the Biomaterials Annotator.

lexical and semantic resources across domains, and thus to date there are no automatic biomaterials-specific NER systems to detect relevant entities of interest.

Here, we report the development of the first biomaterials-specific annotation system, designed to recognize named entities from seventeen different categories, reflecting the complexity and diversity of contemporary biomaterials research. When considering approaches for the design of the Biomaterials Annotator, i.e. lexical versus machine learning-based NER, such as CRF or RNN, it was essential to consider the number of desired annotation categories in the system (17) and the absence of an annotated corpora for text mining efforts for the majority of them. Based on these premises, it was concluded that training a model for each category was impractical. Thus, the system relies on manually curated and validated lexical resources.

To cover entities from different domains, multiple nomenclatures, vocabularies, and especially ontologies were identified and combined. To combine these resources into a single instrument, the Devices, Experimental scaffolds and Biomaterials Ontology (DEB) was used providing the logical schema and the definition of key categories (Hakimi et al., 2020).

The resulting open source-system, the Biomaterials Annotator, along with an annotated collection of biomaterials literature, are publicly available for use and further development at `https://github.com/ProjectDebbie/Biomaterials_annotator`.

2 Previous relevant work

Unlike general purpose NLP systems, biomedical domain-specific tools require advanced approaches to detect classes of interest such as diseases and gene names. In this area, there are several well-known and widely used systems and tools, such as Metamap (Aronson, 2001) and Pubtator (Wei et al., 2013), which were developed using different NER methodologies and approaches, e.g. gazetteers and hand-made rule-based NER; machine learning-based NER that includes Hidden Markov Model, Conditional Random Fields (CRF) and recurrent neural network (RNN); and Hybrid NER (Lee et al., 2003; McCallum and Li, 2003; Song et al., 2004; GuoDong and Jian, 2004; Zhao, 2004; Yeh et al., 2005; Campos et al., 2013; Song et al., 2018; Dang et al., 2018; Kaewphan et al., 2018; Cho and Lee, 2019). In the context of this work, generic text mining tools previously developed for the eTRANSAFE project (Pognan et al., 2021) have been adapted and further developed for the biomaterials domain.

Whilst there are a handful of ontologies in the biomaterials domain (such the nanoparticle ontology NPO (Thomas et al., 2011) and the Bone and Cartilage Tissue Engineering Ontology BCTEO (Viti et al., 2014)), to the best of the our knowledge, the DEB ontology (Hakimi et al., 2020) is the only one that is tailored to link and curate concepts for Biomaterials NER. Therefore, it specifically covers different categories related to the biomaterials domain.

3 Methodology overview

To develop the annotation tool, the workflow in Figure 1 was followed. Various corpora of abstracts were used during the development, covering the general biomaterials literature. These corpora included a collection of manually curated abstracts of the biomedical polymer polydioxanone (Fuenteslópez et al 2021, manuscript in preparation, GitHub repository: `https://github.com/ProjectDebbie/polydioxanone_project`) and a previously published biomaterials gold standard collection (Hakimi et al., 2020), comprising a total of 1222 abstracts. Corpora were passed through four steps, each described in detail below. The first step was a text preprocessing component (section 3.1). This was followed by concept recognition (section 3.2), initially using the MeSH controlled vocabulary and the DEB ontology. Then, the annotations were evaluated by two domain experts, errors were flagged up and additional lexical resources were added through keyword searches. Concept recognition, manual evaluation and curation of lexical resources were performed in an iterative manner during the development phase (section 3.3) over 1000 abstracts. Once the development phase was completed, validation by domain experts was performed on 199 independent abstracts which were not used during the development process (section 4.1). The resulting annotated collection of biomaterials abstracts was published as open source.

3.1 Text preprocessing

To prepare the text for concept recognition, several Natural Language Processing (NLP) steps were performed, namely: tokenization, sentence splitting, part-of-speech tagging and morphological analysis (Figure 2.A). We developed the Standard NLP preprocessing component which

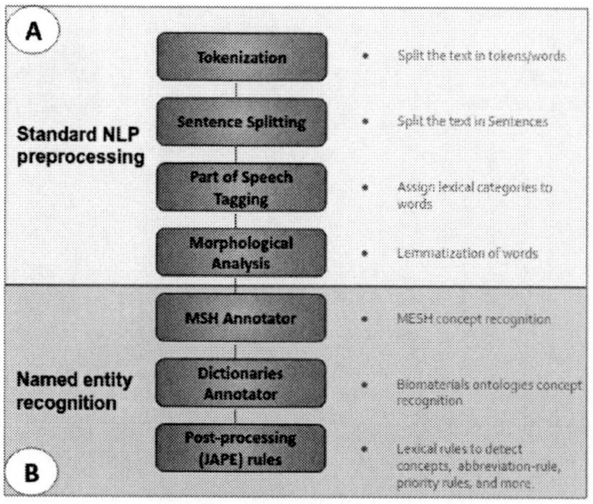

Figure 2: Overview of the components of the Biomaterials Annotator; including the standard preprocessing steps (A) and the biomaterials named entity recognition steps (B).

includes the steps previously outlined. This component is written in JAVA and it uses the Stanford CoreNLP Natural Language Processing open source toolkit. The use of the Stanford CoreNLP API benefits greatly from the provision of a set of stable, robust, high quality linguistic analysis components, which can be easily invoked for common scenarios (Manning et al., 2014). The Standard NLP preprocessing component is available at `https://gitlab.bsc.es/inb/text-mining/generic-tools/nlp-standard-preprocessing`.

3.2 Concept recognition

Here, we developed NER components to detect relevant entities related to the biomaterials domain based on the DEB ontology in conjunction with other open relevant resources, such as the National Cancer Institute Thesaurus (NCIT) and (CHEBI). A comprehensive description of the resources included in this work is described in section 3.3 and Appendix B. Lexical resources were transformed into gazetteers to be used in the NER process (Figure 2.B). Internally, the NER process was divided into three main steps; the MSH Annotator, which annotates relevant categories from the MeSH terminology; the Dictionary Annotator, which annotated predefined categories from the relevant dictionaries; and the Post-processing step in which specific rules were executed. These include entity recognition based on lexical rules and the removal of false positives, among other tasks.

The MSH Annotator is available at `https://github.com/ProjectDebbie/debbie_umls_annotations`; and the Dictionary Annotator and Post-processing rules are available at `https://github.com/ProjectDebbie/DEBBIE_dictionaries_annotations`. These components are instances of the nlp-gate-generic-component (`https://gitlab.bsc.es/inb/text-mining/generic-tools/nlp-gate-generic-component`), a generic component developed in JAVA by our team that uses the General Architecture of Text Engineering (GATE) software (Cunningham et al., 2013) and can be parametrized with gazetteers and specific handmade JAPE (Java Annotation Patterns Engine) rules. Using the Biomaterials Annotator, every recognised entity is labelled with one of the categories (Figure 3.A-B).

The nlp-gate-generic-component was configured to use the GATE Flexible gazetteer, allowing to capture the words present in the text as well as their morphological root value (lemma). This ensures that inflected forms of a word (i.e. plural, singular, -ing forms, tense) can be recognised and analysed as a single item. In addition, the dictionaries used in the Biomaterials Annotator include preferred synonyms, providing the possibility to map terms semantically to a specific primary concept. Thus, the Biomaterials Annotator performs semantic mapping of the annotations by, not only recognizing the category of an entity, but also linking it to the appropriate entry in a well-established resource (Jovanović and Bagheri, 2017). For example, the terms: *"canine"*, *"dogs"* and *"dog"* were all annotated under the 'Species' category; and inside the features of each annotation the preferred term is *"dog"*. This enables the retrieval of all the corresponding terms using the single search term *'dog'*.

To complete the annotation process, the annotator executes JAPE rules for post-processing functions, such as the removal of false positives and the addition of information to each annotation. Added information includes the ontology source, the ontology term id, the lemma and the preferred synonym (Figure 3.C-D). In addition, JAPE rules were run to identify entities using lexical constraints and address the concept recognition of abbreviations. Rule-based entities recognition can use part-of-speech of concepts, as an example; in the case of 'Cell' category, there is a lexical rule defined to detect concepts:
(Token.pos == "JJ" | Token.pos == "NN") Token.root == "cell"
The inclusion of this rule enables the detection of Cell-type concepts that are not present in the dictionaries; e.g. *"neuronal cells"*, *"cancer cell"* and *"osteogenic cells"*. The discovery of such rules is a continuous work; future Biomaterials Annotator versions will improve the lexical rules included to detect relevant concepts.

Another key problem to address is the recognition of abbreviation concepts; to achieve this problem we developed a post-processing rule based on a modified version of Schwartz's algorithm (Schwartz and Hearst, 2003). First, we detect an abbreviation candidate given a text pattern (regex=*"(?:[a-z]*[A-Z][a-z]*)2,"*); subsequently, the Schwartz's algorithm is applied to detect whether there is a definition that matches the abbreviation candidate in the sentence; in such case, if the definition has an entity class assigned to it, we annotate the abbreviation with the same class. As an example, in the following sentence: *"We investigated the potential of human bone marrow derived Mesenchymal stem cells (MSCs) for neuronal differentiation in vitro...."*; the expression *'Mesenchymal stem cells'* is annotated under the 'Cell' category. But the *'MSCs'* abbreviation is not; moreover in the rest of the text the abbreviation is used instead of its long form. The abbreviation-rule detects *'MSCs'* as an abbreviation of *'Mesenchymal stem cells'* and assigns the 'Cell' category to all the *'MSCs'* mentions in the text.

3.3 Terminologies and ontologies curation and manual evaluation

One of the main hurdles to biomaterials concept recognition is the interdisciplinary nature of the domain, with scientific texts containing concepts from various fields such as biology, chemistry, engineering and medicine. A key objective of the Biomaterials Annotator was to identify and combine lexical resources from the different domains in order to cover as many relevant biomaterials concepts as possible. Resources were identified using a manual, bottom-up approach, with cyclic re-iteration, as shown in Figure 1. As a starting point, abstracts were annotated with the automated NER approach described in section 3.2 using the DEB ontology. After each annotation round, manual evaluation was performed by

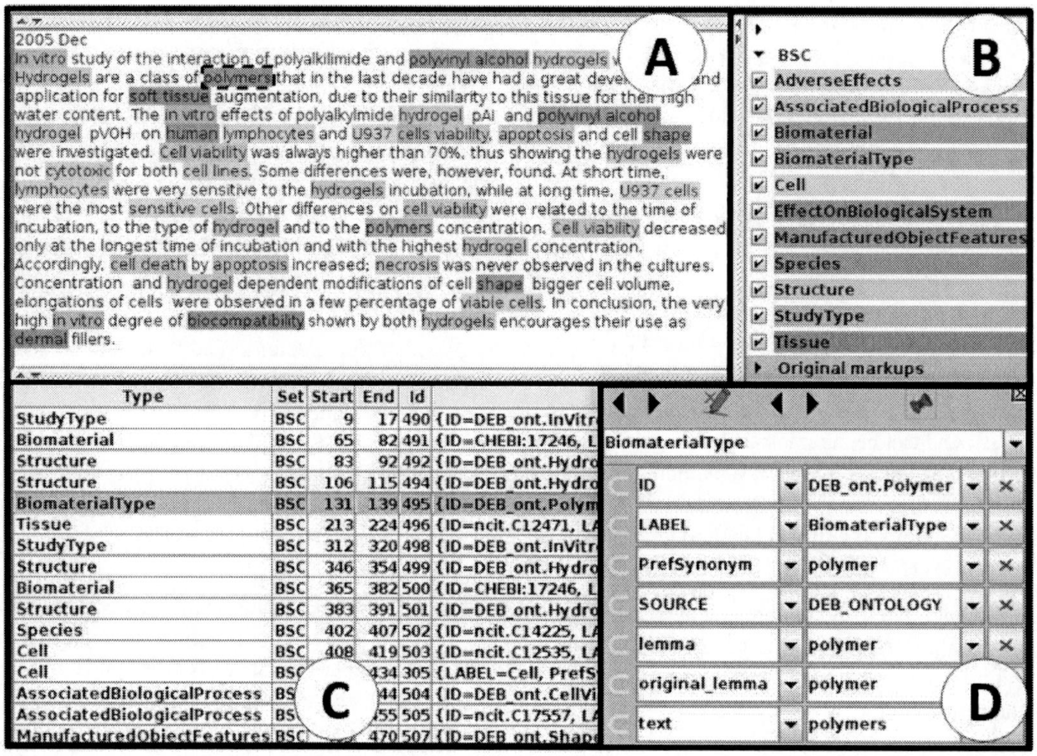

Figure 3: The appearance of an annotated abstract on GATE's user interface. A) Shows the annotated text and in B) colored labels used to tag annotations by their respective category. C) Information regarding each annotation (type, position, features), and in D) a specific example: “polymers”: "BiomaterialType" entity with their corresponding features.

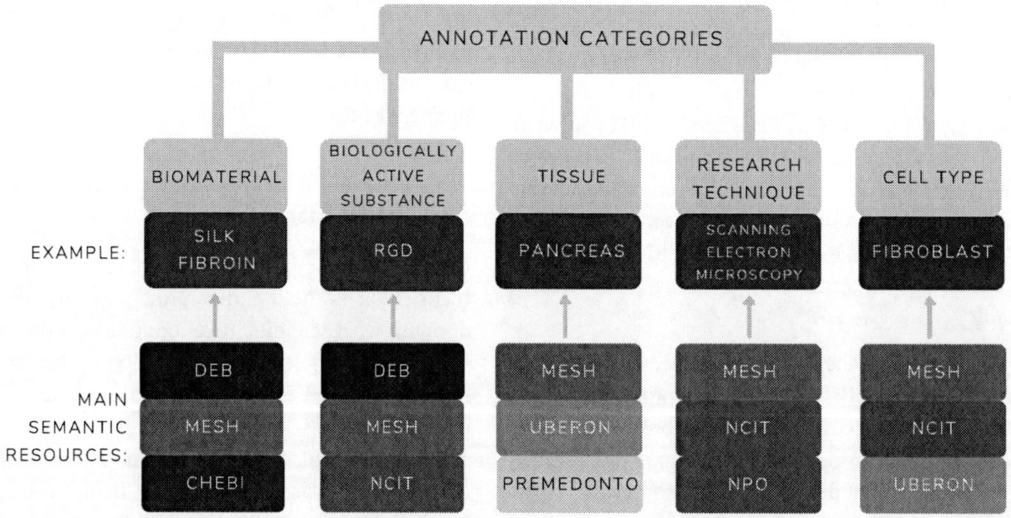

Figure 4: An illustration of part of the annotation schema (showing five out of seventeen categories), which relies on multiple semantic resources for each annotation category. Full details of all categories and resources are in the Appendix A.

two domain experts. The evaluation entailed reviewing samples of 10-20 abstracts in order to flag annotation errors and highlight relevant concepts which were missed by the system. The flagged terms were used for keyword search in the Bioportal (Martínez-Romero et al., 2017) and the UMLS metathesaurus browser (Bodenreider, 2004). Through these searches, specific classes (or 'parent concepts') within relevant ontologies and UMLS 'semantic types' were identified and added to the annotation schema (part of which is shown for illustration in Figure 4). The resources identified belonged to three categories: ontologies, controlled vocabularies and nomenclatures. All the ontologies were open access and downloaded in .owl format from NCBO Bioportal (`http://bioportal.bioontology.org`) (Martínez-Romero et al., 2017). The controlled vocabulary (MeSH) was downloaded for use under license from the UMLS Terminology Services. The GMDN nomenclature was kindly provided in .xml format by the GMDN agency under a license. A summary of all the used resources is in Appendix B. For the resources to be used in the annotation system, relevant classes were imported into a dictionary (gazetteer) containing the following fields: the term, its label (annotation category), the ID and whenever available, a preferred synonym. The extraction of desired classes from the ontologies to dictionary format was done using an implementation of owlready2 (Lamy, 2017) and the code (named owl2dict_light) is available in an open github repository as part of the (`https://github.com/ProjectDebbie/OWL2DICT`). The resulting dictionaries are also available (`https://github.com/ProjectDebbie/DEBBIE_dictionaries_annotations`). These were in turn used by the Dictionary Annotator component for concept recognition as described above in section 3.2.

4 Results

4.1 Expert validation

To measure the efficiency of a text mining system such as the Biomaterials Annotator, it is fundamental to organize and plan a validation stage aimed at indicating the performance of the system. The Biomaterials Annotator was validated through manual verification of the validation set, an independent collection of 199 abstracts. The annotated validation set, resulting from the execution of the Biomaterials Annotator, was manually verified by 9 biomaterials experts. The validation process was performed using the GATE user interface, where annotations made by the system were presented to the biomaterials experts with the possibility of adding missing annotations, removing false annotations and editing annotations. Once the expert had finished the validation of a document, it was saved as a different validated copy.

Two strategies to indicate if two annotations agree or not were considered; a strict approach, in which the annotations agree if they have the same origin and end offset, and a more relaxed or "lenient" approach, where the annotations agree if they overlap at some point. For example, in the partial approach the biomaterials expressions "polyvinyl alcohol" and "polyvinyl" are considered to agree, which does not happen in the strict agreement.

To measure the performance of the NER system, the set validated by the experts was taken as the gold standard and the system's output as the set to be validated. Table 1 shows the recall, precision and F-score, including the strict and lenient approaches, as well as an average between them. The global scores calculated for the system are also presented, obtaining an 0.75 strict F-score, 0.79 lenient F-Score and 0.77 average F-score.

Figure 5 shows the average F-scores calculated for the different categories. Categories with an average F-score above 0.8 are considered categories in which the concepts are satisfactorily covered by the resources used (e.g. Structure, BiomaterialType and Tissue). On the other hand, there are categories with lower scores, and specifically: 'Biomaterial', 'Biologically active substance' and 'Cell'. The categories Biomaterials and Biologically active substance had significantly reduced accuracy because they include many ambiguous concepts. Some materials may act as a biomaterial in one set-up, but can also be measured in terms of cell expression or non-biomaterial use in another set-up (e.g. collagen). In the latter case, the human validator will delete the 'Biomaterial' annotation. Solving this kind of ambiguities will require other strategies, such as specific lexical rules or machine learning approaches. Another factor impeding good quality annotations of Biomaterials is the lack of good quality vocabulary of medical polymers. Polymer and co-polymer naming is notoriously variable, with

Category	Precision - strict	Recall - strict	F-score - strict	Precision - lenient	Recall - lenient	F-score - lenient	Precision - average	Recall - average	F-score - average
Adverse Effects	0.94	0.75	0.82	1	0.8	0.87	0.97	0.77	0.85
Associated Biological Process	0.88	0.68	0.77	0.94	0.73	0.82	0.91	0.71	0.79
Biologically Active Substance	0.58	0.43	0.49	0.7	0.52	0.59	0.64	0.48	0.54
Biomaterial	0.76	0.47	0.57	0.83	0.52	0.63	0.79	0.49	0.6
Biomaterial Type	0.92	0.88	0.9	0.98	0.93	0.95	0.95	0.9	0.92
Cell	0.76	0.59	0.66	0.84	0.65	0.73	0.8	0.62	0.69
Effect On Biological System	0.96	0.69	0.79	1	0.72	0.82	0.98	0.71	0.8
Manufactured Object	0.96	0.86	0.9	0.96	0.86	0.9	0.96	0.86	0.9
Manufactured Object Component	0.91	0.84	0.86	0.91	0.84	0.87	0.91	0.84	0.87
Manufactured Object Features	0.68	0.59	0.62	0.71	0.61	0.65	0.69	0.6	0.64
Material Processing	0.78	0.6	0.67	0.83	0.63	0.71	0.81	0.61	0.69
Medical Application	0.68	0.49	0.57	0.82	0.6	0.69	0.75	0.54	0.63
Research Technique	0.81	0.63	0.71	0.87	0.68	0.76	0.84	0.66	0.73
Species	0.97	0.79	0.87	0.99	0.81	0.89	0.98	0.8	0.88
Structure	0.93	0.77	0.84	0.95	0.79	0.86	0.94	0.78	0.85
Study Type	0.96	0.95	0.96	0.99	0.97	0.98	0.98	0.96	0.97
Tissue	0.8	0.77	0.78	0.85	0.82	0.83	0.82	0.8	0.81
Global	**0.84**	**0.69**	**0.75**	**0.89**	**0.73**	**0.79**	**0.86**	**0.71**	**0.77**

Table 1: The performance of the Biomaterials Annotator in a test set of 199 abstracts validated manually by 9 experts.

some named by their commercial name or abbreviation. To address these inaccuracies, future work will involve expanding relevant ontologies using tools such as Spike (Taub-Tabib et al., 2020), including additional lexical rules, and adding machine learning components.

4.2 Full system implementation and availability

A significant challenge for scientific software applications is providing facilities to share, distribute and run such systems in a simple and convenient way. Furthermore, an important concern is the possibility of replicating the results obtained during the research. In order to accomplish these requirements and follow good practices, we developed the Biomaterials Annotator using Docker as software container technology and Nextflow as the workflow manager. Through the use of Docker, all the subcomponents of the Biomaterials Annotator were individually compartmentalized; hosting their own dependencies and programs that work only inside the isolated container. In addition, the Nextflow workflow manager was used for the automated orchestration and execution of the pipeline. By using this architecture, the entire tool, or any of its individual components, can be easily installed and run in heterogeneous environments. The Biomaterials Annotator is available at `https://github.com/ProjectDebbie/Biomaterials_annotator`.

The Biomaterials Annotator is part of DEBBIE (Database of biomedical materials), a wider system that retrieves abstracts from pubmed, annotates using the Biomaterials Annotator and deposits them in an open access database. DEBBIE is under development and can be accessed at `https://github.com/ProjectDebbie/DEBBIE_pipeline`.

Category	Count
Adverse Effects	657
Associated Biological Process	6231
Biologically Active Substance	7709
Biomaterial	5726
Biomaterial Type	1543
Cell	6839
Effect On Biological System	972
Manufactured Object	5967
Manufactured Object Component	2307
Manufactured Object Features	4200
Material Processing	2728
Medical Application	3868
Research Technique	3701
Species	2089
Structure	4136
Study Type	1806
Tissue	9997
Entities	**70476**
Tokens	**392605**
Sentences	**15979**
Abstracts	**1222**

Table 2: Annotated biomaterials corpus statistics.

4.3 Annotated corpus release

Another key objective was to generate the first annotated corpus with entities related to the biomaterials domain. Such a corpus will facilitate the development and evaluation of text mining models for automated extraction of biomaterials-related data from text.

The biomaterials annotated dataset consists of 1222 biomaterials abstracts describing the evaluation of biomaterials in either a laboratory or a

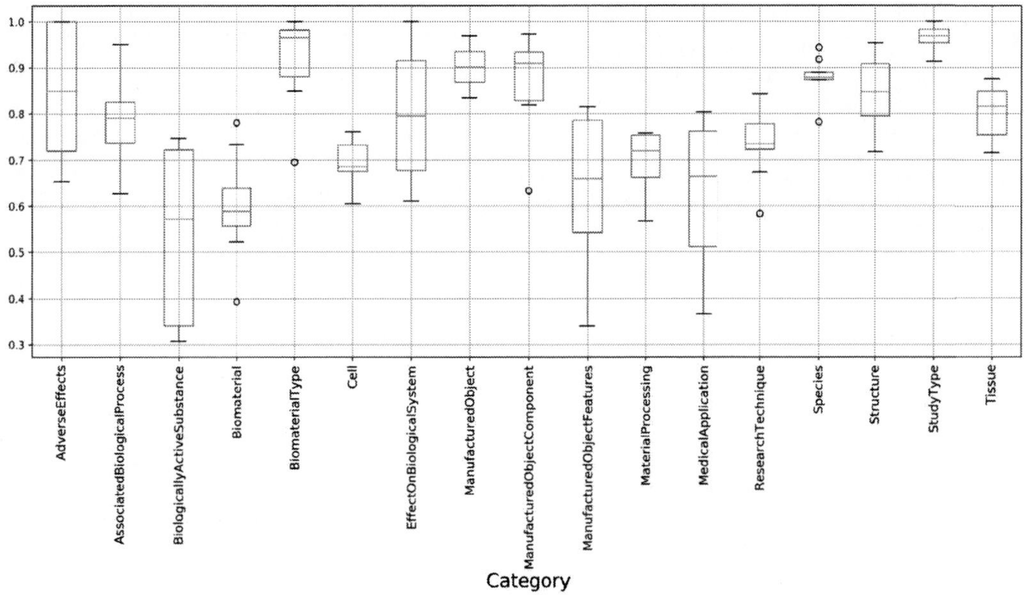

Figure 5: Average F-score of the automated annotations across categories.

clinical setting. Each abstract is individually contained as a separate file under the GATE format. Table 2 shows statistics concerning the number of concepts corresponding to the different categories, as well as the number of total entities, sentences and tokens.

The annotated biomaterials corpus is available and free for use; information to access the corpus can be found at `https://github.com/ProjectDebbie/Biomaterials_annotator`.

5 Conclusions and future directions

In this work we present the Biomaterials Annotator, an ontology-based NER system that identifies 17 domain specific types of concepts and delivers an annotated biomaterials corpus of 1222 MEDLINE articles available for future text mining and machine learning efforts. We have carried out a validation activity to measure the performance of the NER system, with the participation of nine biomaterials experts, obtaining a global average F-score of 0.77.

Future work in the development of the system could involve annotating relations and linking identified concepts to manufactured biomaterials objects. It may also include incorporating additional categories using controlled resources. Improvements to the system will continue in an iterative manner aiming to enhanced performance in key categories such as Biomaterials and Cells. In addition, future versions of the Biomaterials Annotator will be closely related to the DEBBIE system and include additional functionalities and features developed to achieve its main objectives.

The Biomaterials Annotator and the annotated corpus are open source and available to the community to promote future efforts in the field and contribute towards its sustainability.

6 Acknowledgements

This project has received funding from the European Union Horizon 2020 programme under the Marie Skodowska- Curie grant agreement DEBBIE, project number: 751277. O. H. is funded through a Bosch-Aymerich fellowship. J-M.F, S.C-G and J-L.P are partly supported by INB Grant (PT17/0009/0001 - ISCIII-SGEFI / ERDF). M-P. G. acknowledges the ICREA Academia Award from Generalitat de Catalunya. J.C. is partly supported by eTRANSAFE (received funding from the Innovative Medicines Initiative 2 Joint Undertaking under grant agreement No 777365 and support from the European Union's Horizon 2020 research and innovation programme and EFPIA).

References

A. R. Aronson. 2001. Effective mapping of biomedical text to the UMLS Metathesaurus: the MetaMap program. *Proceedings / AMIA ... Annual Symposium. AMIA Symposium*, pages 17–21.

Olivier Bodenreider. 2004. The Unified Medical Language System (UMLS): Integrating biomedical terminology. *Nucleic Acids Research*.

David Campos, Sérgio Matos, and JoséLuís Oliveira. 2013. Current Methodologies for Biomedical Named Entity Recognition. In *Biological Knowledge Discovery Handbook*, pages 839–868. John Wiley Sons, Inc.

Hyejin Cho and Hyunju Lee. 2019. Biomedical named entity recognition using deep neural networks with contextual information. *BMC Bioinformatics*, 20(1):735.

Hamish Cunningham, Valentin Tablan, Angus Roberts, and Kalina Bontcheva. 2013. Getting More Out of Biomedical Documents with GATE's Full Lifecycle Open Source Text Analytics. *PLoS Computational Biology*.

Thanh Hai Dang, Hoang Quynh Le, Trang M. Nguyen, and Sinh T. Vu. 2018. D3NER: Biomedical named entity recognition using CRF-biLSTM improved with fine-tuned embeddings of various linguistic information. *Bioinformatics*, 34(20):3539–3546.

Zhou GuoDong and Su Jian. 2004. Exploring deep knowledge resources in biomedical name recognition. page 96.

Osnat Hakimi, Josep Luis Gelpi, Martin Krallinger, Fabio Curi, Dmitry Repchevsky, and Maria-Pau Ginebra. 2020. The Devices, Experimental Scaffolds, and Biomaterials Ontology (DEB): A Tool for Mapping, Annotation, and Analysis of Biomaterials Data. *Advanced Functional Materials*, 30(16):1909910.

Jelena Jovanović and Ebrahim Bagheri. 2017. Semantic annotation in biomedicine: The current landscape.

Suwisa Kaewphan, Kai Hakala, Niko Miekka, Tapio Salakoski, and Filip Ginter. 2018. Wide-scope biomedical named entity recognition and normalization with CRFs, fuzzy matching and character level modeling. *Database*, 2018(2018):96.

Jean Baptiste Lamy. 2017. Owlready: Ontology-oriented programming in Python with automatic classification and high level constructs for biomedical ontologies. *Artificial Intelligence in Medicine*, 80:11–28.

Ki-Joong Lee, Young-Sook Hwang, and Hae-Chang Rim. 2003. Two-phase biomedical NE recognition based on SVMs.

Christopher Manning, Mihai Surdeanu, John Bauer, Jenny Finkel, Steven Bethard, and David McClosky. 2014. The Stanford CoreNLP Natural Language Processing Toolkit. In *Proceedings of 52nd Annual Meeting of the Association for Computational Linguistics: System Demonstrations*, pages 55–60, Stroudsburg, PA, USA. Association for Computational Linguistics.

Marcos Martínez-Romero, Clement Jonquet, Martin J. O'Connor, John Graybeal, Alejandro Pazos, and Mark A. Musen. 2017. NCBO Ontology Recommender 2.0: An enhanced approach for biomedical ontology recommendation. *Journal of Biomedical Semantics*.

Andrew McCallum and Wei Li. 2003. Early results for named entity recognition with conditional random fields, feature induction and web-enhanced lexicons. In *Proceedings of the Seventh Conference on Natural Language Learning at HLT-NAACL 2003*, pages 188–191.

François Pognan, Thomas Steger-Hartmann, Carlos Díaz, Niklas Blomberg, Frank Bringezu, Katharine Briggs, Giulia Callegaro, Salvador Capella-Gutierrez, Emilio Centeno, Javier Corvi, Philip Drew, William C. Drewe, José M. Fernández, Laura I. Furlong, Emre Guney, Jan A. Kors, Miguel Angel Mayer, Manuel Pastor, Janet Piñero, Juan Manuel Ramírez-Anguita, Francesco Ronzano, Philip Rowell, Josep Saüch-Pitarch, Alfonso Valencia, Bob van de Water, Johan van der Lei, Erik van Mulligen, and Ferran Sanz. 2021. The etransafe project on translational safety assessment through integrative knowledge management: Achievements and perspectives. *Pharmaceuticals*, 14(3).

Ariel S. Schwartz and Marti A. Hearst. 2003. A simple algorithm for identifying abbreviation definitions in biomedical text. *Pacific Symposium on Biocomputing. Pacific Symposium on Biocomputing*.

Hye Jeong Song, Byeong Cheol Jo, Chan Young Park, Jong Dae Kim, and Yu Seop Kim. 2018. Comparison of named entity recognition methodologies in biomedical documents. *BioMedical Engineering Online*, 17(Suppl 2).

Yu Song, Eunju Kim, Gary Geunbae Lee, and Byoungkee Yi. 2004. POSBIOTM-NER in the shared task of BioNLP/NLPBA 2004.

Hillel Taub-Tabib, Micah Shlain, Shoval Sadde, Dan Lahav, Matan Eyal, Yaara Cohen, and Y. Goldberg. 2020. Interactive extractive search over biomedical corpora. *ArXiv*, abs/2006.04148.

Dennis G. Thomas, Rohit V. Pappu, and Nathan A. Baker. 2011. NanoParticle Ontology for cancer nanotechnology research. *Journal of Biomedical Informatics*.

Federica Viti, Silvia Scaglione, Alessandro Orro, and Luciano Milanesi. 2014. Guidelines for managing data and processes in bone and cartilage tissue engineering. *BMC Bioinformatics*, 15(Suppl 1):S14.

Chih Hsuan Wei, Hung Yu Kao, and Zhiyong Lu. 2013. PubTator: a web-based text mining tool for assisting biocuration. *Nucleic acids research*, 41(Web Server issue).

Alexander Yeh, Alexander Morgan, Marc Colosimo, and Lynette Hirschman. 2005. BioCreAtIvE task 1A: Gene mention finding evaluation. *BMC Bioinformatics*, 6(SUPPL.1):1–10.

Shaojun Zhao. 2004. Named entity recognition in biomedical texts using an HMM model. (Grefenstette 1994):84.

A Semantic resources

Table 3: List of semantic resources used by the Biomaterials Annotator

	Semantic Resource Name	Acronym	Scope and relevance	Type
1	Chemical Methods Ontology	CHMO	Methods used to collect chemical experiments data.	Ontology
2	Chemical Entities of Biological Interest	CHEBI	Compounds of biological relevance, macromolecules.	Ontology
3	The Devices, Experimental Scaffolds and Biomaterials Ontology	DEB	Biomaterials-related concepts, materials, structures, material processing.	Ontology
4	EDAM Bioimaging Ontology	EDAM-BIOIMAGING	Imaging and sample preparation techniques.	Ontology
5	Global Medical Device Nomenclature	GMDN	Full names of medical devices.	Nomenclature
6	Interlinking ontology of biological concepts	IOBC	Biological concepts including biological phenomena, diseases, molecular functions, research imaging techniques.	Ontology
7	Medical Subject Headings	MeSH	A hierarchically organized vocabulary produced by the NLM.	Controlled vocabulary
8	National Cancer Institute Thesaurus	NCIT	Vocabulary for clinical care, translational and basic research.	Controlled vocabulary
9	Nanoparticle ontology	NPO	The description, preparation, and characterization of nanomaterials.	Ontology
10	Ontology for Biomedical Investigations	OBI	Biomedical protocols, instruments, data generated, materials, analysis performed.	Ontology
11	Ontology of Nuclear Toxicity	ONTOTOXNUC	Models, chemicals, tools, research techniques and models.	Ontology
12	Precision Medicine Ontology	PREMEDONTO	Human disease terms, genomic, molecular, phenotype, related medical vocabulary.	Ontology
13	Uber Anatomy Ontology	UBERON	An integrated cross-species anatomy ontology	Ontology

B Annotation categories

Table 4: Annotation categories, their respective semantic resources and imported classes

	Annotation category	Definition	Resource and imported classes
1	Biomaterial	A non-drug raw material or substance suitable for inclusion in systems which augment or replace the function of bodily tissues or organs.	DEB: Biomaterials CHEBI: Macromolecule MeSH: Biomedical or Dental Material
2	Biomaterial Types	Classification or nature of biomaterials.	DEB: Biomaterial Type
3	Biologically Active Substance	Substance included in a manufactured object in order to impart a biological activity.	DEB: Biologically Active Substance MeSH: amino acid, peptide, protein Biologically Active Substance Pharmacologic Substance NCIT: Protein Domain
4	Manufactured Object	A physical object created by hand or machine.	DEB: Manufactured Object MeSH: Medical device GMDN: Full nomenclature
5	Manufactured Object Component	A part, region or component referred to as a distinct unit, such as a surface or a layer.	DEB: Manufactured Object Component
6	Medical Application, Disease or condition	Intended use, context, function or outcome of the manufactured object.	DEB: Medical Application MeSH: Disease or Syndrome Therapeutic or Preventive Procedure Anatomical Abnormality
7	Manufactured Object Features	Characteristics inherent or given during processing to a manufactured object or its components.	DEB: Manufactured Object Features MeSH: Chemical Viewed Structurally
8	Structure	The configuration, form or texture associated with a manufactured object or its components.	DEB: Structure
9	Associated Biological Process	A cellular or biological process that the manufactured object is designed to cause or support, or is measured to affect.	DEB: Associated Biological Process MeSH: Organ or Tissue Function Molecular Function Cell Function Biological function NCIT: Cellular Process
10	Material Processing	A planned process which results in physical changes in a specified input material.	DEB: Material Processing CHMO: Material Processing
11	Cell	The reported cell line or primary cell type.	MeSH: Cell NCIT: Cell UBERON: Bone cell, cardiocyte circulating cell connective tissue cell epithelial cell
12	Species	The species and /or breed used in the study.	MeSH: Mammal
13	Tissue	A tissue or an organ mentioned in the study as the target or test system for the biomaterial object or medical device.	MeSH: Tissue, Body Location or organ Body part, organ or organ component UBERON: Tissue PREMEDONTO:Body Part, Organ, Organ System

Table: Continued

	Annotation category	Definition	Resource and imported classes
14	Adverse Effects	An unfavourable or unintended disease, sign, or symptom (including an abnormal laboratory finding) that is temporally associated with the use of a medical device or biomaterial.	DEB: Adverse Effects MeSH: Pathologic Function
15	Research Technique	The reported laboratory technique or instrument used in an experimental study.	MeSH: Laboratory Procedure, Molecular Biology Research Technique DEB: Research Technique NCIT: Research Technique NPO: Instrument IOBC: Microscope OBI: Assay EDAM: Imaging, Sample preparation ONTOTOXNUC: Outil
16	Effect On Biological System	The effect associated with manufactured object in a specific test system (cells, tissue or organism).	DEB: Effect On Biological System
17	Study Type	The study set up, such as in vitro, in vivo, or clinical.	DEB: Study Type

Keyphrase Extraction from Scientific Articles via Extractive Summarization

Chrysovalantis-Giorgos Kontoulis and **Eirini Papagiannopoulou** and **Grigorios Tsoumakas**
School of Informatics, Aristotle University of Thessaloniki, 54124 Thessaloniki, Greece
{ckontoul,epapagia,greg}@csd.auth.gr

Abstract

Automatically extracting keyphrases from scholarly documents leads to a valuable concise representation that humans can understand and machines can process for tasks, such as information retrieval, article clustering and article classification. This paper is concerned with the parts of a scientific article that should be given as input to keyphrase extraction methods. Recent deep learning methods take titles and abstracts as input due to the increased computational complexity in processing long sequences, whereas traditional approaches can also work with full-texts. Titles and abstracts are dense in keyphrases, but often miss important aspects of the articles, while full-texts on the other hand are richer in keyphrases but much noisier. To address this trade-off, we propose the use of extractive summarization models on the full-texts of scholarly documents. Our empirical study on 3 article collections using 3 keyphrase extraction methods shows promising results.

1 Introduction

Automatic keyphrase extraction is the process of identifying representative phrases in a document that summarize its content. Keyphrases are important pieces of information for many applications, including information retrieval (Ji et al., 2019; Boudin et al., 2020), text classification (Meng et al., 2019), text summarization (Song et al., 2019), entity recognition (Du et al., 2018) and event detection (Hossny et al., 2020).

This work focuses on keyphrase extraction from scholarly documents. In particular, we consider an interesting issue in this domain, which concerns the part of a scientific article that should be given as input to keyphrase extraction methods.

Table 1 shows representative supervised and unsupervised keyphrase extraction methods from the most popular categories of the task (deep learning, traditional supervised, graph-based, and statistics-based), along with the parts of academic articles that they consider, among Title+Abstract (TA), Full-text (F) and other Specific Parts (S/P).

Approaches	TA	F	S/P
Deep Learning			
Meng et al. (2017)	✓		
Basaldella et al. (2018)	✓		
Chen et al. (2018)	✓		
Ye and Wang (2018)	✓		
Wang et al. (2018)	✓		
Patel and Caragea (2019)	✓		
Chan et al. (2019)	✓		
Alzaidy et al. (2019)	✓		
Chen et al. (2019)	✓		
Çano and Bojar (2019)	✓		
Zhu et al. (2020)	✓		
Zhou et al. (2020)	✓		
Zahedi et al. (2020)	✓		
Traditional Supervised			
Witten et al. (1999)	✓	✓	
Medelyan et al. (2009)	✓	✓	
Nguyen and Luong (2010)	✓	✓	✓
Caragea et al. (2014)	✓	✓	
Wang and Li (2017)	✓	✓	
Graph-based			
Mihalcea and Tarau (2004)*	✓	✓	
Wan and Xiao (2008)*	✓	✓	
Bougouin et al. (2013)	✓	✓	
Sterckx et al. (2015)	✓	✓	
Boudin (2018)	✓	✓	
Mahata et al. (2018)	✓	✓	
Statistics-based			
TfIdf	✓	✓	
El-Beltagy and Rafea (2009)	✓	✓	
Campos et al. (2020)	✓	✓	

Table 1: Types of textual content, i.e., Title+Abstract (TA), Full-text (F), and Specific Parts (S/P) of the document, used by supervised and unsupervised keyphrase extraction approaches in the training and evaluation process. Approaches with an asterisk (*) are evaluated on TAs and Fs in Hasan and Ng (2010).

We can see that recent deep learning keyphrase extraction and generation methods take titles and abstracts as input, due to the complexity in pro-

Proceedings of the Second Workshop on Scholarly Document Processing, pages 49–55

cessing larger sequences. Traditional supervised learning methods, as well as unsupervised ones can handle full-texts, but this does not necessarily lead to better results compared to using just titles and abstracts. Papagiannopoulou and Tsoumakas (2018) show that graph-based methods achieve better accuracy when titles and abstracts are used, while the strong baseline TfIdf works best with full-text. Florescu and Caragea (2017) and Boudin (2018) show that keyphrases generally occur in positions very close to the beginning of a scholarly document. Nguyen and Luong (2010) show that title and abstracts have the highest density of keyphrases, followed by the conclusions, introduction and related work sections.

It appears that there is a trade-off between using titles and abstracts versus using full-texts of academic papers as input to keyphrase extraction methods. Full-texts provide richer information, including more keyphrases, but at the same time they are much more noisy compared to the titles and abstracts. Motivated from this observation, our scientific question is whether using automated summarization models on the full-text of a scientific article can lead to textual information that is richer than titles and abstracts, yet less noisy than full-texts.

Towards answering this question, we present some first steps employing extractive summarization. Our main goals are to: a) investigate the dynamics of summarization in keyphrase extraction, paving the way for the research community to develop approaches combining techniques from both tasks (e.g., via multi-task learning) and b) provide some guidelines to practitioners of the field suggesting better utilization of the full-texts. Our empirical study provides strong evidence that the full-text extractive summaries manage to capture keyphrases, which in most cases improve the performance of state-of-the-art supervised and unsupervised keyphrase extraction methods (regarding the F_1 score) on three datasets compared to the conventional use of abstracts and full-texts.

2 Our Approach and Alternatives

We are interested in finding out whether we can improve the signal-to-noise ratio of the input given to keyphrase extraction approaches by applying automated summarization on the full-text of scientific articles. As a first step towards investigating this hypothesis, we focus on *extractive summarization* models.

We generate extractive summaries from the corresponding full-texts using the pre-trained distillated RoBERTa model *distilroberta-base-ext-sum* from the TransformerSum[1] library. Distillated RoBERTa is a version of *RoBERTa* (Liu et al., 2019), which is based on DistilBERT (Sanh et al., 2019). It is a lighter, faster and smaller variant of the original RoBERTa, that achieves a time speed-up of 50%, while retaining 95% performance of the original model.

Furthermore, we investigate the utility of alternative input types, such as the first three paragraphs of the document that include the title, the abstract and a part of the document's introduction. We experiment with two different paragraph lengths in words, i.e., 220 and 400.

Our investigation includes the standard input types, i.e., title+abstract and full-text, too. For deep learning methods, we split full-texts into sentences and paragraphs, as they cannot handle their whole length at once due to memory limitations.

Finally, we explore an ensemble approach to keyphrase extraction, which involves the late fusion of two input types: the standard title plus abstract and the title plus the extractive summary. We apply keyphrase extraction methods to these two input types independently and then consider the union of the extracted keyphrases.

Table 2 presents all these approaches along with their abbreviations, which will be used in the rest of our work.

Abbr.	Description
TA	Abstract
ABSE	Abstract in Sentences
F	Full-text
FP	Full-text in Paragraphs
FS	Full-text in Sentences
TS	Extractive Summary
AS	Abstract ∪ Extractive Summary
$3P_{220}$	First 3 Paragraphs - length in words: 220
$3P_{400}$	First 3 Paragraphs - length in words: 400

Table 2: Descriptions of the different approaches along with their abbreviations. The title is part of the input in all cases.

3 Experimental Setup

Our empirical study includes three keyphrase extraction methods: TfIdf, as a baseline method, MultipartiteRank (MR) (Boudin, 2018), as a strong

[1] https://github.com/HHousen/TransformerSum

graph-based method, and Bi-LSTM-CRF (BLC) (Alzaidy et al., 2019), as a strong neural model. Due to the lack of publicly available code for a BLC model tailored to keyphrase extraction, we proceeded to our own implementation, which we make publicly available along with all experiments in this paper[2].

BLC is trained using the train and validation sets from (Meng et al., 2017). Specifically, we trained both models described in (Alzaidy et al., 2019), i.e., the BLC_{TA} on the documents' abstracts and the BLC_{ABSE} on the abstracts' sentences (used only with test datasets that their text is split in sentences and only for the model comparison). Experiments were performed on a Ryzen 5 3600 CPU with 16GB RAM. Training the model on title and abstract takes approximately 24 hours for a total of 5 epochs, while training on title and abstract split in sentences takes about 5 hours to complete.

These keyphrase extraction methods are evaluated on three well-known datasets that contain full-text articles from the computer science domain: SemEval (Kim et al., 2010), NUS (Nguyen and Kan, 2007), and ACM (Krapivin et al., 2008). These datasets contain 244, 211, and 2304 documents, respectively (we merged the train and test sets of the SemEval dataset).

We compute F_1 (F_1@10 for unsupervised methods) according to both the exact (E) and partial (P) (Rousseau and Vazirgiannis, 2015) string match to determine the number of correctly matched phrases with the golden ones for a document. We also apply stemming to the methods' output and the article's golden phrases as a pre-processing step before the evaluation process. We employ the authors' and readers' (in case they are available) keyphrases as a gold evaluation standard for all dataset collections.

Finally, we use a two-sided Wilcoxon signed-rank test to check the statistical significance of the results in terms of the most popular exact match evaluation between the proposed input types and the conventional ones, at a significance level of 0.05. We denote with a "*" the statistical significance with TA and with a "†" the statistical significance with ABSE or F (in cases there is an improvement).

[2]https://github.com/intelligence-csd-auth-gr/keyphrase-extraction-via-summarization

4 Results and Discussion

Table 3 gives the percentage and actual number (in parentheses) of keyphrases that appear inside each textual content type (F, $3P_{400}$, $3P_{220}$, TS, TA) for each of the 3 datasets (SemEval, NUS, ACM). We can see that full-texts contain the highest percentage of keyphrases, as expected. Note that this number is less than 1, as a small percentage of the keyphrases that authors or readers assign to papers do not appear inside the paper's full-text. The percentages of $3P_{400}$ and $3P_{220}$ are high too. Extractive summaries contain less keyphrases than the previous content types, but more than titles+abstracts. This is a positive sign, which combined with low amount of noise, could lead to improved keyphrase extraction results.

	SemEval	NUS	ACM
F	0.857 (3239)	0.878 (2157)	0.738 (9079)
$3P_{400}$	0.668 (2523)	0.696 (1710)	0.665 (8172)
$3P_{220}$	0.582 (2197)	0.624 (1533)	0.616 (7572)
TS	0.518 (1956)	0.576 (1415)	0.573 (7041)
TA	0.439 (1658)	0.514 (1264)	0.530 (6518)
$Total_{KPs}$	3778	2458	12296

Table 3: Percentage of keyphrases, along with actual number of keyphrases inside parentheses, that are found in each textual content type (TA, F, TS, $3P_{220}$, $3P_{400}$) for each of the 3 datasets (SemEval, NUS, ACM). The last row shows the total number of keyphrases per dataset ($Total_{KPs}$).

One disadvantage of extractive summaries, is that they require an additional pre-processing step compared to the rest pre-existing textual content types. The average time to generate the extractive summary per document in the machine used for the experiments is 2.21, 2.13, and 2.34 seconds for the SemEval, NUS, and ACM datasets, respectively. This is not high for offline applications, while for online ones, higher scale hardware and/or more efficient architectures could be employed.

4.1 Bi-LSTM-CRF

Table 4 shows the results of our implementation of the BLC model, along with the ones published in (Alzaidy et al., 2019) for the kp20k test set from (Meng et al., 2017). BLC solves a sequence classification task: for each word, it outputs a binary label indicating whether this word belongs to a keyphrase or not. The evaluation of BLC in (Alzaidy et al., 2019) was based on the F_1-score of this binary sequence classification task that BLC solves, which we also compute for our implementation. We also show the results of our implementation in terms of the exact and partial evaluation approaches.

	S	E	P
Our BLC$_{TA}$	0.381	0.137	0.408
Original BLC$_{TA}$	0.418	-	-
Our BLC$_{ABSE}$	0.288	0.150	0.301
Original BLC$_{ABSE}$	0.356	-	-

Table 4: F_1 based on sequence (S), exact (E) and partial (P) evaluation for the original BLC approach and our implementation.

The results of the two BLC$_{TA}$ implementations are close to each other. The difference could be attributed to two things: a) the pre-processing of the data, which is not described in detail in (Alzaidy et al., 2019), and b) the fact that Alzaidy et al. (2019) might have not included the title in their experiments, as this is not clear in the paper. For BLC$_{ABSE}$, the difference is larger which might be a result of the above and the selected hyper-parameters, which we fine-tuned on BLC$_{TA}$.

Table 5 shows the results of BLC with the standard and proposed input types. Results indicate no significant improvement using extractive summaries compared to titles and abstracts, even though TS includes more keyphrases across all datasets (see Table 3). However, this evaluation may be slightly unfair to TS as input to BLC, since the model used the original documents' abstracts for training. TAs and TSs may have substantial differences in their syntax, structure, etc. Nevertheless, AS performs better than TA, meaning that TS manages to introduce unseen keyphrases to TA, which seems promising for the potential of extractive summarization.

	SemEval		NUS		ACM	
BLC	E	P	E	P	E	P
TA	0.103	0.196	0.129	0.270	0.148	0.325
ABSE	**0.161**	0.325	**0.182**	**0.360**	**0.179**	**0.387**
FP	0.157*	**0.349**	0.144*	0.319	0.082	0.241
FS	0.132*	0.316	0.102	0.226	0.068	0.175
TS	0.097	0.192	0.128	0.265	0.139	0.317
AS	0.118*	0.226	0.145	0.300	0.151*	0.345
3P$_{220}$	0.143*	0.264	0.168*	0.337	0.157*	0.352
3P$_{400}$	0.088	0.187	0.102	0.239	0.138	0.336

Table 5: F_1 based on exact (E) and partial (P) evaluation approach for BLC on 3 different datasets (SemEval, NUS, ACM) using various textual content types as input, i.e., TA, ABSE, FP, FS, TS, AS, 3P$_{220}$, 3P$_{400}$.

In addition, our findings show that we achieve higher F_1-scores when we predict on the abstracts split into sentences rather than the entire abstract. This indicates the inability of the model to retain past information from longer text excerpts, which is a common problem for RNNs. Note that for all the results of the experiments in Table 5, we utilize only the BLC$_{TA}$ model, even on the text excerpts split in sentences as it showed superior performance than the BLC$_{ABSE}$.

Moreover, FP and 3P$_{220}$ seem to be better alternatives to TA, as they constitute richer sources in keyphrases, and the trained BLC$_{TA}$ model can utilize them properly. Finally, the FS approach fails to detect the full-text's keyphrases due to the combination of noise and the disparity of important context, which is a result of the extreme fragmentation of long texts to sentences.

4.2 Unsupervised methods

Tables 6 and 7 show that the unsupervised methods TfIdf and MR certainly benefit from the extractive summaries (TS) as they outperform the conventional approaches (TA, F) (except for the MR method on NUS where the TS's F_1-score is slightly lower than the F's one). 3P$_{200}$ and 3P$_{400}$ approaches, in most cases, do not improve the corresponding methods' accuracy. Although the introductory parts of a document contain many keyphrases, they are also quite noisy due to general descriptions related to the document's topics.

	SemEval		NUS		ACM	
TfIdf	E	P	E	P	E	P
TA	0.143	0.312	0.179	0.377	0129	0.351
F	0.140	0.289	0.193	0.347	0.112	0.285
TS	**0.162***†	0.325	**0.201***	0.388	**0.143***†	**0.361**
AS	0.160*†	0.349	0.190	**0.393**	0.129	0.349
3P$_{220}$	0.134	0.325	0.139	0.317	0.083	0.245
3P$_{400}$	0.160*†	**0.362**	0.171	0.361	0.099	0.277

Table 6: F_1 @ 10 based on exact (E) and partial (P) evaluation approach for TfIdf on 3 different datasets (SemEval, NUS, ACM) using various textual content types as input, i.e., TA, F, TS, AS, 3P$_{220}$, 3P$_{400}$.

5 Conclusions and Future Work

Our work set out to investigate whether using automated summarization, as a pre-processing step, can lead to improved results in the task of keyphrase extraction from scholarly documents. Our empirical study shows that unsupervised approaches improve

	SemEval		NUS		ACM	
MR	E	P	E	P	E	P
TA	0.137	0.344	0.154	0.376	0.116	0.354
F	0.135	0.343	**0.158**	**0.396**	0.100	0.333
TS	0.145	0.358	0.157	0.383	**0.117**†	**0.360**
AS	**0.150***†	**0.367**	**0.158**	0.376	0.110†	0.339
$3P_{220}$	0.128	0.335	0.125	0.309	0.077	0.247
$3P_{400}$	0.134	0.351	0.135	0.324	0.083	0.261

Table 7: F_1@10 based on exact (E) and partial (P) evaluation approach for MR on 3 different datasets (SemEval, NUS, ACM) using various input types, i.e., TA, F, TS, AS, $3P_{220}$, $3P_{400}$.

their accuracy using extractive summaries as input, highlighting the full-text's useful information for the task and showing a positive relationship between the tasks of extractive summarization and keyphrase extraction.

It is worth noting that even though the gains on the exact match F_1-scores seem to be moderate, this does not necessarily reflect the actual performance gain. Considering that exact match scores are generally low due to the strict nature of the method, a moderate increase in performance leads to considerable percentage gain over the initial performance.

As future work, an interesting direction would be to experiment with additional summarization methods, including abstractive ones as well as their combination with extractive ones. In addition, we could experiment with additional recent and state-of-the-art keyphrase extraction methods, including methods building on top of contextual embeddings (Sahrawat et al., 2020).

References

Rabah Alzaidy, Cornelia Caragea, and C. Lee Giles. 2019. Bi-lstm-crf sequence labeling for keyphrase extraction from scholarly documents. In *The World Wide Web Conference, WWW 2019, San Francisco, CA, USA, May 13-17, 2019*, pages 2551–2557. ACM.

Marco Basaldella, Elisa Antolli, Giuseppe Serra, and Carlo Tasso. 2018. Bidirectional LSTM recurrent neural network for keyphrase extraction. In *Digital Libraries and Multimedia Archives - 14th Italian Research Conference on Digital Libraries, IRCDL 2018, Udine, Italy, January 25-26, 2018, Proceedings*, volume 806 of *Communications in Computer and Information Science*, pages 180–187. Springer.

Florian Boudin. 2018. Unsupervised keyphrase extraction with multipartite graphs. In *Proceedings of the 2018 Conference of the North American Chapter of the Association for Computational Linguistics: Human Language Technologies, Volume 2 (Short Papers)*, pages 667–672, New Orleans, Louisiana. Association for Computational Linguistics.

Florian Boudin, Ygor Gallina, and Akiko Aizawa. 2020. Keyphrase generation for scientific document retrieval. In *Proceedings of the 58th Annual Meeting of the Association for Computational Linguistics*, pages 1118–1126, Online. Association for Computational Linguistics.

Adrien Bougouin, Florian Boudin, and Béatrice Daille. 2013. TopicRank: Graph-based topic ranking for keyphrase extraction. In *Proceedings of the Sixth International Joint Conference on Natural Language Processing*, pages 543–551, Nagoya, Japan. Asian Federation of Natural Language Processing.

Ricardo Campos, Vítor Mangaravite, Arian Pasquali, Alípio Jorge, Célia Nunes, and Adam Jatowt. 2020. Yake! keyword extraction from single documents using multiple local features. *Inf. Sci.*, 509:257–289.

Erion Çano and Ondřej Bojar. 2019. Keyphrase generation: A text summarization struggle. In *Proceedings of the 2019 Conference of the North American Chapter of the Association for Computational Linguistics: Human Language Technologies, Volume 1 (Long and Short Papers)*, pages 666–672, Minneapolis, Minnesota. Association for Computational Linguistics.

Cornelia Caragea, Florin Adrian Bulgarov, Andreea Godea, and Sujatha Das Gollapalli. 2014. Citation-enhanced keyphrase extraction from research papers: A supervised approach. In *Proceedings of the 2014 Conference on Empirical Methods in Natural Language Processing (EMNLP)*, pages 1435–1446, Doha, Qatar. Association for Computational Linguistics.

Hou Pong Chan, Wang Chen, Lu Wang, and Irwin King. 2019. Neural keyphrase generation via reinforcement learning with adaptive rewards. In *Proceedings of the 57th Annual Meeting of the Association for Computational Linguistics*, pages 2163–2174, Florence, Italy. Association for Computational Linguistics.

Jun Chen, Xiaoming Zhang, Yu Wu, Zhao Yan, and Zhoujun Li. 2018. Keyphrase generation with correlation constraints. In *Proceedings of the 2018 Conference on Empirical Methods in Natural Language Processing*, pages 4057–4066, Brussels, Belgium. Association for Computational Linguistics.

Wang Chen, Yifan Gao, Jiani Zhang, Irwin King, and Michael R. Lyu. 2019. Title-guided encoding for keyphrase generation. In *The Thirty-Third AAAI Conference on Artificial Intelligence, AAAI 2019, The Thirty-First Innovative Applications of Artificial Intelligence Conference, IAAI 2019, The Ninth AAAI Symposium on Educational Advances in Artificial Intelligence, EAAI 2019, Honolulu, Hawaii, USA,*

January 27 - February 1, 2019, pages 6268–6275. AAAI Press.

Jingcheng Du, Yaoyun Zhang, Jianhong Luo, Yuxi Jia, Qiang Wei, Cui Tao, and Hua Xu. 2018. Extracting psychiatric stressors for suicide from social media using deep learning. *BMC Medical Informatics Decis. Mak.*, 18(S-2):77–87.

Samhaa R. El-Beltagy and Ahmed A. Rafea. 2009. Kp-miner: A keyphrase extraction system for english and arabic documents. *Inf. Syst.*, 34(1):132–144.

Corina Florescu and Cornelia Caragea. 2017. PositionRank: An unsupervised approach to keyphrase extraction from scholarly documents. In *Proceedings of the 55th Annual Meeting of the Association for Computational Linguistics (Volume 1: Long Papers)*, pages 1105–1115, Vancouver, Canada. Association for Computational Linguistics.

Kazi Saidul Hasan and Vincent Ng. 2010. Conundrums in unsupervised keyphrase extraction: Making sense of the state-of-the-art. In *COLING 2010, 23rd International Conference on Computational Linguistics, Posters Volume, 23-27 August 2010, Beijing, China*, pages 365–373. Chinese Information Processing Society of China.

Ahmad Hany Hossny, Lewis Mitchell, Nick Lothian, and Grant Osborne. 2020. Feature selection methods for event detection in twitter: a text mining approach. *Soc. Netw. Anal. Min.*, 10(1):61.

Xiaonan Ji, Han-Wei Shen, Alan Ritter, Raghu Machiraju, and Po-Yin Yen. 2019. Visual exploration of neural document embedding in information retrieval: Semantics and feature selection. *IEEE Trans. Vis. Comput. Graph.*, 25(6):2181–2192.

Su Nam Kim, Olena Medelyan, Min-Yen Kan, and Timothy Baldwin. 2010. SemEval-2010 task 5 : Automatic keyphrase extraction from scientific articles. In *Proceedings of the 5th International Workshop on Semantic Evaluation*, pages 21–26, Uppsala, Sweden. Association for Computational Linguistics.

Mikalai Krapivin, Aliaksandr Autayeu, and Maurizio Marchese. 2008. Large dataset for keyphrases extraction. In *Technical Report DISI-09-055*. Trento, Italy.

Yinhan Liu, Myle Ott, Naman Goyal, Jingfei Du, Mandar Joshi, Danqi Chen, Omer Levy, Mike Lewis, Luke Zettlemoyer, and Veselin Stoyanov. 2019. Roberta: A robustly optimized BERT pretraining approach. *CoRR*, abs/1907.11692.

Debanjan Mahata, John Kuriakose, Rajiv Ratn Shah, and Roger Zimmermann. 2018. Key2vec: Automatic ranked keyphrase extraction from scientific articles using phrase embeddings. In *Proceedings of the 2018 Conference of the North American Chapter of the Association for Computational Linguistics: Human Language Technologies, NAACL-HLT, New Orleans, Louisiana, USA, June 1-6, 2018, Volume 2 (Short Papers)*, pages 634–639. Association for Computational Linguistics.

Olena Medelyan, Eibe Frank, and Ian H. Witten. 2009. Human-competitive tagging using automatic keyphrase extraction. In *Proceedings of the 2009 Conference on Empirical Methods in Natural Language Processing*, pages 1318–1327, Singapore. Association for Computational Linguistics.

Rui Meng, Sanqiang Zhao, Shuguang Han, Daqing He, Peter Brusilovsky, and Yu Chi. 2017. Deep keyphrase generation. In *Proceedings of the 55th Annual Meeting of the Association for Computational Linguistics (Volume 1: Long Papers)*, pages 582–592, Vancouver, Canada. Association for Computational Linguistics.

Yu Meng, Jiaming Shen, Chao Zhang, and Jiawei Han. 2019. Weakly-supervised hierarchical text classification. In *The Thirty-Third AAAI Conference on Artificial Intelligence, AAAI 2019, The Thirty-First Innovative Applications of Artificial Intelligence Conference, IAAI 2019, The Ninth AAAI Symposium on Educational Advances in Artificial Intelligence, EAAI 2019, Honolulu, Hawaii, USA, January 27 - February 1, 2019*, pages 6826–6833. AAAI Press.

Rada Mihalcea and Paul Tarau. 2004. Textrank: Bringing order into text. In *Proceedings of the 2004 Conference on Empirical Methods in Natural Language Processing , EMNLP 2004, A meeting of SIGDAT, a Special Interest Group of the ACL, held in conjunction with ACL 2004, 25-26 July 2004, Barcelona, Spain*, pages 404–411. ACL.

Thuy Dung Nguyen and Min-Yen Kan. 2007. Keyphrase extraction in scientific publications. In *Asian Digital Libraries. Looking Back 10 Years and Forging New Frontiers, 10th International Conference on Asian Digital Libraries, ICADL 2007, Hanoi, Vietnam, December 10-13, 2007, Proceedings*, volume 4822 of *Lecture Notes in Computer Science*, pages 317–326. Springer.

Thuy Dung Nguyen and Minh-Thang Luong. 2010. WINGNUS: Keyphrase extraction utilizing document logical structure. In *Proceedings of the 5th International Workshop on Semantic Evaluation*, pages 166–169, Uppsala, Sweden. Association for Computational Linguistics.

Eirini Papagiannopoulou and Grigorios Tsoumakas. 2018. Local word vectors guiding keyphrase extraction. *Inf. Process. Manag.*, 54(6):888–902.

Krutarth Patel and Cornelia Caragea. 2019. Exploring word embeddings in crf-based keyphrase extraction from research papers. In *Proceedings of the 10th International Conference on Knowledge Capture, K-CAP 2019, Marina Del Rey, CA, USA, November 19-21, 2019*, pages 37–44. ACM.

François Rousseau and Michalis Vazirgiannis. 2015. Main core retention on graph-of-words for single-document keyword extraction. In *Advances in Information Retrieval - 37th European Conference on IR*

Research, ECIR 2015, Vienna, Austria, March 29 - April 2, 2015. Proceedings, volume 9022 of *Lecture Notes in Computer Science*, pages 382–393.

Dhruva Sahrawat, Debanjan Mahata, Haimin Zhang, Mayank Kulkarni, Agniv Sharma, Rakesh Gosangi, Amanda Stent, Yaman Kumar, Rajiv Ratn Shah, and Roger Zimmermann. 2020. Keyphrase extraction as sequence labeling using contextualized embeddings. In *Advances in Information Retrieval - 42nd European Conference on IR Research, ECIR 2020, Lisbon, Portugal, April 14-17, 2020, Proceedings, Part II*, volume 12036 of *Lecture Notes in Computer Science*, pages 328–335. Springer.

Victor Sanh, Lysandre Debut, Julien Chaumond, and Thomas Wolf. 2019. Distilbert, a distilled version of BERT: smaller, faster, cheaper and lighter. *CoRR*, abs/1910.01108.

Shengli Song, Haitao Huang, and Tongxiao Ruan. 2019. Abstractive text summarization using LSTM-CNN based deep learning. *Multim. Tools Appl.*, 78(1):857–875.

Lucas Sterckx, Thomas Demeester, Johannes Deleu, and Chris Develder. 2015. Topical word importance for fast keyphrase extraction. In *Proceedings of the 24th International Conference on World Wide Web Companion, WWW 2015, Florence, Italy, May 18-22, 2015 - Companion Volume*, pages 121–122. ACM.

Xiaojun Wan and Jianguo Xiao. 2008. Single document keyphrase extraction using neighborhood knowledge. In *Proceedings of the Twenty-Third AAAI Conference on Artificial Intelligence, AAAI 2008, Chicago, Illinois, USA, July 13-17, 2008*, pages 855–860. AAAI Press.

Liang Wang and Sujian Li. 2017. PKU_ICL at SemEval-2017 task 10: Keyphrase extraction with model ensemble and external knowledge. In *Proceedings of the 11th International Workshop on Semantic Evaluation (SemEval-2017)*, pages 934–937, Vancouver, Canada. Association for Computational Linguistics.

Yanan Wang, Qi Liu, Chuan Qin, Tong Xu, Yijun Wang, Enhong Chen, and Hui Xiong. 2018. Exploiting topic-based adversarial neural network for cross-domain keyphrase extraction. In *IEEE International Conference on Data Mining, ICDM 2018, Singapore, November 17-20, 2018*, pages 597–606. IEEE Computer Society.

Ian H. Witten, Gordon W. Paynter, Eibe Frank, Carl Gutwin, and Craig G. Nevill-Manning. 1999. KEA: practical automatic keyphrase extraction. In *Proceedings of the Fourth ACM conference on Digital Libraries, August 11-14, 1999, Berkeley, CA, USA*, pages 254–255. ACM.

Hai Ye and Lu Wang. 2018. Semi-supervised learning for neural keyphrase generation. In *Proceedings of the 2018 Conference on Empirical Methods in Natural Language Processing*, pages 4142–4153, Brussels, Belgium. Association for Computational Linguistics.

Amin Ghazi Zahedi, Morteza Zahedi, and Mansoor Fateh. 2020. A deep extraction model for an unseen keyphrase detection. *Soft Comput.*, 24(11):8233–8242.

Tao Zhou, Yuxiang Zhang, and Haoxiang Zhu. 2020. Multi-level memory network with crfs for keyphrase extraction. In *Advances in Knowledge Discovery and Data Mining - 24th Pacific-Asia Conference, PAKDD 2020, Singapore, May 11-14, 2020, Proceedings, Part I*, volume 12084 of *Lecture Notes in Computer Science*, pages 726–738. Springer.

Xun Zhu, Chen Lyu, Donghong Ji, Han Liao, and Fei Li. 2020. Deep neural model with self-training for scientific keyphrase extraction. *Plos one*, 15(5):e0232547.

Argument Mining for Scholarly Document Processing: Taking Stock and Looking Ahead

Khalid Al-Khatib*
Leipzig University, Germany
khalid.alkhatib@uni-leipzig.de

Tirthankar Ghosal*
Charles University, MFF, ÚFAL, CZ
ghosal@ufal.mff.cuni.cz

Yufang Hou
IBM Research, Ireland
yhou@ie.ibm.com

Anita de Waard
Elsevier, USA
a.dewaard@elsevier.com

Dayne Freitag
SRI International, USA
freitag@ai.sri.com

Abstract

Argument mining targets structures in natural language related to interpretation and persuasion. Most scholarly discourse involves interpreting experimental evidence and attempting to persuade other scientists to adopt the same conclusions, which could benefit from argument mining techniques. However, While various argument mining studies have addressed student essays and news articles, those that target scientific discourse are still scarce. This paper surveys existing work in argument mining of scholarly discourse, and provides an overview of current models, data, tasks, and applications. We identify a number of key challenges confronting argument mining in the scientific domain, and suggest some possible solutions and future directions.

1 Introduction

Scientific papers aim to present verifiable evidence for a series of stated claims, anchoring these claims in experiments, data, and references. However, the interpretation of such objective sources of evidence is often ambiguous and subjective. Thus, much of scientific communication is essentially persuasive and uses an argumentative structure to establish the relevance, validity, and novelty of an author's main claims and conclusions (Pelclova and Weilun, 2018). This argumentation takes the form of a dialogue between the author and her readers, in which new knowledge is proposed and an attempt made to persuade the readers to accept and follow particular claims (Fahy, 2008; Hyland, 2014). However, most current research on automatic document processing ignores this argumentative context and treats statements that are persuasive, tentative, or speculative to be factual. This risks overstating the certainty of claims and hypotheses, and bypasses the rhetorical aspect of scientific discourse (see e.g. (Gross and Chesley, 2012)).

Computational argumentation is a recent and growing field of research concerned with the computational analysis and generation of natural language arguments and argumentative discourses. Over the past decade, this area has attracted researchers seeking to tackle different tasks including argument mining, argument quality assessment, and argument generation (for an overview, see e.g. (Stede et al., 2018)). The most studied task is *argument mining*, i.e., the identification of argumentative units, argument components (e.g., conclusion and premise), and structures of text documents. However, despite a wealth of Natural Language Processing (NLP) research on extracting information from scientific literature—including entity extraction (Augenstein et al., 2017; Hou et al., 2019), relation identification (Luan et al., 2018), question answering (Demner-Fushman and Lin, 2007), and summarization (Erera et al., 2019)—relatively few attempts have been made to model argumentative structures in science.

This paper argues for an increased focus of the NLP community on argument mining in scientific documents. To encourage work at the intersection of Scholarly Discourse Processing and Argument Mining, we provide a brief overview of current work in this field, and discusses the most used models, data, methods, and applications. We discuss a number of challenges in mining the argumentative structure of scientific documents and propose some promising future directions.

2 Argumentation in Scientific Discourses

To support future efforts on argument mining of scientific documents, we present a survey of the literature from 2000 to the present, summarized in Table 1 in the Appendix. To attempt to create a somewhat comprehensive overview, we concentrated on papers published by the NLP commu-

*These authors contributed equally

Proceedings of the Second Workshop on Scholarly Document Processing, pages 56–65
June 10, 2021.

nity[2]. To obtain this list, we used Google Scholar (https://scholar.google.com/) to find papers on "Argumentation Mining on Scientific Papers", "Argumentation Mining on Research Papers", and "Argumentative Zoning on Scientific Papers". We also traced the references of some pivotal papers from the proceedings of Argument Mining workshops[3].

For each paper, we identified the *Domain* of study (i.e., a specific scientific domain, full-text or abstracts), the *Objectives* of the work, and the *Methods* used. Furthermore, the papers can be categorized under four areas of study, discussed, in turn, below.

Corpus Creation and New Annotation Schemes A number of studies propose an annotation scheme for mining argumentative discourse in the science domain. Many of these studies follow the well-known argumentation model of Toulmin (Toulmin, 1958). Toulmin's model targets the structure of an argument, modelling it as a *claim* that is supported by *data* following some *warrants*, which can be supported by *backing*. The model has also two optional components: *qualifiers* and *rebuttals*.

Examples of the studies that adopt Toulmin's model are Green (2014) and Lauscher et al. (2018b). The former proposes the scheme of premise (i.e., data and warrant) and conclusion. The latter's scheme includes background claim, own claim, and data, which is used to annotate 40 publications from computer graphics.

Another model that is often used is that of *argumentation schemes* (Walton et al., 2008). Argumentation schemes target the structure of an argument, where the argument is modeled as a set of propositions, i.e., a conclusion and one or more premises, with a pattern that manifests the logical inference between the conclusion and its premise. Walton et al. (2008) proposed around 60 different schemes including 'argument from cause to effect' and 'argument from example', among others. An example of this approach is Green (2015a), where ten schemes were selected and annotated in a corpus of biomedical genetics articles.

Other studies focus on identifying argumentative discourse roles, especially *argumentative zones* (Teufel and Moens, 2002), assigning roles such as 'aim' and 'background' to large text spans (usually paragraphs). Following this approach, several corpora have been constructed for biomedical papers (Guo et al., 2011), as well as papers in chemistry, computational linguistics (Yang and Li, 2018), and agriculture (Teufel, 2014).

Inspired by the theory of Freeman (2011), some studies annotate the argumentative relations between arguments. For instance, Lauscher et al. (2018a) consider the relations of 'support', 'contradicts', and 'same claim'. Kirschner et al. (2015), in another study, consider the relations of 'support', 'attack', 'detail', and 'sequence', which were annotated in 24 articles belong to the domain of educational and developmental.

Automatic Argument Unit Identification Much work in argument mining focuses on identifying *Argumentative Discourse Units* (ADUs). An ADU is a text span that plays a specific role in an argument. In this way, argument unit identification resembles named entity recognition or discourse segment type identification. Green (2017b) extracted argumentative units from biomedical and biological articles using a semantic rule-based approach. Lauscher et al. (2018a) and Lauscher et al. (2018c) proposed several neural multi-task learning models based on Bi-LSTM to identify premises and conclusions. Other papers propose different approaches to identify argumentative zones, including supervised and weakly-supervised approaches with a rich set of linguistics features (e.g., (Guo et al., 2011)). Identifying the 'claim' unit is tackled in several papers such as Achakulvisut et al. (2019), which employs transfer learning on top of a discourse tagging model using a pre-trained BilSTM-CRF to identify claims in biomedical abstracts. Extracting 'evidence' has been tackled in other studies, e.g. Li et al. (2019) extracted evidence in biomedical publications with sentence-level sequential labelling, using BiLSTM-CRF and attention.

Automatic Argument Structure Identification If unit identification resembles entity recognition, *argument structure identification* is akin to relation extraction: this work aims to find typed relationships between ADUs. This more challenging task has been addressed by relatively few studies: Accuosto and Saggion (2020) extend existing discourse parsing models to address this problem on

[2]In this paper, we focus our research on papers related to argument mining for scholarly document processing and exclude less central topics such as citation analysis: we hope that future scholars can help augment our work with these and similar related approaches

[3]See https://2021.argmining.org/ and links from there for a full list of past workshops

computational linguistics abstracts and identify the argumentative discourses of computational linguistics abstracts using lexical and ELMo embeddings, while Song et al. (2019) analyze the argument structure of information science and biomedical science articles through sequential pattern mining.

Applications To date, much of the application-oriented work has focused on scientific article summarization. An exception is Feltrim and Teufel (2004), which had the goal of developing tools for scientific writing for the computer science domain. Other efforts aim to identify claims and evidence, to enable claim-evidence based representations of collections of documents, such as (de Waard et al., 2009), (Groza et al., 2011) and (Li et al., 2021). The goal here is to allow the reader to traverse the reasoning behind a scientific claim to either experimental evidence in the paper itself, or to reasoning for data provided in cited papers. Recently, Yu et al. (2020) study the problem of correlation-to-causation exaggeration in press releases by comparing claims made in news articles and the corresponding scientific papers.

3 Challenges

In this section, we describe a few challenges that are relevant to argument mining in the scientific literature. Although not only specific for the scientific domain, these are hurdles that need to be faced in future research to allow progress to be made.

Argumentation Modeling As described above, various argument models have been proposed (Stede et al., 2018). The selection of which model fits scientific documents is a crucial and challenging research question.

Most previous studies in argument mining of scientific documents utilize either Toulmin's model or argumentation schemes. However, none of these models seems to be a perfect fit: Toulmin's warrants and rebuttals are not common to scholarly argumentation[4], and none of the other argument schemes take the specific nature of scholarly argumentation into account. Adapting these models for use seems to be an essential step to achieve feasible annotation and identification of argument structures in scholarly discourse.

Domain Knowledge Science communication encompasses a variety of domains, topics, and methodologies organized into research communities, each following its own standards regarding the structuring of documents and the arguments they contain (Weinstein, 1990). These community conventions present a barrier to understanding for non-specialists and computational models alike. An important open question, therefore, is whether argument mining techniques must be tailored to individual scientific communities, or whether a unified model can be adapted to address domain-specific features of scientific argumentation.

Scientific Document Type Scientific communication involves a variety of document types, including reviews, methods papers, and experimental reports, among others [5]. Each type concentrates on specific aspects of the discussed topic and usually provides particular types of evidence.

Analogous to the previous point, an open question is whether different document types require different models, or whether they can be accommodated by a single representation and modeling approach tailored to different argument structures.

Enthymemes An enthymeme is the implicit (unstated) premise or conclusion in an argument. Because enthymemes are supposedly known by the target audience (or easily constructed using common knowledge), enthymeme are rarely a problem for humans. However, to the extent that shared knowledge is required which is not found in the document, this offers a challenge for argument mining techniques.

As an example, Green (2014) conducted a manual inspection of several arguments in the biomedical genetics research literature, showing that arguments with enthymemes are common there and suggested explicitly providing domain knowledge for reconstructing enthymemes.

Subjective Interpretation A common dilemma in argument mining is that an argumentative text may have multiple valid interpretations of its structure. This is a concern for scientific documents, where the connection between a claim and its evidence can be implicit, i.e., the author leaves this connection to the readers' interpretations.

In particular, experimental papers can follow a line of reasoning that makes e.g. 'biological sense',

[4]For example, Lauscher et al. (2018b) conducted an expert annotation of the argumentative structures of a small set of scientific publications based on Toulmin's model. The annotation results show that warrant, backing, qualifier, and rebuttal are not observed in the publications.

[5]For more examples of the types, see https://coling2018.org/index.html%3Fp=156.html

i.e. where a specific experiment follows another experiment to address a potential alternate interpretation of the previous experiment. For a non-biologist, this reasoning is unclear, and the reason for these subsequent results are generally never explicitly stated in the text.

Context-Dependence Context plays a key role in text mining in general and argument mining in particular. Scientific documents are at least as complex as other genres where argument plays a role, such as persuasive essays, to fulfil both the persuasive role and the presentation of objectivity which scientific writing demands (Vazquez Orta and Giner, 2009-11). More specifically, selecting the optimal boundaries of argumentative units in scientific documents is known to be challenging (Green, 2014; Stab et al., 2014). For instance, the distance between a claim and its premise may be particularly wide in scientific discourse, e.g., the claim which is stated in one section can be supported by a premise in a different section.

4 Discussion

In summary, we have provided a brief overview of current work and a summary of issues that need to be addressed to make headway in the automated argument mining for scholarly documents. We hope to have shown that more research is needed in this field to enable better representation of the persuasive aspects of scholarly communication. This can help provide a more realistic representation of how scientific knowledge is obtained, and how authors aim to persuade readers of the validity of claims. In particular, seeing scholarly discourse as a pragmatic discourse, i.e. one that humans undertake with interpersonal, as well as informative goals, can allow richer representations of the knowledge structures underlying scientific progress.

As noted, applications of argument mining in scientific discourse, such as summarization and aids to technical writing, to date have been limited to those that are relatively robust to errors, a partial consequence of the immaturity of the field. In particular, these applications are mostly insensitive to the *factual* content of scientific arguments. Meanwhile, a relatively mature community continues to expand models and methods for information extraction in various scientific domains, usually with no attention to the argumentative context in which the target facts are presented. Because a correct understanding and use of facts is critical to scientific understanding and progress, we see an opportunity for many innovative applications at the intersection of fact and argument. For example, models capable of determining the *salience* of individual facts in a domain could provide the basis for highly precise forms of scientific information retrieval, or even offer forms of automation that assist scientists in maximizing the pertinence of their experiments.

To achieve this vision at scale, the argument mining community must grapple with the problem of increasing scientific domain specialization. It is crucial that we separate the invariant features of scientific argumentation from those that vary with field and specialization, and that we investigate effective methods of cross-domain transfer. To this end, the field should seek consensus regarding how scientific argumentation should be formalized and strive for broad-coverage reference corpora annotated under guidelines optimized for high inter-annotator agreement.

To support these efforts, we suggest a greater collaboration between participants of the scholarly document processing and argument mining domains, with a particular focus on creating shared models and shared and accessible corpora to spur on research. We hope such conversations can commence at this workshop and others, to inspire and unite members of both communities with natural language processing and improve sharing and improving the outputs of science and scholarship.

5 Conclusion

This paper endeavors at promoting the collaboration between the communities of scholarly discourse processing and computational argumentation, arguing for the ultimate importance of more extensive research on *argument mining in scientific documents*. Particularly, we address the current contributions on argument mining for scientific documents by surveying about 40 papers that approach different aspects and tasks such as proposing annotation schemes, creating corpora, and identifying argumentative discourse units as well as argumentative relations in scientific documents. Furthermore, we describe various challenges for mining argumentative structures of scientific documents and suggest some strategic directions in order to accomplish remarkable benefits on a wide range of downstream applications such as scientific writing assistance, scientific articles summarization, and quality assessment.

References

Pablo Accuosto and Horacio Saggion. 2019. Transferring knowledge from discourse to arguments: A case study with scientific abstracts. In *Stein B, Wachsmuth H, editors. Proceedings of the 6th Workshop on Argument Mining; 2019 Aug 1; Florence, Italy. Stroudsburg: Association for Computational Linguistics; 2019. p. 41-51.* ACL (Association for Computational Linguistics).

Pablo Accuosto and Horacio Saggion. 2020. Mining arguments in scientific abstracts with discourse-level embeddings. *Data & Knowledge Engineering*, 129:101840.

Titipat Achakulvisut, Chandra Bhagavatula, Daniel Acuna, and Konrad Kording. 2019. Claim extraction in biomedical publications using deep discourse model and transfer learning. *arXiv preprint arXiv:1907.00962*.

Mohammed Alliheedi, Robert E Mercer, and Robin Cohen. 2019. Annotation of rhetorical moves in biochemistry articles. In *Proceedings of the 6th Workshop on Argument Mining*, pages 113–123.

Isabelle Augenstein, Mrinal Das, Sebastian Riedel, Lakshmi Vikraman, and Andrew McCallum. 2017. SemEval 2017 task 10: ScienceIE - extracting keyphrases and relations from scientific publications. In *Proceedings of the 11th International Workshop on Semantic Evaluation (SemEval-2017)*, pages 546–555, Vancouver, Canada. Association for Computational Linguistics.

Danish Contractor, Yufan Guo, and Anna Korhonen. 2012. Using argumentative zones for extractive summarization of scientific articles. In *Proceedings of COLING 2012*, pages 663–678.

Dina Demner-Fushman and Jimmy Lin. 2007. Answering clinical questions with knowledge-based and statistical techniques. *Computational Linguistics*, 33(1):63–103.

Shai Erera, Michal Shmueli-Scheuer, Guy Feigenblat, Ora Peled Nakash, Odellia Boni, Haggai Roitman, Doron Cohen, Bar Weiner, Yosi Mass, Or Rivlin, Guy Lev, Achiya Jerbi, Jonathan Herzig, Yufang Hou, Charles Jochim, Martin Gleize, Francesca Bonin, Francesca Bonin, and David Konopnicki. 2019. A summarization system for scientific documents. In *Proceedings of the 2019 Conference on Empirical Methods in Natural Language Processing and the 9th International Joint Conference on Natural Language Processing (EMNLP-IJCNLP): System Demonstrations*, pages 211–216, Hong Kong, China. Association for Computational Linguistics.

Kathleen Fahy. 2008. Writing for publication: Argument and evidence. *Women and Birth*, 21(3):113–117.

Syeed Ibn Faiz and Robert E Mercer. 2014. Extracting higher order relations from biomedical text. In *Proceedings of the First Workshop on Argumentation Mining*, pages 100–101.

Valéria D Feltrim and Simone Teufel. 2004. Automatic critiquing of novices' scientific writing using argumentative zoning. In *Proc. AAAI spring symposium exploring affect and attitude in text*.

Valéria D Feltrim, Simone Teufel, Maria Graças V das Nunes, and Sandra M Aluísio. 2006. Argumentative zoning applied to critiquing novices' scientific abstracts. In *Computing Attitude and Affect in Text: Theory and Applications*, pages 233–246. Springer.

J. Freeman. 2011. Argument structure: Representation and theory. In *Argumentation Library*.

Heather Graves, Roger Graves, Robert E Mercer, and Mahzereen Akter. 2014. Titles that announce argumentative claims in biomedical research articles. In *Proceedings of the First Workshop on Argumentation Mining*, pages 98–99.

Nancy Green. 2014. Towards creation of a corpus for argumentation mining the biomedical genetics research literature. In *Proceedings of the first workshop on argumentation mining*, pages 11–18.

Nancy Green. 2015a. Identifying argumentation schemes in genetics research articles. In *Proceedings of the 2nd Workshop on Argumentation Mining*, pages 12–21.

Nancy Green. 2017a. Manual identification of arguments with implicit conclusions using semantic rules for argument mining. In *Proceedings of the 4th Workshop on Argument Mining*, pages 73–78.

Nancy Green. 2018a. Proposed method for annotation of scientific arguments in terms of semantic relations and argument schemes. In *Proceedings of the 5th Workshop on Argument Mining*, pages 105–110.

Nancy L Green. 2015b. Annotating evidence-based argumentation in biomedical text. In *2015 IEEE International Conference on Bioinformatics and Biomedicine (BIBM)*, pages 922–929. IEEE.

Nancy L Green. 2017b. Argumentation mining in scientific discourse. In *CMNA@ ICAIL*, pages 7–13.

Nancy L Green. 2018b. Towards mining scientific discourse using argumentation schemes. *Argument & Computation*, 9(2):121–135.

A. Gross and Paula Chesley. 2012. Hedging, stance and voice in medical research articles.

Tudor Groza, Siegfried Handschuh, and Stefan Decker. 2011. Capturing rhetoric and argumentation aspects within scientific publications. In *Journal on data semantics XV*, pages 1–36. Springer.

Yufan Guo, Anna Korhonen, and Thierry Poibeau. 2011. A weakly-supervised approach to argumentative zoning of scientific documents. In *Empirical Methods in Natural language Processing (EMNLP)*.

Yufan Guo, Ilona Silins, Roi Reichart, and Anna Korhonen. 2012. Crab reader: A tool for analysis and visualization of argumentative zones in scientific literature. In *Proceedings of COLING 2012: Demonstration Papers*, pages 183–190.

Yufang Hou, Charles Jochim, Martin Gleize, Francesca Bonin, and Debasis Ganguly. 2019. Identification of tasks, datasets, evaluation metrics, and numeric scores for scientific leaderboards construction. In *Proceedings of the 57th Annual Meeting of the Association for Computational Linguistics*, pages 5203–5213, Florence, Italy. Association for Computational Linguistics.

Hospice Houngbo and Robert E Mercer. 2014. An automated method to build a corpus of rhetorically-classified sentences in biomedical texts. In *Proceedings of the first workshop on argumentation mining*, pages 19–23.

Ken Hyland. 2014. Introductory chapter:dialogue, community and persuasion in research writing. In Luz Gil-Salom and Carmen Soler-Monreal, editors, *Dialogicity in Written Specialised Genres*, Dialogicity in Written Specialised Genres, pages 1–20. John Benjamins.

Christian Kirschner, Judith Eckle-Kohler, and Iryna Gurevych. 2015. Linking the thoughts: Analysis of argumentation structures in scientific publications. In *Proceedings of the 2nd Workshop on Argumentation Mining*, pages 1–11.

Anne Lauscher, Goran Glavaš, and Kai Eckert. 2018a. Arguminsci: A tool for analyzing argumentation and rhetorical aspects in scientific writing. Association for Computational Linguistics.

Anne Lauscher, Goran Glavaš, and Simone Paolo Ponzetto. 2018b. An argument-annotated corpus of scientific publications. In *Proceedings of the 5th Workshop on Argument Mining*, pages 40–46.

Anne Lauscher, Goran Glavaš, Simone Paolo Ponzetto, and Kai Eckert. 2018c. Investigating the role of argumentation in the rhetorical analysis of scientific publications with neural multi-task learning models. In *Proceedings of the 2018 Conference on Empirical Methods in Natural Language Processing*, pages 3326–3338.

Xiangci Li, Gully Burns, and Nanyun Peng. 2019. Scientific discourse tagging for evidence extraction. *arXiv e-prints*, pages arXiv–1909.

Xiangci Li, Gully Burns, and Nanyun Peng. 2021. Scientific discourse tagging for evidence extraction. In *Proceedings of the 16th Conference of the European Chapter of the Association for Computational Linguistics: Main Volume*, pages 2550–2562, Online. Association for Computational Linguistics.

Yi Luan, Luheng He, Mari Ostendorf, and Hannaneh Hajishirzi. 2018. Multi-task identification of entities, relations, and coreference for scientific knowledge graph construction. In *Proceedings of the 2018 Conference on Empirical Methods in Natural Language Processing*, pages 3219–3232, Brussels, Belgium. Association for Computational Linguistics.

Jana Pelclova and Lu Wei-lun. 2018. Persuasion in public discourse: cognitive and functional perspectives. *Discourse approaches to politics, society, and culture*.

José María González Pinto, Serkan Celik, and Wolf-Tilo Balke. 2019. Learning to rank claim-evidence pairs to assist scientific-based argumentation. In *International Conference on Theory and Practice of Digital Libraries*, pages 41–55. Springer.

Ningyuan Song, Hanghang Cheng, Huimin Zhou, and Xiaoguang Wang. 2019. Argument structure mining in scientific articles: a comparative analysis. In *2019 ACM/IEEE Joint Conference on Digital Libraries (JCDL)*, pages 339–340. IEEE.

Christian Stab, Christian Kirschner, Judith Eckle-Kohler, and Iryna Gurevych. 2014. Argumentation mining in persuasive essays and scientific articles from the discourse structure perspective. In *Proceedings of the Workshop on Frontiers and Connections between Argumentation Theory and Natural Language Processing, Forlì-Cesena, Italy, July 21-25, 2014*, volume 1341 of *CEUR Workshop Proceedings*. CEUR-WS.org.

M. Stede, J. Schneider, and G. Hirst. 2018. *Argumentation Mining*. Synthesis Lectures on Human Language Technologies. Morgan & Claypool Publishers.

Manfred Stede, Maite Taboada, and Debopam Das. 2017. Annotation guidelines for rhetorical structure. *Manuscript. University of Potsdam and Simon Fraser University*.

Simone Teufel. 2014. Scientific argumentation detection as limited-domain intention recognition. In *ArgNLP*.

Simone Teufel and Marc Moens. 1999. Discourse-level argumentation in scientific articles: human and automatic annotation. In *Towards Standards and Tools for Discourse Tagging*.

Simone Teufel and Marc Moens. 2002. Summarizing scientific articles: experiments with relevance and rhetorical status. *Computational linguistics*, 28(4):409–445.

Stephen E. Toulmin. 1958. *The Uses of Argument*. Cambridge University Press.

Ignacio Vazquez Orta and Diana Giner. 2009-11. Writing with conviction: the use of boosters in modelling persuasion in academic discourses.

Anita de Waard, S Buckingham Shum, Annamaria Carusi, Jack Park, Matthias Samwald, and Ágnes Sándor. 2009. Hypotheses, evidence and relationships: The hyper approach for representing scientific knowledge claims.

Douglas Walton, Chris Reed, and Fabrizio Macagno. 2008. *Argumentation Schemes*. Cambridge University Press.

Mark Weinstein. 1990. Towards an account of argumentation in science. *Argumentation*, 4(3):269–298.

An Yang and Sujian Li. 2018. SciDTB: Discourse dependency TreeBank for scientific abstracts. In *Proceedings of the 56th Annual Meeting of the Association for Computational Linguistics (Volume 2: Short Papers)*, pages 444–449, Melbourne, Australia. Association for Computational Linguistics.

Antonio Jimeno Yepes, James G Mork, and Alan R Aronson. 2013. Using the argumentative structure of scientific literature to improve information access. In *Proceedings of the 2013 Workshop on Biomedical Natural Language Processing*, pages 102–110.

Bei Yu, Jun Wang, Lu Guo, and Yingya Li. 2020. Measuring correlation-to-causation exaggeration in press releases. In *Proceedings of the 28th International Conference on Computational Linguistics*, pages 4860–4872, Barcelona, Spain (Online). International Committee on Computational Linguistics.

A Appendix

Please follow in the next page.

Table 1: Argumentation Mining Literature on Scientific Discourse

Reference	Domain	Objectives	Methods	Additional Contribution
Manual Argument Analysis				
Green (2015b)	Biomedical articles	Analyzed evidence based arguments in four full-text articles on genetic variants that may cause human health problems and created a preliminary catalog of argumentation schemes		
Green (2017a)	Biomedical articles	Evaluate human analysts' ability to identify the argumentation scheme and premises of an argument having an implicit conclusion		
Green (2018b)	Biomedical research articles	Explores how arguments in a research article occur within a narrative of scientific discovery and how they are related to each other		
Green (2018a)	Biomedical Genetics articles	Provide a method for semantic representation of arguments that can be used in empirical studies of scientific discourse as well as to support applications such as argument mining		
Graves et al. (2014)	Biomedical articles	Analyses article title as a potential source of claims and finds that frequency of verbs in titles of experimental research articles has increased over time		
Corpus Creation and New Annotation Schemes				
Green (2014)	Biomedical Genetics articles	Argument annotation scheme: Premise (Data, Warrant) and Conclusion		Theoretical challenges to create an argument corpora
Green (2015a)	Biomedical Genetics articles	Identification of argumentation schemes with specification of ten semantically distinct argumentation schemes		Annotation guidelines for argumentation corpora
Teufel and Moens (1999)	Chemistry, Computational Linguistics	Detect argument zones in scientific articles	Proposed a scheme and annotated 15 argument zone categories for 39 papers (5,374 sentences)	
Kirschner et al. (2015)	Scientific articles (Educational and Developmental Psychology)	New annotation scheme to identify argumentative relations - support, attack, detail, sequence		Study of the annotation strategy across 24 articles, an annotation tool, a new graph-based inter-annotation measure
Lauscher et al. (2018b)	Computer Graphics scientific publications	Proposed a new argument-annotated dataset of scientific publications	Adapted Toulmin's model for argumentative components: Background Claim, Own Claim, Data. Relation between argumentative components: support, contradicts, same claim	Investigation on link between argumentative nature of scientific publications and rhetorical aspects such as discourse categories or citation contexts.
Alliheedi et al. (2019)	Biochemistry articles	Determine rhetorical moves in the argument structure of biomedical articles	Annotated method sections of 105 text files based on a new annotation scheme for identifying the structured representation of knowledge in a set of sentences describing the experimental procedures	
Guo et al. (2012)	Biomedical papers	Introduce a tool for analysis and visualizing argument structure (based on AZ), and also facilitate expert AZ annotation	Used HTML, JavaScript, PHP, XML for the annotation tool; SVM classifier using features from Guo et al. (2011)	Interactive annotation via active learning; CRAB Reader allows user to define AZ schemes; AZ can be performed on each word, sentence, paragraph, document level
Yang and Li (2018)	Scientific abstracts from ACL Anthology	Construct a domain-specific discourse treebank annotated on scientific articles	798 segmented abstracts were labelled by 5 annotators in 6 months. 506 abstracts were annotated more than twice separately by different annotators. In total, SciDTB contains 798 unique abstracts with 63% labelled more than once and 18,978 discourse relations.	Provide several baselines for scientific discourse dependency tree parsing
Automatic Argument Unit Identification				
Green (2017b)	Biomedical, Biological articles	Argumentation extraction	Semantic rule-based approach	Demonstrates the need for a richer model of inter-argument relationships in biomedical/biological research articles.

Reference	Domain	Objectives	Methods	Additional Contribution
Lauscher et al. (2018a)	Computer Graphics scientific publications	A toolkit for rhetorical analysis of argument component identification, discourse role classification, subjective aspect classification, citation context classification, summary relevance classification	Token-level sequence labelling, sentence-level classification using Bi-lSTM	Command-line tool, RESTful API, web application
Lauscher et al. (2018c)	Computer Graphics scientific publications	Proposed two neural multi-task learning (MTL) models for argumentative analysis based on the tasks in (Lauscher et al., 2018a)	Bi-LSTM based simple MTL model for sentence-level classification, hierarchical MTL for sequence labelling	Adapted Toulmin's model for argumentative components: Background Claim, Own Claim, Data. Relation between argumentative components: support, contradicts, same claim
Teufel (2014)	Chemistry, Computational Linguistics, Agriculture	Views scientific argumentation detection as limited-domain intent recognition	Model based on recognition of 28 rhetorical moves in text	
Guo et al. (2011)	Biomedical abstracts	Investigating a weakly-supervised approach for AZ detection when a limited amount of training data is available	Features like location, word bi-gram, verb, verb cues, PoS, grammatical relations, subj/obj, voice are used with ASVM, ASSVM, TSVM, SSCRF	Conclusion that location of AZs are super important, directions to facilitate easy porting of AZ schemes to new NLP tasks and domains
Li et al. (2019)	Biomedical publications	Automatic evidence extraction using scientific discourse tagging based on classification by de Waard et al. (2009)	sentence-level sequential labelling using BiLSTM-CRF + Attention	Leveraging scientific discourse tagging for evidence fragment detection
Achakulvisut et al. (2019)	Biomedical abstracts	Automated claim extraction	Neural discourse tagging model based on a pre-trained BiISTM+CRF followed by transfer learning and fine tuning on a expert annotated dataset	New dataset of 1,500 expert-annotated biomedical abstracts indicating whether the sentence presents a scientific claim.
Houngbo and Mercer (2014)	Biomedical articles	Identify the components of IMRaD rhetorical structure in biomedical papers	Applied a few heuristics to construct a corpus and used machine learning techniques (Naive Bayes and SVM) to classify sentences into Method,Result or Conclusion	
Pinto et al. (2019)	Biomedical papers	Claim-evidence matching as a learning to rank problem where goal is to find evidence in the form of a paper to make a natural language claim appear credible; to assist scientific argumentation	Rhetoric Classification Task and Claim-Evidence Rank Task using NB-BoW, SVM-BoW, CNN on data from a Wikipedia dump with word2vec trained on PubMed Central UMLS, SemMedDB databases	Augmenting "prestige" meta-data features for a paper improved performance, to rank claim-evidence pairs, a model should account for other semantic properties beyond simple content-matching
Faiz and Mercer (2014)	Biomedical papers	Extraction of connections or "higher order relations" between *biomedical relations* (relationship between biomedical entities). The higher order relation conveys a causal sense, which indicates that the latter relation causes the earlier one.	In the first stage, the authors use a discourse relation parser to extract the explicit discourse relations from text. In the second stage, the authors analyze each extracted explicit discourse relation to determine whether it can produce a higher order relation.	Pilot evaluation on AIMed corpus for protein-protein interaction prediction: identify the full argument extent which contain the biomedical entities
Yepes et al. (2013)	MEDLINE/PubMed abstracts	An evaluation of several learning algorithms to label abstract text with argumentative labels, based on structured abstracts available in MEDLINE/PubMed	Naive Bayes, SVM, Logistic Legression, CRF, AdaBoostM1 as classifiers for the argumentation labels on abstract text. In addition to textual features, the position of the sentence or paragraph from the beginning of the abstract is used	A data set to compare and evaluate GeneRIF indexing approaches. The sentence annotation are: Expression, Function, Isolation, Non-GeneRIF, Other, Reference, and Structure on MEDLINE articles.
		Automatic Argument Structure Identification		
Stab et al. (2014)	Scientific articles	Identification of argumentation structures	Argument unit identification and relation extraction	An evaluation dataset of 20 scientific full-texts annotated with argument relations 'support', 'attack', 'sequence'
Feltrim et al. (2006)	Brazilian PhD Theses	A system to detect argumentative structures in text	The annotation scheme has the following rhetorical categories: Background, Gap, Purpose, Methodology, Results, Conclusion and Outline. A Naive Bayes classifier to identify the argumentative units	Porting of Argumentative Zoning (AZ) from English to Portuguese. A pilot system to demonstrate the effectiveness of AZ for a critiquing tool to support academic writing
Accuosto and Saggion (2020)	Computational linguistics abstracts	Argument unit identification and relation extraction	Explore two transfer learning approaches in which discourse parsing is used as an auxiliary task when training argument mining models	Propose a new annotation schema and use it to augment a corpus of computational linguistics abstracts that had previously been annotated with discourse units and relations
Song et al. (2019)	Information Science and Biomedical articles	Apply sequential pattern mining to analyse the common argument structure in two scientific domains (Information science and biomedical science)		

Reference	Domain	Objectives	Methods	Additional Contribution
		Applications		
Accuosto and Saggion (2019)	Computational Linguistics abstracts	Leverage existing discourse parsing RST annotations (Stede et al., 2017) to identify argumentative components and relations	Transfer learning to improve the performance of argument mining tasks trained with a small corpus of 60 abstracts by leveraging the discourse annotations available in the full SciDTB () corpus; sequence labelling task with dependency-based word embeddings, contextualized ElMo, RST encodings, GloVe	Enrich a subset of SciDTB with additional layer of argumentation, EDUs as minimal span for annotation, pilot task to predict acceptance/rejection using automatically identified argumentative components and relations
Contractor et al. (2012)	Biomedical papers	Leveraging on AZ features for extractive summarization of scientific articles	Used AZ categories as features in final sentence selection process + additionally used verbs, tf-idf, citation and reference occurrences, locative features for classification to generate initial set of candidate sentences. Then performed k-Means cluatering to group similar sentences and select the centroid from each group to generate the summary (redundancy elimination)	Demonstrated the efficacy of weakly-supervised AZ classifier for less training data by Guo et al. (2011) for scientific article summary extraction
Teufel and Moens (2002)	Computational Linguistics papers	Summarize scientific articles by concentrating on the rhetorical status of statements in an article	Developed an algorithm to select content from articles and classify them into rhetorical categories which integrate argumentation structure in scientific papers	
Feltrim and Teufel (2004)	Brazilian PhD Theses in Computer Science	Integrated Argumentative Zoning into an automatic Critiquing Tool for Scientific Writing in Portuguese (SciPo)	Implemented a set of 7 features, derived from the 16 used by (Teufel and Moens, 2002), Naive Bayes as the classifier	Port the feature detection stage of AZ from English to Portuguese, a human annotation experiment to verify the reproducibility of the annotation scheme, intrinsic evaluation of AZ-part of SciPo
Groza et al. (2011)	Production and Manufacturing, Biomedical, Law/Legal	The authors present SALT (Semantically Annotated LATEX), a semantic authoring framework that enables the externalization of the argumentation and rhetoric captured in scientific publication's content.	The annotation framework is a layered organization of three ontologies: the Document Ontology - capturing the linear structure of the publication, the Rhetorical Ontology - modeling the rhetorical and argumentation, and the Annotation Ontology - linking the rhetoric and argumentation to the publication's structure and content.	A LATEX and MS-Word plugin for semantic annotation of scientific publications as per SALT scheme
de Waard et al. (2009)		Proposal to extract knowledge from articles to allow the construction of a system where a specific scientific claim is connected, through trails of meaningful relationships, to experimental evidence. To improve access to collections of scientific papers represented as networks of collection of claims that have a defined epistemic value, with links to experimental evidence and argumentative relationships to other statements and evidence. The authors coin this conceptual approach 'Hypotheses, Evidence and Relationships' (HypER).		
Yu et al. (2020)	PubMed papers and news articles	Study exaggeration in press releases	Developed a new corpus and trained models that can identify causal claims in the main statements in a press release. By comparing the claims made in a press release with the corresponding claims in the original research paper, the authors found that 22% of press releases made exaggerated causal claims from correlational findings in observational studies.	
Li et al. (2021)	Biomedical papers	demonstrate the benefit of leveraging scientific discourse tags for downstream tasks such as claim-extraction and evidence fragment detection	Develop a sentence-level sequence tagging model to label discourse types for each sentence in a paragraph	

Bootstrapping Multilingual Metadata Extraction: A Showcase in Cyrillic

Johan Krause and **Igor Shapiro** and **Tarek Saier** and **Michael Färber**
Institute AIFB, Karlsruhe Institute of Technology (KIT), Karlsruhe, Germany
{johan.krause,igor.shapiro}@student.kit.edu
{tarek.saier,michael.faerber}@kit.edu

Abstract

Applications based on scholarly data are of ever increasing importance. This results in disadvantages for areas where high-quality data and compatible systems are not available, such as non-English publications. To advance the mitigation of this imbalance, we use Cyrillic script publications from the CORE collection to create a high-quality data set for metadata extraction. We utilize our data for training and evaluating sequence labeling models to extract title and author information. Retraining GROBID on our data, we observe significant improvements in terms of precision and recall and achieve even better results with a self developed model. We make our data set covering over 15,000 publications as well as our source code freely available.[1]

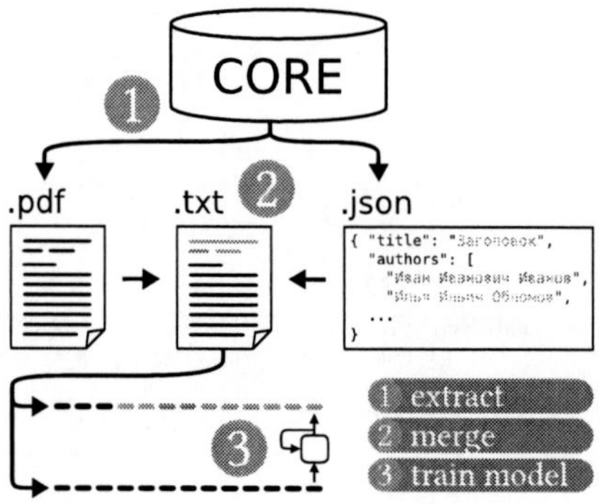

Figure 1: Schematic overview of our approach.

1 Introduction

The use of scholarly data becomes more and more important as the rate of academic publications keeps increasing and automated processing gains relevance, such as scientometric analysis and scholarly recommendation (Sigurdsson, 2020; Zhang et al., 2020). Consequentially, limitations of scholarly data and approaches based thereon directly translate into disadvantages for the affected publications, in terms of, for example, discoverability and impact. One particular limitation of scholarly data nowadays is an underrepresentation of non-English content (Vera-Baceta et al., 2019; Moskaleva and Akoev, 2019). While supporting multiple languages poses challenges, such as language-specific preprocessing requirements (Grave et al., 2018; McCann, 2020), disregarding non-English work is problematic (Amano et al., 2016; Lynch et al., 2021). To further the availability of high-quality scholarly data beyond the anglophone publication record, we showcase the creation and application of a data set for training and evaluating sequence labeling tasks on Cyrillic publications.

Recent years have seen an increased focus on multilinguality in natural language processing approaches, such as language models (Devlin et al., 2019) and data sets (Caswell et al., 2021). Furthermore, there are efforts to specifically support languages that use non-Latin scripts (Roark et al., 2020; Pfeiffer et al., 2021). With regards to Cyrillic script languages, approaches concerned with named entity linking in Web documents (Piskorski et al., 2021), as well as approaches to extracting keywords from scientific texts (Bolshakova et al., 2019) exist. Model training for these types of information extraction tasks is increasingly done using automatically generated high-quality training data. This has, for example, been done for tasks such as text extraction from scholarly PDF files (Bast and Korzen, 2017), identification of publication components such as figures and tables in scanned documents (Ling and Chen, 2020), and the parsing of bibliographic references (Grennan and Beel, 2020; Thai et al., 2020).

We extend this approach to non-English scholarly data. To this end, we use Cyrillic script documents from the CORE data set (Knoth and Zdrahal, 2012) to train and evaluate sequence labeling mod-

[1] See https://github.com/IllDepence/sdp2021.

Proceedings of the Second Workshop on Scholarly Document Processing, pages 66–72
June 10, 2021.

els for identifying publications' metadata (title and authors) in unlabeled text, as illustrated in Figure 1.

Overall, the contributions we make with this paper are as follows.

1. We showcase an effective method for creating high-quality data for training and evaluating metadata extraction sequence labeling models on multilingual scholarly data.

2. We provide a data set for Cyrillic, comprising 15,553 publications spanning three languages and 27 years.

3. We create sequence labeling models that outperform available methods on Cyrillic data.

2 Data Set Creation

2.1 Data Selection

Although many large scholarly data sets exist nowadays, most are restricted in terms of language coverage, language related metadata, or availability of full text documents. The PubMed Central Open Access Subset,[2] for example, only contains Latin script publications,[3] the Semantic Scholar Open Research Corpus (Lo et al., 2020) is restricted to English, and the Microsoft Academic Graph (Sinha et al., 2015; Wang et al., 2019) contains no full texts. Furthermore, none of the aforementioned offers metadata on publications' language. We chose to use the CORE data set[4] (Knoth and Zdrahal, 2012)—a large scholarly data set consisting of PDF documents and metadata aggregated from institutional and subject repositories—for our approach because it is not restricted by language, offers full papers and partly provides language metadata.

To obtain Cyrillic script publications, we first filter the whole collection for the language labels of four Cyrillic script languages, namely Russian, Ukrainian, Bulgarian, and Macedonian, resulting in 23,850 documents. Noticing that a lot of the items we identified are clustered in certain ID ranges of CORE, we extend our data to roughly 48,000 papers by applying language detection on the PDF files of documents adjacent in the set of CORE IDs. After removal of duplicates (papers with different CORE ID but identical PDF) we end up with 27,755 documents.

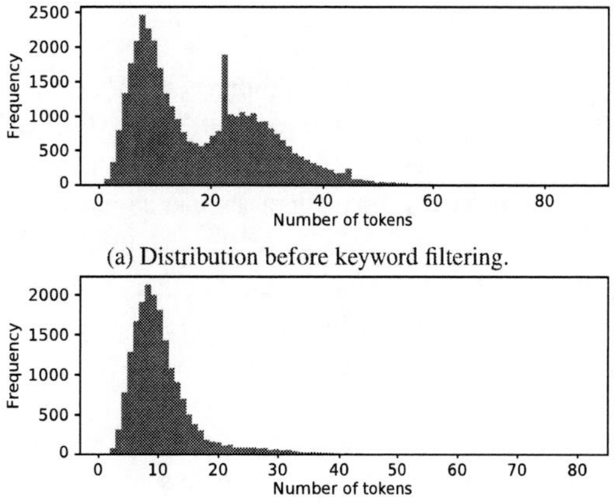

(a) Distribution before keyword filtering.

(b) Distribution after keyword filtering.

Figure 2: Change in document title length due to keyword filtering.

Examination of our data at this point reveals that it contains documents other than scientific papers, such as lecture notes, lecture schedules, and untypically long documents such as whole conference proceedings. To remove these, we perform two filtering steps. First, we remove documents whose title contains either of the words студентів (UKR: "student"), Конспект лекцій (UKR: "lecture schedule"), Програма (RUS: "program", as in study program) and Диплом (RUS: "diploma"), leaving around 22,000 documents and changing the distribution of document title lengths as shown in Figure 2. Second, we drop documents whose length exceeds the 95% quantile (68 pages). Finally, we remove papers for which CORE does not provide basic metadata, and papers for which the plain text was not extractable from the PDF. This leaves us with 15,553 papers, which form the basis for our work and the provided Cyrillic data set.

2.2 Data Preparation

To prevent having to remove large portions of the identified Cyrillic papers due to missing metadata (see previous section), we decide to focus on publications' *title* and list of *authors*. In order to create training data for sequence labeling tasks, we obtain the JSON metadata and PDF of each of the selected publications from CORE. From the PDF, we extract the plain text contained in the first page using *PDFMiner*[5], identify the title and authors from the JSON metadata and insert labels accordingly (see Section 3.2.1 for details).

[2]See `https://www.ncbi.nlm.nih.gov/pmc/tools/openftlist/`.

[3]See `https://www.ncbi.nlm.nih.gov/pmc/about/faq/#q16`.

[4]Specifically, we use the *2018-03-01 full text data set* version of CORE containing 123,988,821 documents.

[5]See `https://github.com/euske/pdfminer`.

2.3 Data Set

The resulting data set comprises *15,553 papers* spanning *27 years* and *three languages*. For each paper, we provide ground truth sequence labeling output in TEI[6] format and as annotated plain text.[7]

A detailed breakdown of languages, obtained using fastText (Joulin et al., 2016, 2017) language detection is shown in Table 1. Languages with less than five occurrences throughout the data set are not included. The distribution of papers by publication year is shown in Figure 3. A breakdown of the topics[8] covered by the data set is shown in Table 2. Analysing the origin of papers, we note that 90% originate from either the "A.N.Beketov KNUME Digital Repository"[9] or the "Zhytomyr State University Library."[10]

Language	#Documents
Ukrainian	11,708
Russian	3,786
Bulgarian	54

Table 1: Distribution of languages.

Topic	#Documents
Engineering	2,472
Economics	2,429
Urban Planning/Infrastructure	2,263
Education	2,255
Other (Linguistics, Zoology, Psychology ...)	6,134

Table 2: Distribution of topics.

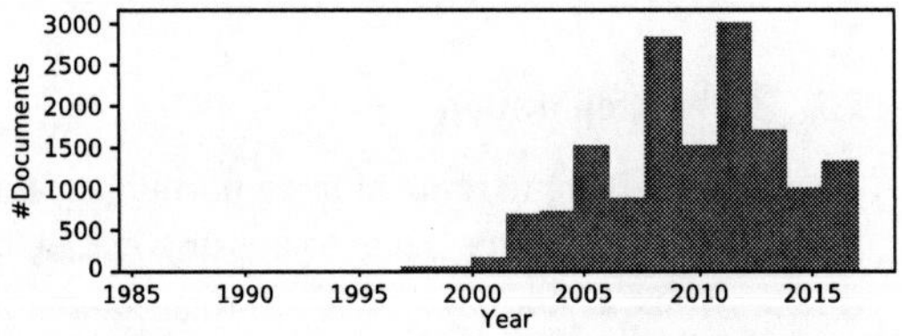

Figure 3: Distribution of publication years of the final data set.

[6]See `https://tei-c.org/`.

[7]See `https://zenodo.org/record/4708696`.

[8]For details of how topics were determined see `https://github.com/IllDepence/sdp2021`.

[9]See `https://eprints.kname.edu.ua/`.

[10]See `http://eprints.zu.edu.ua/`.

3 Application

To assess the utility of our data set, we use it to retrain GROBID (Lopez, 2008–2021), a widely used metadata extraction tool (Nasar et al., 2018), as well as a standalone sequence labeling model, and evaluate their performance against an off-the-shelf version of GROBID.

3.1 GROBID Training

GROBID utilizes several models for different tasks, each of which can be retrained. Our use case—the extraction of title and author information—concerns the *header* model, which is based on conditional random fields (CRF). Retraining the header model from scratch using our data set, we note that for a significant portion of PDFs, GROBID is not able to produce plain text on which the CRF would then be applied. Because of this, we are only able to use 9,620 papers (62% of the data set) for retraining.

3.2 Standalone Sequence Labeling Model

3.2.1 Data Preprocessing

For our standalone model we decide to label the textual content of the first page of each paper using four tags, namely *Author*, *B-title* (beginning of the title, i.e. the first title token), *I-title* (tokens inside the title) and *Misc* (everything else).

To this end, we extract the plain text from the PDF using *PDFMiner*, tokenize the text according to whitespace, and replace newlines with a `NEWLINE` token. The publication's title is then identified using the JSON metadata and each token labeled accordingly. `NEWLINE` tokens within a sequence of title tokens are preserved.

For the matching of authors, we split the author strings from the metadata into surname and given names. We first locate the surnames in the token sequence, and label the occurrence closest to the title as *Author*. Because given names can appear written-out as well as abbreviated in the form of initials, we heuristically identify the latter as follows. Given an identified surname, we search within a window of eight tokens before and after the surname[11] for uppercase characters followed by a period. Matching initials are then labeled accordingly. Written-out given names are normally

[11]Eight being given in the edge case where a surname is followed by a separating comma, two initials and a newline somewhere in-between. E.g.: "`<surname>,␣<initial>.␣<newline><initial>.`".

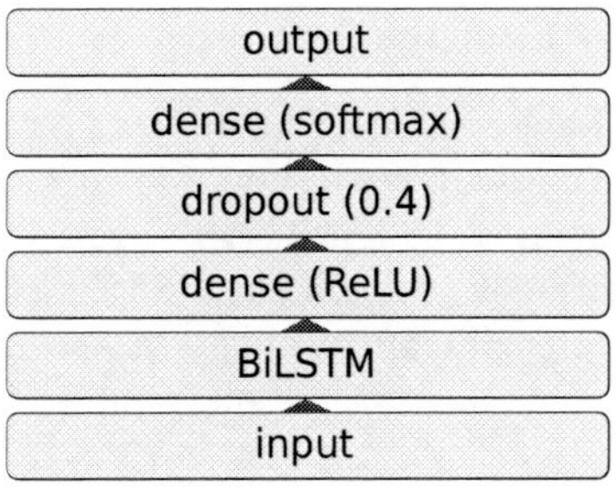

Figure 4: Network architecture.

matched just like surnames.

From the tokens we derive vectorized embeddings using *fastText*. Following Chiu and Nichols (2016) we use representations with 100 dimensions. In addition to the embeddings, we add five additional feature dimensions to the word vectors as done by Huang et al. (2015). These contain information about whether a token is uppercase, capitalized, contains punctuation, contains a line break or is styled like an author initial (uppercase and ending in a period character).

3.2.2 Model Training

For our standalone model we choose to use a BiLSTM network, as is commonly done for sequence labeling tasks (Huang et al., 2015).

We trim input sequences to the first 1,000 tokens, resulting in an input space of $1,000 \times 105$ dimensions per document, as each token is represented by a 100-dimensional vector with a set of five added features per token. The output space is of equal length and contains a one-hot-encoded representation of one of the four labels *Author*, *B-title*, *I-title* and *Misc*.

Because title and authors only make up a small fraction of the words at the beginning of a publication, tokens with the *Misc* label make up a majority of our data. To prevent the trivial prediction of the *Misc* label playing too much of a role in training, each input word token is given an individual, heuristically determined weight value of either 1 for *Misc.* or 5 for *Author* and **-title* labels.

The final network, as shown in Figure 4, consists of a BiLSTM layer followed by a ReLU activated dense layer, a dropout layer and a final dense layer with softmax activation. For training, categorical cross entropy serves as the model's loss function and recall is employed as the target metric. Furthermore, the Adam optimizer (Kingma and Ba, 2017) with a learning rate of 0.0001 is used.

Model	Precision	Recall	F1
GROBID vanilla	0.06	0.06	0.06
GROBID retrained	**0.85**	0.81	0.83
BiLSTM	0.84	**0.96**	**0.90**

Table 3: Overall evaluation scores.

Model$_{label}$	Precision	Recall	F1
GROBID retr.$_{title}$	**0.90**	0.90	0.90
BiLSTM$_{title}$	0.88	**0.96**	**0.92**
GROBID retr.$_{author}$	**0.81**	0.74	0.77
BiLSTM$_{author}$	0.80	**0.95**	**0.87**
GROBID retr.$_{misc}$	-	-	-
BiLSTM$_{misc}$	0.99	0.99	0.99

Table 4: Evaluation scores per label.

4 Evaluation

To assess the performance of both the off-the-shelf and retrained GROBID as well as the standalone BiLSTM model, we perform five-fold cross-validations and measure the overall precision, recall, and F1 score.[12]

Because GROBID retraining is only possible on roughly two thirds of our data (see Section 3.1) we evaluate the off-the-shelf ("vanilla") GROBID model on the same subset in order to maximize comparability of the evaluation results.

Regarding the comparability to our standalone BiLSTM model, a key difference lies in the fact that we use four labels (*Author*, *B-title*, *I-title* and *Misc*) instead of GROBID's two (*Author* and *Title*). To adjust for this difference, we decide to disregard the *Misc* label and combine the two types of **-title* label by a weighted average.

The overall evaluation scores resulting from this are shown in Table 3. We note that off-the-shelf GROBID is only able to determine a small fraction of title and author tokens correctly. Retraining GROBID using our training data, however, significantly improves the performance from an F1 score of 0.06 to 0.83, on par with GROBID's performance on English documents (Nasar et al., 2018). Our standalone BiLSTM model outperforms the retrained GROBID due to significantly higher recall with a F1 score of 0.90. Looking at the evaluation results per label for the retrained GROBID and standalone BiLSTM model, as shown in Table 4, we can see that the largest performance difference

[12]Since off-the-shelf GROBID does not have to be retrained, it is simply evaluated on 100% of the data instead of five folds.

Language	Precision	Recall	F1
Ukrainian	0.83	0.95	0.89
Russian	**0.88**	**0.97**	**0.92**
Bulgarian	0.51	0.70	0.58

Table 5: BiLSTM evaluation scores per language.

is given in the recall of the author label (measuring 0.74 and 0.95 respectively).

For further assessment of the BiLSTM model's performance, we evaluate its predictions per language as shown in Table 5. We can observe that the model achieves higher scores for Russian documents compared to the results for Ukrainian. This is especially notable since the amount of Ukrainian documents in the data set is significantly higher than that of Russian papers. One possible explanation of this performance gap could be a more consistent structure among the Russian documents. Performance on the 50 Bulgarian documents within the data set is comparatively low. While this could likely be due to the vast majority of the respective training data being in a different language, the informativeness of the score itself has to be considered keeping in mind that there are merely 50 documents for testing available.

5 Conclusion

Inspired by recent approaches creating high-quality data for training and evaluating information extraction tasks involving scholarly publications, we utilize this approach to tackle the problem of underrepresented non-English scholarly (training) data. To this end, we use Cyrillic script documents found in the CORE data set to train sequence labeling models for identifying publications' metadata.

We create a data set of *15,553 papers* spanning *27 years* and *three languages*. Using this data set, we retrain GROBID and thereby greatly improve its performance. Furthermore, we train and evaluate a separate sequence labeling model that is less constrained by PDF parsing restrictions (see Section 3.1), showing even better overall performance results than the retrained GROBID model.

By showcasing the use of freely available non-English publications to improve the availability of high-quality data and models covering areas beyond the anglophone publication record, we hope to inspire similar efforts for other languages. For our own approach, we plan to extend it to the extraction of bibliographic references in the future.

Author Contributions

Johan Krause and Igor Shapiro: Data curation, Formal Analysis, Investigation, Methodology, Software, Writing – original draft. Tarek Saier: Conceptualization, Data curation, Supervision, Writing – original draft, Writing – review & editing. Michael Färber: Supervision, Writing – review & editing.

References

Tatsuya Amano, Juan P. González-Varo, and William J. Sutherland. 2016. Languages are still a major barrier to global science. *PLOS Biology*, 14(12):1–8.

Hannah Bast and Claudius Korzen. 2017. A Benchmark and Evaluation for Text Extraction from PDF. In *2017 ACM/IEEE Joint Conference on Digital Libraries (JCDL)*, pages 1–10.

Elena Bolshakova, Natalia Efremova, and Kirill Ivanov. 2019. Terminological information extraction from russian scientific texts: Methods and applications. In *Proceedings of Third Workshop "Computational linguistics and language science"*, volume 4, pages 95–106.

Isaac Caswell, Julia Kreutzer, Lisa Wang, Ahsan Wahab, Daan van Esch, Nasanbayar Ulzii-Orshikh, Allahsera Auguste Tapo, Nishant Subramani, Artem Sokolov, Claytone Sikasote, Monang Setyawan, Supheakmungkol Sarin, Sokhar Samb, Benoît Sagot, Clara E. Rivera, Annette Rios, Isabel Papadimitriou, Salomey Osei, Pedro Javier Ortiz Suárez, Iroro Fred Ọ̀nọ̀mẹ̀ Orife, Kelechi Ogueji, Rubungo Andre Niyongabo, Toan Nguyen, Mathias Müller, André Müller, Shamsuddeen Hassan Muhammad, Nanda Muhammad, Ayanda Mnyakeni, Jamshidbek Mirzakhalov, Tapiwanashe Matangira, Colin Leong, Nze Lawson, Sneha Kudugunta, Yacine Jernite, Mathias Jenny, Orhan Firat, Bonaventure F. P. Dossou, Sakhile Dlamini, Nisansa de Silva, Sakine Çabuk Ballı, Stella Biderman, Alessia Battisti, Ahmed Baruwa, Ankur Bapna, Pallavi Baljekar, Israel Abebe Azime, Ayodele Awokoya, Duygu Ataman, Orevaoghene Ahia, Oghenefego Ahia, Sweta Agrawal, and Mofetoluwa Adeyemi. 2021. Quality at a Glance: An Audit of Web-Crawled Multilingual Datasets. In *Proceedings of the AfricaNLP Workshop*.

Jason P.C. Chiu and Eric Nichols. 2016. Named Entity Recognition with Bidirectional LSTM-CNNs. *Transactions of the Association for Computational Linguistics*, 4:357–370.

Jacob Devlin, Ming-Wei Chang, Kenton Lee, and Kristina Toutanova. 2019. BERT: Pre-training of Deep Bidirectional Transformers for Language Understanding. In *Proceedings of the 2019 Conference of the North American Chapter of the Association for Computational Linguistics*, pages 4171–4186, Minneapolis, Minnesota. Association for Computational Linguistics.

Edouard Grave, Piotr Bojanowski, Prakhar Gupta, Armand Joulin, and Tomas Mikolov. 2018. Learning Word Vectors for 157 Languages.

Mark Grennan and Joeran Beel. 2020. Synthetic vs. Real Reference Strings for Citation Parsing, and the Importance of Re-training and Out-Of-Sample Data for Meaningful Evaluations: Experiments with GROBID, GIANT and Cora. In *Proceedings of the 8th International Workshop on Mining Scientific Publications*.

Zhiheng Huang, Wei Xu, and Kai Yu. 2015. Bidirectional LSTM-CRF Models for Sequence Tagging. *Baidu research*.

Armand Joulin, Edouard Grave, Piotr Bojanowski, Matthijs Douze, Hérve Jégou, and Tomas Mikolov. 2016. Fasttext.zip: Compressing text classification models.

Armand Joulin, Edouard Grave, Piotr Bojanowski, and Tomas Mikolov. 2017. Bag of tricks for efficient text classification. In *Proceedings of the 15th Conference of the European Chapter of the Association for Computational Linguistics: Volume 2, Short Papers*, pages 427–431, Valencia, Spain. Association for Computational Linguistics.

Diederik P. Kingma and Jimmy Ba. 2017. Adam: A Method for Stochastic Optimization.

Petr Knoth and Zdenek Zdrahal. 2012. CORE: three access levels to underpin open access. *D-Lib Magazine*, 18(11/12).

Meng Ling and Jian Chen. 2020. DeepPaperComposer: A Simple Solution for Training Data Preparation for Parsing Research Papers. In *Proceedings of the First Workshop on Scholarly Document Processing*, pages 91–96. Association for Computational Linguistics.

Kyle Lo, Lucy Lu Wang, Mark Neumann, Rodney Kinney, and Daniel Weld. 2020. S2ORC: The Semantic Scholar Open Research Corpus. In *Proceedings of the 58th Annual Meeting of the Association for Computational Linguistics*, pages 4969–4983. Association for Computational Linguistics.

Patrice Lopez. 2008–2021. GROBID. `https://github.com/kermitt2/grobid`.

Abigail J. Lynch, Álvaro Fernández-Llamazares, Ignacio Palomo, Pedro Jaureguiberry, Tatsuya Amano, Zeenatul Basher, Michelle Lim, Tuyeni Heita Mwampamba, Aibek Samakov, and Odirilwe Selomane. 2021. Culturally diverse expert teams have yet to bring comprehensive linguistic diversity to intergovernmental ecosystem assessments. *One Earth*, 4(2):269–278.

Paul McCann. 2020. fugashi, a Tool for Tokenizing Japanese in Python. In *Proceedings of Second Workshop for NLP Open Source Software (NLP-OSS)*, pages 44–51, Online. Association for Computational Linguistics.

Olga Moskaleva and Mark Akoev. 2019. Non-English language publications in Citation Indexes - quantity and quality. In *Proceedings 17th International Conference on Scientometrics & Informetrics*, volume 1, pages 35–46, Italy. Edizioni Efesto.

Zara Nasar, Syed Waqar Jaffry, and Muhammad Kamran Malik. 2018. Information extraction from scientific articles: a survey. *Scientometrics*, 117(3):1931–1990.

Jonas Pfeiffer, Ivan Vulić, Iryna Gurevych, and Sebastian Ruder. 2021. UNKs Everywhere: Adapting Multilingual Language Models to New Scripts.

Jakub Piskorski, Bogdan Babych, Zara Kancheva, Olga Kanishcheva, Maria Lebedeva, Michał Marcińczuk, Preslav Nakov, Petya Osenova, Lidia Pivovarova, Senja Pollak, Pavel Přibáň, Ivaylo Radev, Marko Robnik-Sikonja, Vasyl Starko, Josef Steinberger, and Roman Yangarber. 2021. Slav-NER: the 3rd Cross-lingual Challenge on Recognition, Normalization, Classification, and Linking of Named Entities across Slavic Languages. In *Proceedings of the 8th Workshop on Balto-Slavic Natural Language Processing*, pages 122–133, Kiyv, Ukraine. Association for Computational Linguistics.

Brian Roark, Lawrence Wolf-Sonkin, Christo Kirov, Sabrina J. Mielke, Cibu Johny, Isin Demirsahin, and Keith Hall. 2020. Processing South Asian Languages Written in the Latin Script: the Dakshina Dataset. In *Proceedings of the 12th Language Resources and Evaluation Conference*, pages 2413–2423, Marseille, France. European Language Resources Association.

Steinn Sigurdsson. 2020. The future of arXiv and knowledge discovery in open science. In *Proceedings of the First Workshop on Scholarly Document Processing*, pages 7–9, Online. Association for Computational Linguistics.

Arnab Sinha, Zhihong Shen, Yang Song, Hao Ma, Darrin Eide, Bo-June (Paul) Hsu, and Kuansan Wang. 2015. An Overview of Microsoft Academic Service (MAS) and Applications. In *Proceedings of the 24th International Conference on World Wide Web*, WWW '15 Companion, pages 243–246. ACM.

Dung Thai, Zhiyang Xu, Nicholas Monath, Boris Veytsman, and Andrew McCallum. 2020. Using bibtex to automatically generate labeled data for citation field extraction. In *Automated Knowledge Base Construction*.

Miguel-Angel Vera-Baceta, Michael Thelwall, and Kayvan Kousha. 2019. Web of Science and Scopus language coverage. *Scientometrics*, 121(3):1803–1813.

Kuansan Wang, Zhihong Shen, Chiyuan Huang, Chieh-Han Wu, Darrin Eide, Yuxiao Dong, Junjie Qian, Anshul Kanakia, Alvin Chen, and Richard Rogahn. 2019. A Review of Microsoft Academic Services for Science of Science Studies. *Frontiers in Big Data*, 2:45.

Yu Zhang, Min Wang, Morteza Saberi, and Elizabeth Chang. 2020. Knowledge fusion through academic articles: a survey of definitions, techniques, applications and challenges. *Scientometrics*, 125(3):2637–2666.

The Effect of Pretraining on Extractive Summarization for Scientific Documents

Yash Gupta[1] **Pawan Sasanka Ammanamanchi**[2] **Shikha Bordia**[3] **Arjun Manoharan**[3]
Deepak Mittal[3] **Ramakanth Pasunuru**[4] **Manish Shrivastava**[2]
Maneesh Singh[3] **Mohit Bansal**[4] **Preethi Jyothi**[1*]
[1]Indian Institute of Technology, Bombay, [2]International Institute of Information Technology, Hyderabad
[3]Verisk Analytics ,[4]University of North Carolina, Chapel Hill

Abstract

Large pretrained models have seen enormous success in extractive summarization tasks. We investigate, here, the influence of pretraining on a BERT-based extractive summarization system for scientific documents. We derive performance improvements using an intermediate pretraining step that leverages existing summarization datasets and report state-of-the-art results on a recently released scientific summarization dataset, SCITLDR. We systematically analyze the intermediate pretraining step by varying the size and domain of the pretraining corpus, changing the length of the input sequence in the target task and varying target tasks. We also investigate how intermediate pretraining interacts with contextualized word embeddings trained on different domains.

1 Introduction

Text summarization is a quintessential NLP task that involves generating a coherent and succinct summary of an article containing the most salient information from the original article. Summarization systems are particularly useful for scientific articles that tend to be long and rich in technical content. Summarization can arguably reduce information overload on researchers and facilitate the quick retrieval of relevant papers from vast amounts of scientific literature. Broadly, summarization techniques can be categorized as extractive or abstractive. While abstractive systems treat the summarization problem as a natural language generation task and produce new phrases and sentences directly in the summary, extractive techniques select salient phrases or sentences verbatim from the original document to create a summary. Maynez et al. (2020), Kryscinski et al. (2020), Huang et al. (2020) report factual hallucinations in abstractive summarization. Durmus et al. (2020) highlight the trade-off between faithfulness and abstractiveness. Since for the scientific summarization task, it is critical to be factually-accurate and be faithful to the source document, we focus on extractive summarization of scientific articles.

Large pretrained language models (e.g. BERT (Devlin et al., 2019)) have been successfully used for many NLP tasks including summarization (Liu and Lapata, 2019), using the following, now widely-adopted, two-step approach:

Pretraining. Start with a pretrained model like BERT and suitably adapt its architecture to fit the target task.

Finetuning. Finetune the model using a labeled dataset for the target task.

Recent work shows the benefits of interspersing the pretraining and finetuning steps with an intermediate pretraining step (Phang et al., 2018),(Vu et al., 2020). This intermediate step often involves supervised pretraining using labeled datasets from different domains for a task that is related to or is the same as the target task. While the efficacy of such pretraining approaches have been studied in prior work for natural language understanding tasks (like entailment, question answering, etc. (Vu et al., 2020)), the effect of pretraining on summarization has been far less explored.

In this work, we explore the benefits of intermediate pretraining using existing summarization datasets for a target task involving the summarization of scientific articles. We obtain improvements in performance over state-of-the-art extractive summarization baseline systems on a new sci-

*Correspondence to pjyothi@cse.iitb.ac.in

Proceedings of the Second Workshop on Scholarly Document Processing, pages 73–82
June 10, 2021. ©2021 Association for Computational Linguistics

entific summarization benchmark, SCITLDR (Cachola et al., 2020). We also make the following key observations:

- Intermediate pretraining using labeled summarization datasets (even when containing articles that are very different in domain from scientific articles) is very beneficial to low-resource target tasks like SCITLDR. We also derive additional benefits by filtering the intermediate pretraining data to only retain a subset of articles (based on a similarity metric) that best matches the target task.
- While starting with a BERT-based model pretrained on scientific articles (e.g., SCIBERT(Beltagy et al., 2019)) offers a small advantage compared to the standard BERT-based model as an initialization, this advantage is eclipsed by the effect of intermediate pretraining which is much more significant.
- The benefits from intermediate pretraining diminish with access to sufficiently large amounts of finetuning data in the target task. We also observe a trend of diminishing returns with the intermediate pretraining, as we increase the amount of pretraining data.

2 Related Work

Transfer Learning Pretrained language models like BERT(Devlin et al., 2019) are trained on self-supervised training objectives over large amount of unlabelled text corpus. As shown in (Phang et al., 2018), (Zhang and Bowman, 2018), (Phang et al., 2020), the pretrained knowledge in these models can be leveraged by domain and task adaptive pre-training before finetuning the model to the desired target task. Gururangan et al. (2020), Chakrabarty et al. (2019), Beltagy et al. (2019) finetune language models on the domains of interest and show improvements on the respective in-domain tasks.

Summarization Recent works in summarization MatchSum (Zhong et al., 2020), BERTSUM (Liu and Lapata, 2019), STEPwise ETCSum (Narayan et al., 2020) use pretrained language models. BART (Lewis et al., 2020), PEGASUS (Zhang et al., 2020) use variants of self-supervised training objectives on massive amounts of text corpora and compute to achieve stellar performance on summarization tasks. While most of the recent works focus on improving state-of-the-art results on news datasets like CNN/DailyMail and XSum, improving summarization on scientific documents is an overlooked area.

Intermediate Pretraining Howard and Ruder (2018) first introduced the idea of intermediate pre-training in NLP and its benefits on the 6 tasks of classification. The benefits of this in summarization has been shown by Yu et al. (2021) where in they finetune BART (Lewis et al., 2020) on XSUM (Narayan et al., 2018) and show its results on low resource domain adaptation benchmark for summarization . We show the effects of intermediate pretraining in the context of scientific document summarization.

Scientific Summarization Cachola et al. (2020) introduce the SCITLDR task and benchmark a variety of summarization models such as MatchSum and BERTSUM on the task. Impressive results were reported by Pilault et al. (2020), Zaheer et al. (2020) on scientific datasets like Pubmed, arXiv using compute-intensive transformer based models. We report results on Pubmed and SCITLDR where our models use significantly less compute and achieve superior results on SCITLDR over BERTSUM and MatchSum.

Cross task learning Lebanoff et al. (2018), Mao et al. (2020) use methods that adapt single document summarization task to multi document summarization setup, namely using the CNN/Daily Mail (CNN/DM) dataset. While it is similar to the idea of the intermediate finetuning used in this paper, the end task is different and are tested over a different set of metrics. Zhong et al. (2019) conducts some experiments with supervised pretrained knowledge transfer, we do extensive experiments in the context of scientific summarization.

3 Base Model

In this paper, we base our experiments on the BERTSUM (Liu and Lapata, 2019) architecture that uses BERT embeddings and formulates extractive summarization as a sentence classification problem. The intermediate pretraining step uses data from a summarization task that is different from the target task and could also be from a different domain. We also experiment with replacing pretrained BERT embeddings with SCIBERT embeddings (Beltagy et al., 2019).

BERTSUM Model We use the extractive model proposed by Liu and Lapata (2019) as our base model. It uses a BERT-based encoder (Devlin et al.,

2019) to obtain sentence level representations of a document using the [CLS] token at the beginning of each sentence. Several transformer layers are stacked to represent the discourse. These transformer layers are jointly fine-tuned with BERT on a sentence classification task with a sigmoid layer as the final output predicting whether or not each sentence in the input document should be in the summary. The loss of the model is a cross-entropy loss for binary classification.

Using SciBERT Embeddings Beltagy et al. (2019) finetune BERT-Base on scientific documents from the biomedical and computer science domains. To leverage the stylistic variation and adapt to domain knowledge specific to scientific articles, we examine the effects of replacing BERT embeddings in the BERTSUM model with SciBERT embeddings.

4 Experimental Setup

4.1 Summarization Datasets

We evaluate the models on two scientific summarization benchmark datasets— Pubmed (Cohan et al., 2018) and SciTLDR (Cachola et al., 2020). We use the CNN/DM (Hermann et al., 2015) dataset for intermediate pretraining.

SciTLDR. SciTLDR is a curated corpus containing computer science articles, with each article having one or more reference TLDR's or one-sentence summaries. The inputs could either be abstract-only (SciTLDR-A) or the abstract, introduction and conclusion sections of the article (SciTLDR-AIC). We present results for both settings and use the splits specified in (Cachola et al., 2020).

Pubmed. The Pubmed dataset consists of scientific articles from PubMed.org. We used the splits and preprocessing steps from (Zhong et al., 2020), wherein the introduction is used as the article and the abstract is used as the summary.

CNN/DM. The CNN/DM dataset consists of news articles and highlights from *CNN* and *Daily Mail* news articles, on diverse topics including sports, health, business, etc. The standard splits are used for training, validation and testing without anonymizing the entities. Appendix A contains more detailed statistics about all the three datasets used in this work.

For intermediate pretraining, we also experiment with a subset of articles from Pubmed and CNN/DM together (henceforth referred to as MIXED) that are most similar to our target tasks, SciTLDR-A and SciTLDR-AIC (Guo et al., 2020). We derive BERT-base embeddings for each Pubmed and CNN/DM article via [CLS] tokens. Then, we select 83K articles (roughly 35K and 48K articles from Pubmed and CNN/DM, respectively) with the smallest averaged L2 distance between embeddings of the Pubmed/CNN/DM articles and the SciTLDR target tasks.[1]

4.2 Models and Implementation Details

Our extractive summarization system uses the BERT-based architecture by (Liu and Lapata, 2019) described in Section 3. For intermediate pretraining, we use one of CNN/DM, Pubmed or MIXED. The finetuning step involves data from one of three target tasks, SciTLDR-A, SciTLDR-AIC and Pubmed. For all training steps, we set the dropout rate to 0.1 and learning rate to 2e-3, which are the reported parameters in (Liu and Lapata, 2019) for CNN/DM. We use a batch size of 3000 for all experiments involving CNN/DM during pretraining. The best model is selected on the basis of validation ROUGE scores for one-line summaries on the validation set. This is done to select the model with the best "extreme" summarization capability. When evaluating on Pubmed, the number of sentences extracted is set to 6, as reported in (Zhong et al., 2020). For fine-tuning on SciTLDR-A as well as SciTLDR-AIC, the batch size is set to 100 and the number of extracted sentences to form the final summary is 1.

Evaluation Metrics. The SciTLDR tasks have multiple reference summaries for each test article. We compute ROUGE scores between the summary generated by our system and each of the reference summaries. We consider the reference with the maximum ROUGE-1 score as the main gold summary used in further evaluations. We choose ROUGE-1 (R1), ROUGE-2 (R2) and ROUGE-L (RL) as our main evaluation metrics, as is typically done for summarization tasks. To determine the best possible performance from an extractive summarization system, we also compute oracle scores by choosing a sentence from each test article with the highest R1 score across all reference summaries and averaging these scores across the test articles.

[1]We select 83K articles in MIXED, which is the size of Pubmed, to examine the effect of varying pretraining corpora of a fixed size.

	SciTldr-A			SciTldr-AIC		
	R1	R2	RL	R1	R2	RL
Oracle	49.2	26.0	39.9	53.7	29.9	43.9
MatchSum† (BERT-base)	42.7	20.0	34.0	38.6	16.4	30.1
			Our Models			
Pretraining Datasets			**Using BERT**			
-	39.71	18.91	32.63	36.99	16.14	29.64
Pubmed (83K)	41.49	19.57	33.40	40.82	18.98	32.84
CNN/DM (83K)	41.69	19.55	33.44	41.93	20.10	33.95
Mixed (83K)	**42.32**	**20.50**	**34.30**	**42.78**	**21.06**	**34.83**
CNN/DM (Full)	42.26	20.32	34.09	42.21	20.24	34.19
			Using SciBERT			
-	39.93	18.50	32.32	37.16	15.94	29.65
CNN/DM (83K)	40.60	19.04	32.93	40.74	19.09	32.95
Pubmed (83K)	41.10	19.33	32.87	40.61	18.69	32.68
CNN/DM (Full)	40.66	19.08	32.59	41.25	19.40	33.37

Table 1: Max ROUGE scores for SciTldr on test sets. † Results from (Cachola et al., 2020)

	Pubmed		
	R1	R2	RL
Oracle	45.12	20.33	40.19
MatchSum† (BERT-base)	41.21	14.91	36.75
	Our Models		
Pretraining Datasets	**Using BERT**		
-	40.65	14.85	36.18
CNN/DM (Full)	40.77	14.92	36.29
	Using SciBERT		
-	**41.08**	**15.16**	**36.59**
CNN/DM (Full)	40.59	14.76	36.12

Table 2: Mean ROUGE scores for Pubmed test sets.† Results from (Zhong et al., 2020)

Dataset Size	R1	R2	RL
83K articles	41.93	20.10	33.95
176K articles	**42.27**	**20.37**	**34.32**
286K articles	42.21	20.24	34.19

Table 3: Results by varying the size of the pretraining dataset CNN/DM while finetuning on SciTldr-AIC.

	SciTldr-AIC			Pubmed		
Input Length	R1	R2	RL	R1	R2	RL
512	42.21	20.24	34.19	40.65	14.85	36.18
1024	42.21	20.34	34.35	42.44	16.39	37.86
1500	**42.23**	**20.65**	**34.41**	**42.65**	**16.59**	**38.03**

Table 4: Results by varying the input sequence length while finetuning. The pretraining dataset is CNN/DM for SciTldr-AIC and none for Pubmed.

5 Results and Discussion

Table 1 and Table 2 show our main results. In the first two rows, we present results from the state-of-the-art MatchSum system (Zhong et al., 2020) and oracle scores. The remaining rows show pretraining results using BERT and SciBERT embeddings in the BERTSUM model. Without any intermediate pretraining, SciBERT offers a small advantage over BERT on Pubmed and is statistically comparable to BERT on both SciTldr tasks. With pretraining and using BERT, we observe significant improvements in performance regardless of the pretraining corpora used. (We significantly outperform MatchSum on SciTldr-AIC.) With keeping the size of the pretraining corpus fixed at 83K articles, pretraining with Mixed gives the best results showing that it is beneficial to selectively choose articles in the pretraining corpus that best match the target tasks. Unlike for the low-resource SciTldr target tasks, intermediate pretraining does not benefit Pubmed showing that its effect diminishes when sufficient amounts of finetuning data are available for the target task.

With pretraining and replacing BERT with SciBERT, we observe a deterioration in performance indicated by the drop in ROUGE scores (especially with CNN/DM). The SciBERT initialization appears to be counterproductive when using CNN/DM during intermediate pretraining. It is more beneficial to start with BERT, rather than SciBERT, and pretrain on CNN/DM before the final finetuning step.

Additionally, we undertake two ablation experiments. 1) We investigate the effect of varying amounts of pretraining data. We vary the size of CNN/DM to 83K, 176K and 286K articles and analyse the finetuning results on SciTldr-AIC with BERT embeddings. As shown in Table 3, R1, R2 and RL scores increase on moving from 83K to 176K articles but performance stagnates with a further increase in the size of the pretraining corpus. 2) During finetuning, we experiment with truncating the input sequence lengths of SciTLDR-AIC and Pubmed at 512, 1024 and 1500 tokens, as shown in Table 4. We initialize the model with BERT embeddings for the first 512 tokens and repeat the last set of weights for the remaining input tokens. We observe that the ROUGE scores improve with longer input lengths, with a sizeable boost for Pubmed.

6 Conclusions and Future Work

In this paper, we present a systematic investigation of the benefits of transfer learning via pretraining for extractive summarization of scientific articles. We show improvements in ROUGE scores for the SciTLDR benchmark using an intermediate pretraining that uses existing summarization datasets. We obtain additional benefits by filtering these existing datasets to construct a pretraining corpus that best matches the target task. This suggests the need for further explorations in future work on different criteria to be used for selective pretraining and how it could benefit both extractive and abstractive summarization.

References

Iz Beltagy, Kyle Lo, and Arman Cohan. 2019. SciBERT: A pretrained language model for scientific text. In *Proceedings of the 2019 Conference on Empirical Methods in Natural Language Processing and the 9th International Joint Conference on Natural Language Processing (EMNLP-IJCNLP)*, pages 3615–3620, Hong Kong, China. Association for Computational Linguistics.

Isabel Cachola, Kyle Lo, Arman Cohan, and Daniel Weld. 2020. TLDR: Extreme summarization of scientific documents. In *Findings of the Association for Computational Linguistics: EMNLP 2020*, pages 4766–4777, Online. Association for Computational Linguistics.

Tuhin Chakrabarty, Christopher Hidey, and Kathy McKeown. 2019. IMHO fine-tuning improves claim detection. In *Proceedings of the 2019 Conference of the North American Chapter of the Association for Computational Linguistics: Human Language Technologies, Volume 1 (Long and Short Papers)*, pages 558–563, Minneapolis, Minnesota. Association for Computational Linguistics.

Arman Cohan, Franck Dernoncourt, Doo Soon Kim, Trung Bui, Seokhwan Kim, Walter Chang, and Nazli Goharian. 2018. A discourse-aware attention model for abstractive summarization of long documents. In *Proceedings of the 2018 Conference of the North American Chapter of the Association for Computational Linguistics: Human Language Technologies, Volume 2 (Short Papers)*, pages 615–621, New Orleans, Louisiana. Association for Computational Linguistics.

Jacob Devlin, Ming-Wei Chang, Kenton Lee, and Kristina Toutanova. 2019. BERT: Pre-training of deep bidirectional transformers for language understanding. In *Proceedings of the 2019 Conference of the North American Chapter of the Association for Computational Linguistics: Human Language Technologies, Volume 1 (Long and Short Papers)*, pages 4171–4186, Minneapolis, Minnesota. Association for Computational Linguistics.

Esin Durmus, He He, and Mona Diab. 2020. FEQA: A question answering evaluation framework for faithfulness assessment in abstractive summarization. In *Proceedings of the 58th Annual Meeting of the Association for Computational Linguistics*, pages 5055–5070, Online. Association for Computational Linguistics.

Han Guo, Ramakanth Pasunuru, and Mohit Bansal. 2020. Multi-source domain adaptation for text classification via distancenet-bandits. *ArXiv*, abs/2001.04362.

Suchin Gururangan, Ana Marasović, Swabha Swayamdipta, Kyle Lo, Iz Beltagy, Doug Downey, and Noah A. Smith. 2020. Don't stop pretraining: Adapt language models to domains and tasks.

Karl Moritz Hermann, Tomas Kocisky, Edward Grefenstette, Lasse Espeholt, Will Kay, Mustafa Suleyman, and Phil Blunsom. 2015. Teaching machines to read and comprehend. In C. Cortes, N. D. Lawrence, D. D. Lee, M. Sugiyama, and R. Garnett, editors, *Advances in Neural Information Processing Systems 28*, pages 1693–1701. Curran Associates, Inc.

Jeremy Howard and Sebastian Ruder. 2018. Universal language model fine-tuning for text classification. In *Proceedings of the 56th Annual Meeting of the Association for Computational Linguistics (Volume 1: Long Papers)*, pages 328–339, Melbourne, Australia. Association for Computational Linguistics.

Dandan Huang, Leyang Cui, Sen Yang, Guangsheng Bao, Kun Wang, Jun Xie, and Yue Zhang. 2020. What have we achieved on text summarization? In *Proceedings of the 2020 Conference on Empirical Methods in Natural Language Processing (EMNLP)*, pages 446–469, Online. Association for Computational Linguistics.

Wojciech Kryscinski, Bryan McCann, Caiming Xiong, and Richard Socher. 2020. Evaluating the factual consistency of abstractive text summarization. In *Proceedings of the 2020 Conference on Empirical Methods in Natural Language Processing (EMNLP)*, pages 9332–9346, Online. Association for Computational Linguistics.

Logan Lebanoff, Kaiqiang Song, and Fei Liu. 2018. Adapting the neural encoder-decoder framework from single to multi-document summarization. In *Proceedings of the 2018 Conference on Empirical Methods in Natural Language Processing*, pages 4131–4141, Brussels, Belgium. Association for Computational Linguistics.

Mike Lewis, Yinhan Liu, Naman Goyal, Marjan Ghazvininejad, Abdelrahman Mohamed, Omer Levy, Veselin Stoyanov, and Luke Zettlemoyer. 2020. BART: Denoising sequence-to-sequence pretraining for natural language generation, translation, and comprehension. In *Proceedings of the 58th Annual Meeting of the Association for Computational Linguistics*, pages 7871–7880, Online. Association for Computational Linguistics.

Yang Liu and Mirella Lapata. 2019. Text summarization with pretrained encoders. In *Proceedings of the 2019 Conference on Empirical Methods in Natural Language Processing and the 9th International Joint Conference on Natural Language Processing (EMNLP-IJCNLP)*, pages 3730–3740, Hong Kong, China. Association for Computational Linguistics.

Yuning Mao, Yanru Qu, Yiqing Xie, Xiang Ren, and Jiawei Han. 2020. Multi-document summarization with maximal marginal relevance-guided reinforcement learning. In *Proceedings of the 2020 Conference on Empirical Methods in Natural Language Processing (EMNLP)*, pages 1737–1751, Online. Association for Computational Linguistics.

Joshua Maynez, Shashi Narayan, Bernd Bohnet, and Ryan McDonald. 2020. On faithfulness and factuality in abstractive summarization. In *Proceedings of the 58th Annual Meeting of the Association for Computational Linguistics*, pages 1906–1919, Online. Association for Computational Linguistics.

Shashi Narayan, Shay B. Cohen, and Mirella Lapata. 2018. Don't give me the details, just the summary! topic-aware convolutional neural networks for extreme summarization. In *Proceedings of the 2018 Conference on Empirical Methods in Natural Language Processing*, pages 1797–1807, Brussels, Belgium. Association for Computational Linguistics.

Shashi Narayan, Joshua Maynez, Jakub Adamek, Daniele Pighin, Blaz Bratanic, and Ryan McDonald. 2020. Stepwise extractive summarization and planning with structured transformers. In *Proceedings of the 2020 Conference on Empirical Methods in Natural Language Processing (EMNLP)*, pages 4143–4159, Online. Association for Computational Linguistics.

Jason Phang, Iacer Calixto, Phu Mon Htut, Yada Pruksachatkun, Haokun Liu, Clara Vania, Katharina Kann, and Samuel R. Bowman. 2020. English intermediate-task training improves zero-shot cross-lingual transfer too. In *Proceedings of the 1st Conference of the Asia-Pacific Chapter of the Association for Computational Linguistics and the 10th International Joint Conference on Natural Language Processing*, pages 557–575, Suzhou, China. Association for Computational Linguistics.

Jason Phang, Thibault Févry, and Samuel R. Bowman. 2018. Sentence encoders on stilts: Supplementary training on intermediate labeled-data tasks. *CoRR*, abs/1811.01088.

Jonathan Pilault, Raymond Li, Sandeep Subramanian, and Chris Pal. 2020. On extractive and abstractive neural document summarization with transformer language models. In *Proceedings of the 2020 Conference on Empirical Methods in Natural Language Processing (EMNLP)*, pages 9308–9319, Online. Association for Computational Linguistics.

Tu Vu, Tong Wang, Tsendsuren Munkhdalai, Alessandro Sordoni, Adam Trischler, Andrew Mattarella-Micke, Subhransu Maji, and Mohit Iyyer. 2020. Exploring and predicting transferability across nlp tasks. In *Proceedings of the 2020 Conference on Empirical Methods in Natural Language Processing (EMNLP)*, pages 7882–7926.

Tiezheng Yu, Zihan Liu, and Pascale Fung. 2021. Adaptsum: Towards low-resource domain adaptation for abstractive summarization.

Manzil Zaheer, Guru Guruganesh, Kumar Avinava Dubey, Joshua Ainslie, Chris Alberti, Santiago Ontanon, Philip Pham, Anirudh Ravula, Qifan Wang, Li Yang, and Amr Ahmed. 2020. Big bird: Transformers for longer sequences. In *Advances in Neural Information Processing Systems*, volume 33, pages 17283–17297. Curran Associates, Inc.

Jingqing Zhang, Yao Zhao, Mohammad Saleh, and Peter Liu. 2020. PEGASUS: Pre-training with extracted gap-sentences for abstractive summarization. In *Proceedings of the 37th International Conference on Machine Learning*, volume 119 of *Proceedings of Machine Learning Research*, pages 11328–11339. PMLR.

Kelly Zhang and Samuel Bowman. 2018. Language modeling teaches you more than translation does: Lessons learned through auxiliary syntactic task analysis. In *Proceedings of the 2018 EMNLP Workshop BlackboxNLP: Analyzing and Interpreting Neural Networks for NLP*, pages 359–361, Brussels, Belgium. Association for Computational Linguistics.

Ming Zhong, Pengfei Liu, Yiran Chen, Danqing Wang, Xipeng Qiu, and Xuanjing Huang. 2020. Extractive summarization as text matching. In *Proceedings of the 58th Annual Meeting of the Association for Computational Linguistics*, pages 6197–6208, Online. Association for Computational Linguistics.

Ming Zhong, Pengfei Liu, Danqing Wang, Xipeng Qiu, and Xuanjing Huang. 2019. Searching for effective neural extractive summarization: What works and what's next. In *Proceedings of the 57th Annual Meeting of the Association for Computational Linguistics*, pages 1049–1058, Florence, Italy. Association for Computational Linguistics.

A Appendix

A.1 Dataset Details

Corpus ($\mathcal{C}$)	$\|\mathcal{C}\|$ Train	Val	Test	Source of $\mathcal{C}$	# of Tokens Doc.	Sum.
SciTldr-A	1992 papers (1992 TLDRs)	619 papers (1452 TLDRs)	618 papers (1967 TLDRs)	OpenReview API	159	21
SciTLDR-AIC	1992 papers (1992 TLDRs)	619 papers (1452 TLDRs)	618 papers (1967 TLDRs)	OpenReview API	993	21
CNN/DM (Full) CNN/DM (83k)	287k 83k	-	-	News Articles	685	53
Pubmed	83233	4946	5025	Biomedical Literature	444	209

Table 5: Dataset details of summarization datasets. Unlike the other datasets, SciTLDR consists of multiple reference summaries for each article. SciTLDR-AIC has the highest compression ratio when compared to the other datasets.

A.1.1 SciTLDR

This dataset is built from a combination of TLDRs written by human experts and author-written TLDRs of computer science papers from OpenReview. OpenReview (https://openreview.net/) is one such example where authors are asked to submit TLDRs of their papers, which communicates to both reviewers and users of OpenReview the main content of the paper. SciTLDR has multiple reference summaries for each of the test and validation articles. The additional reference summaries (apart from the author written one) were obtained from human annotators. This is an "extreme" summarisation task as the compression ratio is very high compared to the other datasets i.e. around 47 for the AIC task. While the dataset is inherently abstractive in nature, the extractive oracle scores listed in Table **??** are quite high (in fact, they are much higher than existing abstractive and extractive SoTA scores), which implies there is a lot of scope for extractive summarisation.

A.1.2 CNN/DM

This dataset contains online news articles paired with multi-sentence summaries (which are highlights of the news articles). The dataset is fairly large and also has a high extractive oracle (with ROUGE-1 / ROUGE-2 / ROUGE-L scores of 52.59 / 31.24 / 48.87), although the summaries are not inherently extractive. The compression ratio is much lower compared to SciTLDR i.e. around 13.

A.1.3 Pubmed

This dataset is collected from scientific papers. It has a very low compression ratio i.e. around 2 (which is a direct consequence of using the introduction section as the document and the abstract as the corresponding summary). The summaries are relatively long, compared to SciTLDR and CNN/DM, with around 6 sentences per summary.

A.2 Qualitative Analysis

We present examples of SciTLDR articles and generated summaries to illustrate the effects of pretraining and other design choices (such as varying input lengths and BERT/SciBERT initializations).

A.2.1 Effect of Input Sequence Length on SciTLDR-AIC

Article 1
Good representations facilitate transfer learning and few-shot learning. Motivated by theories of language and communication that explain why communities with large number of speakers have, on average, simpler languages with more regularity, we cast the representation learning problem in terms of learning to communicate.Our starting point sees traditional autoencoders as a single encoder with a fixed decoder partner that must learn to communicate. Generalizing from there, we introduce community-based autoencoders in which multiple encoders and decoders collectively learn representations by being randomly paired up on successive training iterations. Our experiments show that increasing community sizes reduce idiosyncrasies in the learned codes, resulting in more invariant representations with increased reusability and structure. The importance of representation learning lies in two dimensions. First and foremost, representation learning is a crucial building block of a neural model being trained to perform well on a particular task, i.e., representation learning that induces the "right" manifold structure can lead to models that generalize better, and even extrapolate. Another property of representation learning, and arguably the most important one, is that it can facilitate transfer of knowledge across different tasks , essential for transfer learning and few-shot learning among others BID0 . With this second point in mind, we can define good representations as the ones that are reusable, induce the abstractions that capture the "right" type of invariances and can allow for generalizing very quickly to a new task. Significant efforts have been made to learn representations with these properties; one frequently explored direction involves trying to learn disentangled representations BID12 BID6 BID5 BID17), while others focus on general regularization methods BID15 BID18 . In this work, we take a different approach to representation learning, inspired by successful abstraction mechanisms found in nature, to wit human language and communication.Human languages and their properties are greatly affected by the size of their linguistic community BID11 BID19 BID16 BID9 .....
Ground Truth Summaries
Motivated by theories of language and communication, we introduce community-based autoencoders, in which multiple encoders and decoders collectively learn structured and reusable representations. The authors tackle the problem of representation learning, aim to build reusable and structured represenation, argue co-adaptation between encoder and decoder in traditional AE yields poor representation, and introduce community based auto-encoders. The paper presents a community based autoencoder framework to address co-adaptation of encoders and decoders and aims at constructing better representations.
Input Length 512 (ROUGE-1: 18.18, ROUGE-2: 0.00, ROUGE-L: 12.12)
Good representations facilitate transfer learning and few-shot learning .
Input Length 1024 (ROUGE-1: 28.57, ROUGE-2: 0.00, ROUGE-L: 14.29)
Our starting point sees traditional autoencoders as a single encoder with a fixed decoder partner that must learn to communicate.
Input Length 1500 (ROUGE-1: 60.0, ROUGE-2: 49.99, ROUGE-L: 55.99)
Generalizing from there, we introduce community-based autoencoders in which multiple encoders and decoders collectively learn representations by being randomly paired up on successive training iterations.
Article 2
Generative models are important tools to capture and investigate the properties of complex empirical data. Recent developments such as Generative Adversarial Networks (GANs) and Variational Auto-Encoders (VAEs) use two very similar, but *reverse*, deep convolutional architectures, one to generate and one to extract information from data. Does learning the parameters of both architectures obey the same rules? .We exploit the causality principle of independence of mechanisms to quantify how the weights of successive layers adapt to each other. Using the recently introduced Spectral Independence Criterion, we quantify the dependencies between the kernels of successive convolutional layers and show that those are more independent for the generative process than for information extraction, in line with results from the field of causal inference. In addition, our experiments on generation of human faces suggest that more independence between successive layers of generators results in improved performance of these architectures. Deep generative models have proven powerful in learning to design realistic images in a variety of complex domains (handwritten digits, human faces, interior scenes). In particular, two approaches have recently emerged: Generative Adversarial Networks (GANs) BID8 , which train an image generator by having it fool a discriminator that should tell apart real from artificially generated images; and Variational Autoencoders (VAEs) BID15 BID21) that learn both a mapping from latent variables to the data (the decoder) and the converse mapping from the data to the latent variables (the encoder), such that correspondences between latent variables and data features can be easily investigated.....
Ground Truth Summaries
We use causal inference to characterise the architecture of generative models . This paper examines the nature of convolutional filters in the encoder and a decoder of a VAE, and a generator and a discriminator of a GAN. This work exploits the causality principle to quantify how the weights of successive layers adapt to each other.
Input Length 512 (ROUGE-1: 25.92, ROUGE-2: 3.84, ROUGE-L: 14.81)
Using the recently introduced Spectral Independence Criterion, we quantify the dependencies between the kernels of successive convolutional layers and show that those are more independent for the generative process than for information extraction, in line with results from the field of causal inference.
Input Length 1024 (ROUGE-1: 38.46, ROUGE-2: 8.33, ROUGE-L: 23.08)
Generative models are important tools to capture and investigate the properties of complex empirical data.
Input Length 1500 (ROUGE-1: 82.05, ROUGE-2: 75.68, ROUGE-L: 82.05)
We exploit the causality principle of independence of mechanisms to quantify how the weights of successive layers adapt to each other.

Table 6: Articles 1 and 2 have 1068 and 1265 tokens, respectively. We see that increasing the length of the input sequence significantly improves the ROUGE scores.

A.2.2 Effect of Pretraining on SciTLDR-AIC

Article 1
Recent advances in neural Sequence-to-Sequence (Seq2Seq) models reveal a purely data-driven approach to the response generation task. Despite its diverse variants and applications, the existing Seq2Seq models are prone to producing short and generic replies, which blocks such neural network architectures from being utilized in practical open-domain response generation tasks. In this research, we analyze this critical issue from the perspective of the optimization goal of models and the specific characteristics of human-to-human conversational corpora. Our analysis is conducted by decomposing the goal of Neural Response Generation (NRG) into the optimizations of word selection and ordering. It can be derived from the decomposing that Seq2Seq based NRG models naturally tend to select common words to compose responses, and ignore the semantic of queries in word ordering. On the basis of the analysis, we propose a max-marginal ranking regularization term to avoid Seq2Seq models from producing the generic and uninformative responses. The empirical experiments on benchmarks with several metrics have validated our analysis and proposed methodology. Past years have witnessed the dramatic progress on the application of generative sequential models (also noted as seq2seq learning (Sutskever et Despite these promising results, current Sequence-to-Sequence (Seq2Seq) architectures for response generation are still far from steadily generating relevant and coherent replies. The essential issue identified by many studies is the Universal Replies: the model tends to generate short and general replies which contain limited information, such as "That's great!", "I don't know", etc. Nevertheless, most previous analysis over the issue are empirical and lack of statistical evidence. Therefore, in this paper, we conduct an in-depth investigation on the performance of seq2seq models on the NRG task....
Ground Truth Summaries
Analyze the reason for neural response generative models preferring universal replies; Propose a method to avoid it. Investigates the problem of universal replies plaguing the Seq2Seq neural generation models. The paper looks into improving the neural response generation task by deemphasizing the common responses using modification of the loss function and presentation the common/universal responses during the training phase.
Pubmed (ROUGE-1: 20.51, ROUGE-2: 0.00, ROUGE-L: 20.51)
In this research, we analyze this critical issue from the perspective of the optimization goal of models and the specific characteristics of human-to-human conversational corpora.
CNN/DM (ROUGE-1: 34.62, ROUGE-2: 8.00, ROUGE-L: 26.92)
Our analysis is conducted by decomposing the goal of Neural Response Generation (NRG) into the optimizations of word selection and ordering.
CNN/DM+Pubmed (ROUGE-1: 37.50, ROUGE-2: 0.0 , ROUGE-L: 31.25)
Therefore, in this paper, we conduct an in-depth investigation on the performance of seq2seq models on the NRG task.
Article 2
Graph convolutional networks (GCNs) have been widely used for classifying graph nodes in the semi-supervised setting. Previous works have shown that GCNs are vulnerable to the perturbation on adjacency and feature matrices of existing nodes. However, it is unrealistic to change the connections of existing nodes in many applications, such as existing users in social networks. In this paper, we investigate methods attacking GCNs by adding fake nodes. A greedy algorithm is proposed to generate adjacency and feature matrices of fake nodes, aiming to minimize the classification accuracy on the existing ones. In additional, we introduce a discriminator to classify fake nodes from real nodes, and propose a Greedy-GAN algorithm to simultaneously update the discriminator and the attacker, to make fake nodes indistinguishable to the real ones....
Ground Truth Summaries
non-targeted and targeted attack on GCN by adding fake nodes The authors propose a new adversarial technique to add "fake" nodes to fool a GCN-based classifier
Pubmed (ROUGE-1: 23.53, ROUGE-2: 0.0, ROUGE-L: 11.76)
Graph convolutional networks (GCNs) have been widely used for classifying graph nodes in the semi-supervised setting.
CNN/DM (ROUGE-1: 34.15, ROUGE-2: 5.13, ROUGE-L: 24.39)
A greedy algorithm is proposed to generate adjacency and feature matrices of fake nodes, aiming to minimize the classification accuracy on the existing ones.
CNN/DM+Pubmed (ROUGE-1: 52.17, ROUGE-2: 38.09, ROUGE-L: 52.17)
In this paper, we investigate methods attacking GCNs by adding fake nodes.

Table 7: For both the articles, we note an increasing trend in the ROUGE scores with pretraining on Pubmed, CNN/DM and MIXED (i.e., CNN/DM+Pubmed).

A.2.3 Bert vs SCIBERT without pretraining on SciTLDR-AIC

Article 1
In this paper, we introduce a system called GamePad that can be used to explore the application of machine learning methods to theorem proving in the Coq proof assistant. Interactive theorem provers such as Coq enable users to construct machine-checkable proofs in a step-by-step manner. Hence, they provide an opportunity to explore theorem proving with human supervision. We use GamePad to synthesize proofs for a simple algebraic rewrite problem and train baseline models for a formalization of the Feit-Thompson theorem. We address position evaluation (i.e., predict the number of proof steps left) and tactic prediction (i.e., predict the next proof step) tasks, which arise naturally in tactic-based theorem proving. Theorem proving is a challenging AI task that involves symbolic reasoning (e.g., SMT solvers BID2) and intuition guided search. Recent work BID7 Loos et al., 2017; has shown the promise of applying deep learning techniques in this domain, primarily on tasks useful for automated theorem provers (e.g., premise selection) which operate with little to no human supervision. In this work, we aim to move closer to learning on proofs constructed with human supervision.We look at theorem proving in the realm of formal proofs. A formal proof is systematically derived in a formal system, which makes it possible to algorithmically (i.e., with a computer) check these proofs for correctness....
Ground Truth Summaries
We introduce a system called GamePad to explore the application of machine learning methods to theorem proving in the Coq proof assistant. This paper describes a system for applying machine learning to interactive theorem proving, focuses on tasks of tactic prediction and position evaluation, and shows that a neural model outperforms an SVM on both tasks. Proposes that machine learning techniques be used to help build proof in the theorem prover Coq.
Bert Output (ROUGE-1: 34.78, ROUGE-2: 4.55, ROUGE-L: 21.74)
We use GamePad to synthesize proofs for a simple algebraic rewrite problem and train baseline models for a formalization of the Feit-Thompson theorem.
SCIBERT Output (ROUGE-1: 86.27, ROUGE-2: 81.63, ROUGE-L: 86.27)
In this paper, we introduce a system called GamePad that can be used to explore the application of machine learning methods to theorem proving in the Coq proof assistant.

Article 2
We propose a novel method that makes use of deep neural networks and gradient decent to perform automated design on complex real world engineering tasks. Our approach works by training a neural network to mimic the fitness function of a design optimization task and then, using the differential nature of the neural network, perform gradient decent to maximize the fitness. We demonstrate this methods effectiveness by designing an optimized heat sink and both 2D and 3D airfoils that maximize the lift drag ratio under steady state flow conditions. We highlight that our method has two distinct benefits over other automated design approaches. First, evaluating the neural networks prediction of fitness can be orders of magnitude faster then simulating the system of interest. Second, using gradient decent allows the design space to be searched much more efficiently then other gradient free methods. These two strengths work together to overcome some of the current shortcomings of automated design. Automated Design is the process by which an object is designed by a computer to meet or maximize some measurable objective. This is typically performed by modeling the system and then exploring the space of designs to maximize some desired property whether that be an automotive car styling with low drag or power and cost efficient magnetic bearings BID1 BID4 . A notable historic example of this is the 2006 NASA ST5 spacecraft antenna designed by an evolutionary algorithm to create the best radiation pattern (Hornby et al.) . More recently, an extremely compact broadband on-chip wavelength demultiplexer was design to split electromagnetic waves with different frequencies BID17 . While there have been some significant successes in this field the dream of true automated is still far from realized. The main challenges present are heavy computational requirements for accurately modeling the physical system under investigation and often exponentially large search spaces. These two problems negatively complement each other making the computation requirements intractable for even simple problems.Our approach works to solve the current problems of automated design in two ways. First, we learn a computationally efficient representation of the physical system on a neural network. This trained network can be used to evaluate the quality or fitness of the design several orders of magnitude faster. Second, we use the differentiable nature of the trained network to get a gradient on the parameter space when performing optimization. This allows significantly more efficient optimization requiring far fewer iterations then other gradient free methods such as genetic algorithms or simulated annealing....
Ground Truth Summaries
A method for performing automated design on real world objects such as heat sinks and wing airfoils that makes use of neural networks and gradient descent. Neural network (parameterization and prediction) and gradient descent (back propogation) to automatically design for engineering tasks. This paper introduces using a deep network to approximate the behavior of a complex physical system, and then design optimal devices by optimizing this network with respect to its inputs.
Bert Output (ROUGE-1: 16.67, ROUGE-2: 4.35, ROUGE-L: 12.49)
This allows significantly more efficient optimization requiring far fewer iterations then other gradient free methods such as genetic algorithms or simulated annealing.
SCIBERT Output (ROUGE-1: 62.75, ROUGE-2: 40.82, ROUGE-L: 39.22)
We propose a novel method that makes use of deep neural networks and gradient descent to perform automated design on complex real world engineering tasks.

Table 8: For both the articles, we observe clear improvements in ROUGE scores with using SCIBERT as opposed to BERT.

Finding Pragmatic Differences Between Disciplines

Lee Kezar
University of Southern California
Information Sciences Institute
lkezar@isi.edu

Jay Pujara
University of Southern California
Information Sciences Institute
jpujara@isi.edu

Abstract

Scholarly documents have a great degree of variation, both in terms of content (semantics) and structure (pragmatics). Prior work in scholarly document understanding emphasizes semantics through document summarization and corpus topic modeling but tends to omit pragmatics such as document organization and flow. Using a corpus of scholarly documents across 19 disciplines and state-of-the-art language modeling techniques, we learn a fixed set of domain-agnostic descriptors for document sections and "retrofit" the corpus to these descriptors (also referred to as "normalization"). Then, we analyze the position and ordering of these descriptors across documents to understand the relationship between discipline and structure. We report within-discipline structural archetypes, variability, and between-discipline comparisons, supporting the hypothesis that scholarly communities, despite their size, diversity, and breadth, share similar avenues for expressing their work. Our findings lay the foundation for future work in assessing research quality, domain style transfer, and further pragmatic analysis.

1 Introduction

Disciplines such as art, physics, and political science contain a wide array of ideas, from specific hypotheses to wide-reaching theories. In scholarly research, authors are faced with the challenge of clearly articulating a set of those ideas and relating them to each other, with the ultimate goal of expanding our collective knowledge. In order to understand this work, human readers situate meaning in context (Justin Garten and Deghani, 2019). Similarly, methods for scholarly document processing (SDP) have semantic and pragmatic orientations.

The semantic orientation seeks to understand and evaluate the ideas themselves through information extraction (Singh et al., 2016), summarization (Chandrasekaran et al., 2020), automatic fact-checking (Sathe et al., 2020), etc. The pragmatic orientation, on the other hand, seeks to understand the context around those ideas through rhetorical and style analysis (August et al., 2020), corpus topic modeling (Paul and Girju, 2009), quality prediction (Maillette de Buy Wenniger et al., 2020), etc. Although both orientations are essential for understanding, the pragmatics of disciplinary writing are very weakly understood.

In this paper, we investigate the structures of disciplinary writing. We claim that a "structural archetype" (defined in Section 3) can succinctly capture how a community of authors choose to organize their ideas for maximum comprehension and persuasion. Analogous to how syntactic analysis deepens our understanding of a given sentence and document structure analysis deepens our understanding of a given document, structural archetypes, we argue, deepen our understanding of domains themselves.

In order to perform this analysis, we classify sections according to their pragmatic intent. We contribute a data-driven method for deriving the types of pragmatic intent, called a "structural vocabulary", alongside a robust method for this classification. Then, we apply these methods to 19k scholarly documents and analyze the resulting structures.

2 Related Work

We draw from two areas of related work in SDP: interdisciplinary analysis and rhetorical structure prediction.

In interdisciplinary analysis, we are interested in comparing different disciplines, whether by topic modeling between select corpora/disciplines (Paul and Girju, 2009) or by domain-agnostic language modeling (Wang et al., 2020). These comparisons are more than simply interesting; they allow for models that can adapt to different disciplines, helping the generalizability for downstream tasks like

Proceedings of the Second Workshop on Scholarly Document Processing, pages 83–90
June 10, 2021.

information extraction and summarization.

In rhetorical structure prediction, we are interested in the process of implicature, whether by describing textual patterns in an unsupervised way (Ó Séaghdha and Teufel, 2014) or by classifying text as having a particular strategy like "statistics" (Al-Khatib et al., 2017) or "analogy" (August et al., 2020). These works descend from argumentative zoning (Lawrence and Reed, 2020) and the closely related rhetorical structure theory (Mann and Thompson, 1988), which argue that many rhetorical strategies can be described in terms of *units* and their relations. These works are motivated by downstream applications such as predicting the popularity of a topic (Prabhakaran et al., 2016) and classifying the quality of a paper (Maillette de Buy Wenniger et al., 2020).

Most similar to our work is Arnold et al. (2019). Here, the authors provide a method of describing Wikipedia articles as a series of section-like topics (e.g. `disease.symptom`) by clustering section headings into topics and then labeling words and sentences with these topics. We build on this work by using domain-agnostic descriptors instead of domain-specific ones and by comparing structures across disciplines.

3 Methods

In this section, we define structural archetypes (3.1) and methods for classifying pragmatic intent through a structural vocabulary (3.2).

3.1 Structural Archetypes

We coin the term "structural archetype" to focus and operationalize our pragmatic analysis. Here, a "structure" is defined as *a sequence of domain-agnostic indicators of pragmatic intent*, while an "archetype" refers to *a strong pattern across documents*. In the following paragraphs, we discuss the components of this concept in depth.

Pragmatic Intent In contrast to verifiable propositions, "indicators of pragmatic intent" refer to instances of meta-discourse, comments on the document itself (Ifantidou, 2005). There are many examples, including background (comments on what the reader needs in order to understand the content), discussions (comments on how results should be interpreted), and summaries (comments on what is important). These indicators of pragmatic intent serve the critical role of helping readers "digest" material; without them, scholarly documents would only contain isolated facts.

We note that the boundary between pragmatic intent and argumentative zones (Lawrence and Reed, 2020) is not clear. Some argumentative zones are more suitable for the sentence- and paragraph-level (e.g. "own claim" vs. "background claim") while others are interpretative (e.g. "challenge"). This work does not attempt to draw this boundary, and the reader might find overlap between argumentative zoning work and our section types.

Sequences As a sequence, these indicators reflect how the author believes their ideas should best be received in order to remain coherent. For example, many *background* indicators reflects a belief that the framing of the work is very important.

Domain-agnostic archetypes Finally, the specification that indicators must be domain-agnostic and that the structures should be widely-held are included to allow for cross-disciplinary comparisons.

We found that the most straightforward way to implement structural archetypes is through classifying section headings according to their pragmatic intent. With this comes a few challenges: (1) defining a set of domain-agnostic indicators, which we refer to as a "structural vocabulary"; (2) parsing a document to obtain its structure; and (3) finding archetypes from document-level structures. In the proceeding section, we address (1) and (2), and in Section 4 we address (3).

3.2 Deriving a Structural Vocabulary

Although indicators of pragmatic intent can exist on the sentence level, we follow Arnold et al. (2019) and create a small set of types that are loosely related to common section headings (e.g. "Methods"). We call this set a "structural vocabulary" because it functions in an analogous way to a vocabulary of words; any document can be described as a sequence of items that are taken from this vocabulary. There are three properties that the types should satisfy:

A. **domain independence**: types should be used by different disciplines

B. **high coverage**: unlabeled instances should be able to be classified as a particular type.

C. **internal consistency**: types should accurately reflect their instances

Domain Independence As pointed out by Arnold et al. (2019), there exists a "vocabulary mismatch problem" where different disciplines talk about their work in different ways. Indeed, 62% of the sampled headings only appear once and are not good choices for section types. On the other hand, the most frequent headings are a much better choice, especially those that appear in all domains. After merging a few popular variations among the top 20 section headings (e.g. *conclusion* and *summary*, *background* and *related work*), we yield the following types[1]: *introduction* (a section which introduces the reader to potentially new concepts; $n = 10916$), *methods* (a section which details how a hypothesis will be tested; $n = 2116$), *results* (a section which presents findings of the method; $n = 3119$), *discussion* (a section which interprets and summarizes the results; $n = 3118$), *conclusion* (a section which summarizes the entire paper; $n = 7738$), *analysis* (a section which adds additional depth and nuance to the results; $n = 951$), and *background* (a section which connects ongoing work to previous related work; $n = 800$). Figure 2 contains discipline-level counts.

High Coverage We can achieve high coverage by classifying any section as one of these section types through language modeling. Specifically, the hidden representation of a neural language model $h(\cdot)$ can act as an embedding of its input. We use the `[CLS]` tag of SciBERT's hidden layer, selected for its robust representations of scientific literature (Beltagy et al., 2019).

To classify, we define a distance score $d(\cdot)$ for a section s and a type T as the distance between $h(s)$ and the average embedding across all instances of a type, i.e.

$$d(s,T) = \left| h(s) - \frac{\sum_{t \in T} h(t)}{\|T\|} \right|$$

Note that since the embedding is a vector, addition and division are elementwise. Then, we compute the distance for all types in the vocabulary V and select the minimum, i.e.

$$s_{type} = \arg\min_{T \in V}(d(s,T))$$

Internal Consistency Some sections do not adequately fit any section type, so nearest-neighbor classification will result in very inconsistent clusters. We address this problem by imposing a threshold on the maximum distance for $d(\cdot)$. Further, since the types have unequal variance (that is, the ground truth for some types are more consistent than other types), we define a type-specific threshold as half of the distance from the center of T to the furthest member of T, i.e.

$$\text{threshold}_T = 0.5 \cdot \max_{t \in T}(d(t,T))$$

The weight of 0.5 was found to remove outliers appropriately an maximize retrofitting performance (Section 4.2).

We also note that some headings, especially brief ones, leave much room for interpretation and make retrofitting challenging. We address this problem by concatenating tokens of each section's heading and body, up to 25 tokens, as input to the language model. This ensures that brief headings contain enough information to make an accurate representation without including too many details from the body text.

4 Results and Discussion

4.1 Data

We use the Semantic Scholar Open Research Corpus (S2ORC) for all analysis (Lo et al., 2020). This corpus, which is freely available, contains approximately 7.5M PDF-parsed documents from 19 disciplines, including natural sciences, social sciences, arts, and humanities. For our experiments, we randomly sample 1k documents for each discipline, yielding a total of 19k documents.

4.2 Retrofitting Performance

Retrofitting (or normalizing) section headers refers to re-labeling sections with the structural vocabulary. We evaluate retrofitting performance by manually tagging 30 of each section type and comparing the true labels to the predicted values. Our method yields an average F1 performance of 0.76. The breakdown per section type, shown in Table 1, reveals that *conclusion*, *background*, and *analysis* sections were the most difficult to predict. We attribute this to a lack of textual clues in the heading and body, and also a semantic overlap with *introduction* sections. Future work can improve the classifier with more nuanced signals, such as position, length, number of references, etc.

[1]Although *abstract* is extremely common we found it redundant as a section type as it only exists once per paper and in a predictable location.

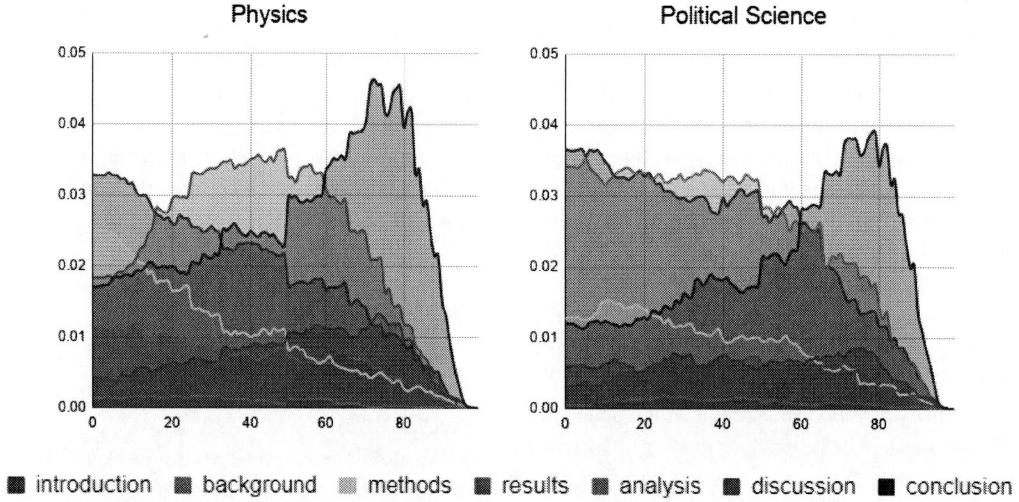

Figure 1: A comparison between the positions (normalized by document length; x axis) and frequencies (y axis) of section types in Physics and Political Science. Comparable distributions of *introduction*, *methods*, *analysis*, *discussion*, and *conclusion*, but different distributions of background and results.

Type	Precision	Recall	F1
introduction	0.77	0.97	0.85
conclusion	0.67	0.72	0.69
discussion	0.88	0.88	0.88
results	0.80	0.85	0.83
methods	0.83	0.91	0.87
background	0.63	0.77	0.69
analysis	0.50	0.61	0.55
overall	**0.72**	**0.88**	**0.76**

Table 1: Type-level and overall performance for section type retrofitting.

4.3 Analyzing Position with Aggregate Frequency

A simple yet expressive way of showing the structural archetypes of a discipline is to consider the frequency of a particular type at any point in the article (normalized by length). This analysis reveals general trends throughout a discipline's documents, such as where a section type is most frequent or where there is homogeneity.

To illustrate the practicality of this analysis, consider the hypothesis that Physics articles are more empirically-motivated while Political Science articles are more conceptually-motivated, i.e. that they are on opposing ends of the *concrete* versus *abstract* spectrum. We operationalize this by claiming that Physics articles have more *methods*, *results*, and *analysis* sections than Political Science. Figure 1 shows the difference between Physics and Political Science at each point in the article. It reveals that not only do Physics articles contain more *methods* and *results*, but also that Physics articles introduce *methods* earlier than Political Science, and that both contain the same amount of *analysis* sections.

4.4 Analyzing Ordering with State Transitions

A more structural analysis of a discipline is to look at the frequency of sequence fragments through computing transition probabilities. As a second example, suppose we have a more nuanced hypothesis: that Psychology papers tend to separate claims and evaluate them sequentially (*methods*, *results*, *discussion*, repeat) whereas Sociology papers tend to evaluate all claims at once. We can operationalize these hypotheses by calculating the transition probability between section s_i and s_{i-1} conditioned on some discipline.

In Table 2, we see evidence that *methods* sections are more likely to be preceded by *results* sections in Psychology than Sociology, implying a new iteration of a cycle. We might conclude that Psychology papers are more likely to have cyclical experiments, but not that Sociology papers conduct multiple experiments in a linear fashion.

Transition Probability	Psych.	Socio.
$P(method \rightarrow method)$	0.31	0.20
$P(results \rightarrow results)$	0.22	0.23
$P(disc \rightarrow disc)$	0.16	0.13
$P(method \rightarrow results)$	0.21	0.10
$P(results \rightarrow disc)$	0.15	0.16
$P(disc \rightarrow method)$	0.23	0.13

Table 2: Transition probabilities for methods, results, and discussion in Psychology and Sociology

5 Conclusion and Future Work

In this paper, we have shown a simple method for constructing and comparing structural archetypes across different disciplines. By classifying the pragmatic intent of section headings, we can visualize structural trends across disciplines. In addition to utilizing a more complex classifier, future directions for this work include (1) further distinguishing between subdisciplines (e.g. abnormal psychology vs. developmental psychology) and document type (e.g. technical report vs. article); (2) learning relationships between structures and measures of research quality, such as reproducibility; (3) learning how to convert one structure into another, with the ultimate goal of normalizing them for easier comprehension or better models; (4) deeper investigations into the selection of a structural vocabulary, such as including common argumentative zoning types or adjusting the scale to the sentence-level; and (5) drawing comparisons, such as by clustering, between different documents based strictly on their structure.

6 Acknowledgements

This work was funded by the Defense Advanced Research Projects Agency with award W911NF-19-20271. The authors would like to thank the reviewers of this paper for their detailed and constructive feedback, and in particular their ideas for future directions.

References

Khalid Al-Khatib, Henning Wachsmuth, Matthias Hagen, and Benno Stein. 2017. Patterns of argumentation strategies across topics. In *Proceedings of the 2017 Conference on Empirical Methods in Natural Language Processing*, pages 1351–1357, Copenhagen, Denmark. Association for Computational Linguistics.

Sebastian Arnold, Rudolf Schneider, Philippe Cudré-Mauroux, Felix A. Gers, and Alexander Löser. 2019. SECTOR: A neural model for coherent topic segmentation and classification. *Transactions of the Association for Computational Linguistics*, 7:169–184.

Tal August, Lauren Kim, Katharina Reinecke, and Noah A. Smith. 2020. Writing strategies for science communication: Data and computational analysis. In *Proceedings of the 2020 Conference on Empirical Methods in Natural Language Processing (EMNLP)*, pages 5327–5344, Online. Association for Computational Linguistics.

Iz Beltagy, Kyle Lo, and Arman Cohan. 2019. SciBERT: A pretrained language model for scientific text. In *Proceedings of the 2019 Conference on Empirical Methods in Natural Language Processing and the 9th International Joint Conference on Natural Language Processing (EMNLP-IJCNLP)*, pages 3615–3620, Hong Kong, China. Association for Computational Linguistics.

Muthu Kumar Chandrasekaran, Guy Feigenblat, Eduard Hovy, Abhilasha Ravichander, Michal Shmueli-Scheuer, and Anita de Waard. 2020. Overview and insights from the shared tasks at scholarly document processing 2020: CL-SciSumm, LaySumm and LongSumm. In *Proceedings of the First Workshop on Scholarly Document Processing*, pages 214–224, Online. Association for Computational Linguistics.

Elly Ifantidou. 2005. The semantics and pragmatics of metadiscourse. *Journal of Pragmatics*, 37(9):1325–1353. Focus-on Issue: Discourse and Metadiscourse.

Kenji Sagae Justin Garten, Brendan Kennedy and Morteza Deghani. 2019. Measuring the importance of context when modeling language comprehension. *Behavioral Research Methods*, 51:480–492.

John Lawrence and Chris Reed. 2020. Argument Mining: A Survey. *Computational Linguistics*, 45(4):765–818.

Kyle Lo, Lucy Lu Wang, Mark Neumann, Rodney Kinney, and Daniel Weld. 2020. S2ORC: The semantic scholar open research corpus. In *Proceedings of the 58th Annual Meeting of the Association for Computational Linguistics*, pages 4969–4983, Online. Association for Computational Linguistics.

Gideon Maillette de Buy Wenniger, Thomas van Dongen, Eleri Aedmaa, Herbert Teun Kruitbosch, Edwin A. Valentijn, and Lambert Schomaker. 2020. Structure-tags improve text classification for scholarly document quality prediction. In *Proceedings of the First Workshop on Scholarly Document Processing*, pages 158–167, Online. Association for Computational Linguistics.

William Mann and Sandra Thompson. 1988. Rhetorical structure theory: Toward a functional theory of text organization. *Text - Interdisciplinary Journal for the Study of Discourse*, 8:243–281.

Diarmuid Ó Séaghdha and Simone Teufel. 2014. Unsupervised learning of rhetorical structure with un-topic models. In *Proceedings of COLING 2014, the 25th International Conference on Computational Linguistics: Technical Papers*, pages 2–13, Dublin, Ireland. Dublin City University and Association for Computational Linguistics.

Michael Paul and Roxana Girju. 2009. Topic modeling of research fields: An interdisciplinary perspective. In *Proceedings of the International Conference RANLP-2009*, pages 337–342, Borovets, Bulgaria. Association for Computational Linguistics.

Vinodkumar Prabhakaran, William L. Hamilton, Dan McFarland, and Dan Jurafsky. 2016. Predicting the rise and fall of scientific topics from trends in their rhetorical framing. In *Proceedings of the 54th Annual Meeting of the Association for Computational Linguistics (Volume 1: Long Papers)*, pages 1170–1180, Berlin, Germany. Association for Computational Linguistics.

Aalok Sathe, Salar Ather, Tuan Manh Le, Nathan Perry, and Joonsuk Park. 2020. Automated fact-checking of claims from Wikipedia. In *Proceedings of the 12th Language Resources and Evaluation Conference*, pages 6874–6882, Marseille, France. European Language Resources Association.

Mayank Singh, Barnopriyo Barua, Priyank Palod, Manvi Garg, Sidhartha Satapathy, Samuel Bushi, Kumar Ayush, Krishna Sai Rohith, Tulasi Gamidi, Pawan Goyal, and Animesh Mukherjee. 2016. OCR++: A robust framework for information extraction from scholarly articles. In *Proceedings of COLING 2016, the 26th International Conference on Computational Linguistics: Technical Papers*, pages 3390–3400, Osaka, Japan. The COLING 2016 Organizing Committee.

Chengyu Wang, Minghui Qiu, Jun Huang, and Xiaofeng He. 2020. Meta fine-tuning neural language models for multi-domain text mining. In *Proceedings of the 2020 Conference on Empirical Methods in Natural Language Processing (EMNLP)*, pages 3094–3104, Online. Association for Computational Linguistics.

A Section Counts Before and After Retrofitting

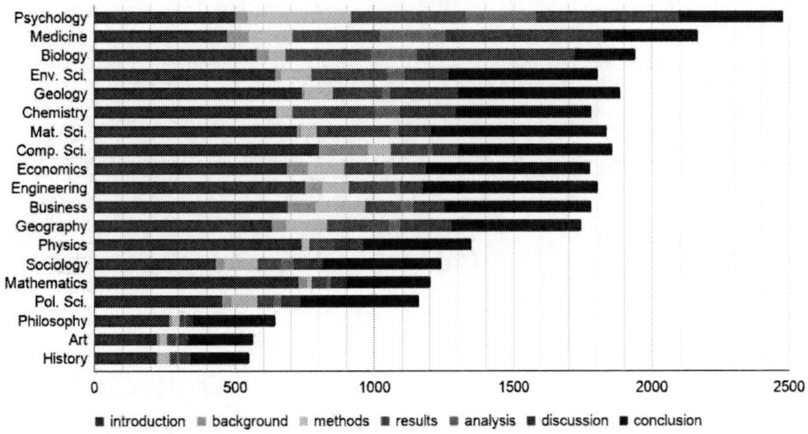

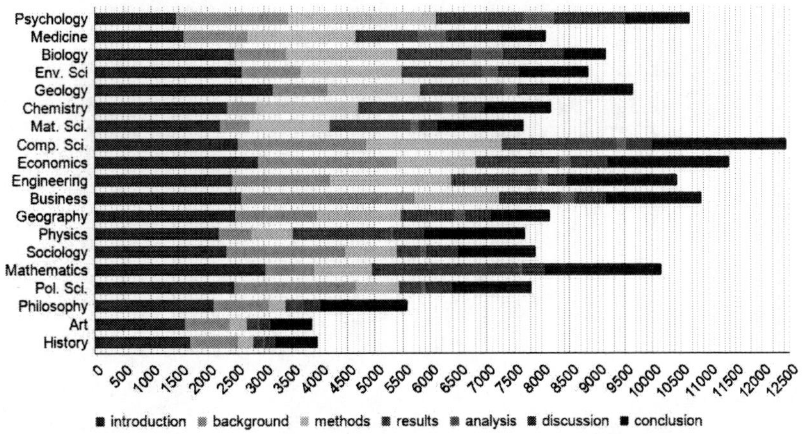

Figure 2: The frequency of the top-7 section headings before (top) and after (bottom) retrofitting.

B Aggregate Frequency for Other Disciplines

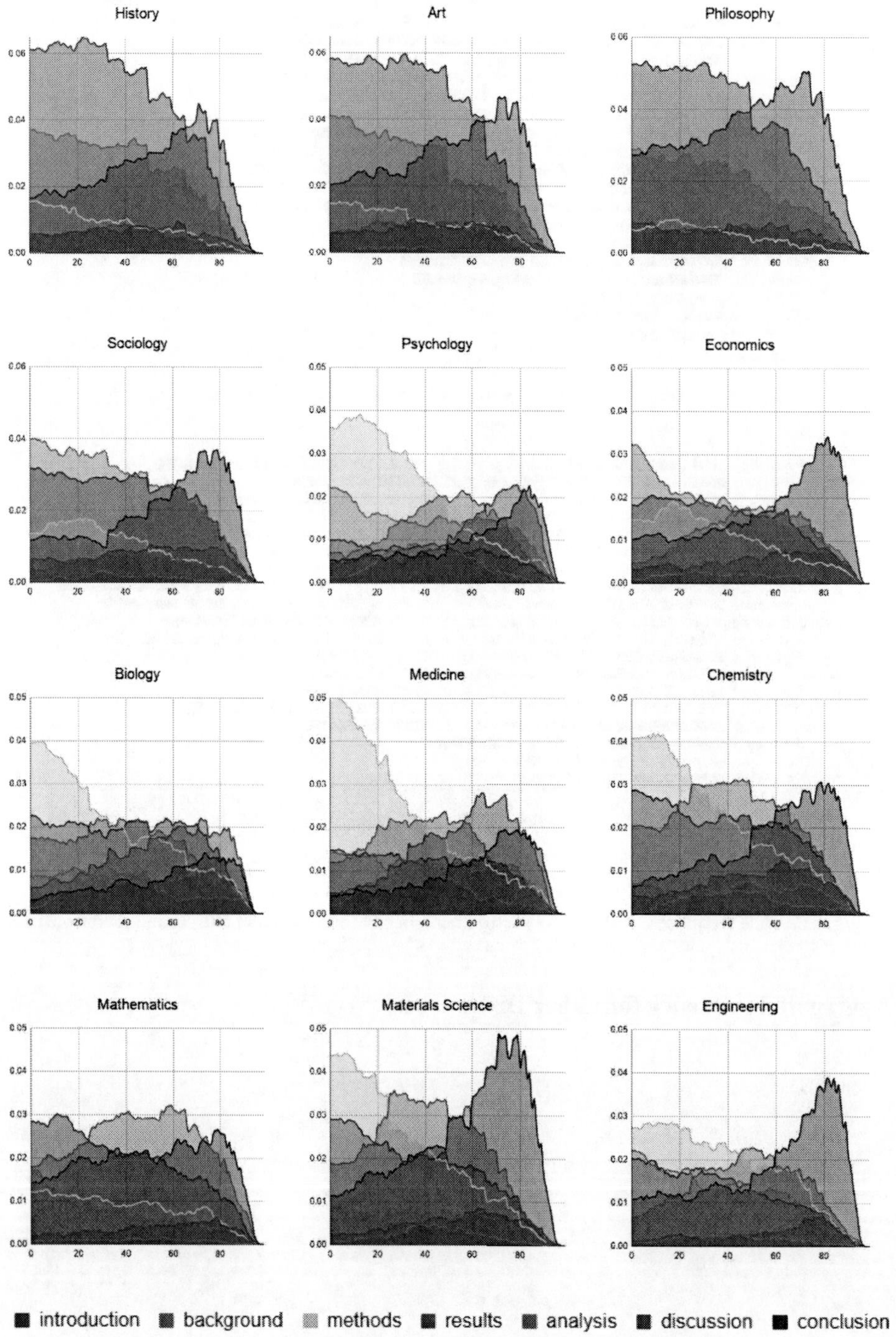

Figure 3: Aggregate Frequency for 12 of the 19 disciplines

Extractive Research Slide Generation Using Windowed Labeling Ranking

Athar Sefid
Pennsylvania State University
atharsefid@gmail.com

Jian Wu
Old Dominion University
j1wu@odu.edu

Prasenjit Mitra
Pennsylvania State University
pum10@psu.edu

C Lee Giles
Pennsylvania State University
clg20@psu.edu

Abstract

Presentation slides describing the content of scientific and technical papers are an efficient and effective way to present that work. However, manually generating presentation slides is labor intensive. We propose a method to automatically generate slides for scientific papers based on a corpus of 5000 paper-slide pairs compiled from conference proceedings websites. The sentence labeling module of our method is based on SummaRuNNer, a neural sequence model for extractive summarization. Instead of ranking sentences based on semantic similarities in the whole document, our algorithm measures importance and novelty of sentences by combining semantic and lexical features within a sentence window. Our method outperforms several baseline methods including SummaRuNNer by a significant margin in terms of ROUGE score.

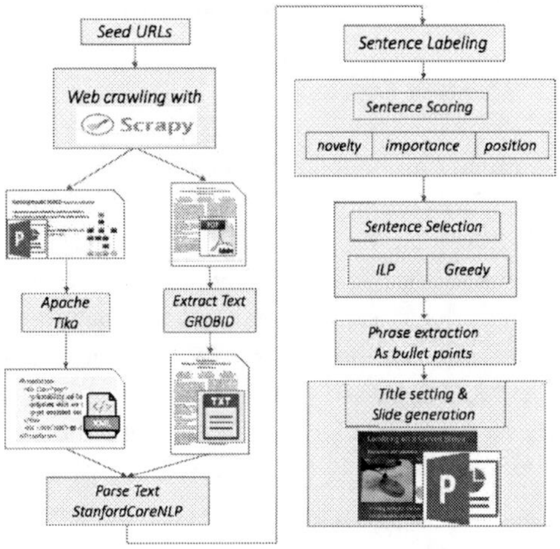

Figure 1: Main components of the model for summarizing the paper and building the slides.

1 Introduction

It has become common practice for researchers to use slides as a visual aid in presenting research findings and innovations. Such slides usually contain bullet points that the researchers believe to be important to show. These bullet points serve both as a reminder to the speaker (when he/she is presenting) and summaries for audiences to understand. Manually creating a set of high-quality slides from an academic paper is time-consuming. We propose a method that automatically selects salient sentences that could be included into the slides, with the purpose of reducing the time and effort for slide generation.

The main challenge for solving this problem is to accurately extract the main points from an academic paper. This is due to the limitations of existing methods to fully encode semantics of sentences and the implicit relations between sentences. Here, we propose an extractive summarizer that identifies the best sentence in a set of consecutive sentence windows. The selection process depends on importance and novelty of the sentence that is modeled by the neural networks. The selected sentences and their frequent noun phrases are then structured in a layered format to make the bullet points of the slides.

Presentation slides are usually created with multiple bullet points organized in a multi-level hierarchical structure, usually with phrases summarizing high level topics at the first level and bullets at the second and other levels for further clarification or details. Statistical analysis on our training data set shows that more than 92% of the bullets are in the first and second level and only 8% are in the third layer. Therefore, we built our presentations in two level bullet points only.

Our contribution is threefold.

- Propose a system that utilizes sentences with high rankings for generating presentation slides for research papers and is used as a starting point in the slide generation process.

Proceedings of the Second Workshop on Scholarly Document Processing, pages 91–96
June 10, 2021.

- Create and provide PS5K, a corpus of 5000 paper-slide pairs in the field of **computer** and **information science**. To the best of our knowledge, this is the largest paper-slide dataset and can be used for training and evaluating slide generation models.

- Propose a novel method to rank sentences within a sentence window, which improved an existing state-of-the-art text-summarization method by a significant margin.

2 Related Work

Summarizing scholarly articles in presentation slides is different from standard text summarization (Xiao and Carenini, 2019), which focuses on generating a paragraph of free text summary out of a longer document. Automatic slide generation can be done by first extracting salient sentences in a hierarchical order and grouping them into slides that are sequentially aligned with the original paper.

PPSGen (Hu and Wan, 2014) was a framework that automatically generated presentation slides from scientific papers. They applied Support Vector Regressor and Integer Linear Programming (ILP) to rank and select important sentences. Wang et al. (2017) generate slides by extracting phrases from papers and learning the hierarchical relationship between pairs of phrases to build the structure of bullet points. Their model is trained on a small set of 175 paper-slide pairs. The slideSeer (Kan, 2007) project crawled more than 10,000 paper-slide pairs using the Google APIs to search for the slide of papers using their title as a search query. The full set of data is not publicly available (only 20 pairs are available). Compared with previous works, our model is trained and tested on a relatively large set of 5000 paper-slide pairs and the dataset will be publicly available for future works. There had been some work on the alignment of presentations slides to the article sections (Hayama et al., 2005; Kan, 2007; Beamer and Girju, 2009).

SummaRuNNer (Nallapati et al., 2017) is a neural extractive summarizer that treats the summarization task as a sequence labeling problem. SummaRuNNer was evaluated on CNN/Daily Mail corpus, which contains news articles that are shorter than research papers. We improve upon the SummaRuNNer model for the summarization of scientific papers.

3 Data

Producing a large dataset for summarization of scientific documents is challenging and requires domain experts to make the summaries. The latest CL-Scisumm 2018 summarization task contains **only 40 NLP papers** with human-annotated reference summaries. Recently, ScisummNet (Yasunaga et al., 2019) expanded the CL-Scisumm to 1000 scientific articles. TalkSum (Lev et al., 2019) summarizes scientific articles based on the transcripts of the presentation talks at conferences.

Using presentation slides made by the authors is promising for the training of deep neural summarization models as more conferences are providing slides with papers.

We crawled more than 5,000 paper-slide pairs from a manually curated list of websites, e.g., usenix.org and aclweb.org. GROBID (Lopez, 2009) is used to get metadata and the body of the text from scientific papers in PDF format. Presentations are transformed form PDF or PPT format to XML by Apache Tika[1]. The Tika XML files are divided into *pages* and the text is extracted using Optical Character Recognition (OCR) tools. Most venues of papers in our dataset are in computational linguistics, system, and system security. In our dataset, there are on average 35 pages of slide per presentation and 8 lines of text per slide page. The majority (75%) of papers are published between 2013 and 2019. We used this dataset (called PS5K) to train summarization models to identify important parts of the input document at the sentence level.

4 Method

Generating slides requires identifying important sentences of the input scientific article and consists of three main steps. The first is to label salient sentences in the paper that are literally similar to corresponding slides. The second is to train the model to rank sentences and the final step selects salient sentences based on the predicted scores, size of the summary and the length of the sentences. Afterwards, frequent noun phrases are extracted from the selected sentences to shape the hierarchical structure of the bullet points. The architecture of our model is shown in Figure 1.

[1]https://tika.apache.org/

4.1 Sentence Labeling

The text in manually generated slides may not be directly extracted from the original paper. Instead, text can be truncated, summarized, or rephrased. Therefore, we need to generate extractive labels for sentences of the input document. The sentence labeling process attempts to identify salient sentences that are semantically similar to the corresponding slides. This generates an *extractive* summary, which will be used as the ground truth for training and evaluation.

The problem is formalized below:

A research paper can be represented as a sequence of n sentences $D = \{s_1, s_2, ...s_n\}$, each having a label $y_i \in \{0, 1\}$, the system predicts $p(y_i = 1)$, probability of including sentence i to the summary.

SummaRuNNer treats the summarization task as a sequence labeling problem, if adding the sentence to the summary improves the ROUGE score, the sentence is labeled with 1, otherwise it is labeled with 0. This method is suitable for news articles such as CNN/DailyMail (Nallapati et al., 2016) where the first couple of sentences in articles usually cover the main content. Scholarly papers usually contain a hierarchical structure of sections. Each section should have its own summary as a part of the summary of the entire paper. Therefore, the labeling process should be adapted to distribute positive labels across all sections of the paper. However, accurately parsing sections of open domain scholarly papers is non-trivial. Therefore, we propose a windowed labeling approach, in which ranking is performed only within a series of non-overlapping text windows, each of which contains w consecutive sentences. A sentence is labeled as 1 if adding the current sentence increases the ROUGE-1 index. The best window size is determined empirically by trying different widow sizes and calculating the ROUGE score between selected sentences and the presentation slides. Section 5 elaborates on the experiments performed to select the best window size.

4.2 Sentence and Document Embedding

The ranking of sentences depends on their salience, novelty, and content similarity to the ground truth. To quantify these characteristics, a document is represented into a vector. We explore two methods to build the embedding for the whole document.

Simple Document Embedding A simple document embedding can be obtained by calculating the average of sentence encodings generated by a Bidirectional Long Short-Term Memory (BiLSTM) (Hochreiter and Schmidhuber, 1997). A sentence s_i can be encoded as $E_{s_i} = [\vec{h_i}, \overleftarrow{h_i}]$ in which E_{s_i} is a concatenation of forward ($\vec{h_i}$) and backward ($\overleftarrow{h_i}$) hidden states of the last token in sentence s_i. The embedding for document D with n sentences is the average of all sentence embeddings:

$$E_D = ReLU(W \times \frac{1}{n}\sum_{i=1}^{n} E_{s_i} + b) \qquad (1)$$

in which $ReLU$ is the activation function, W and b are parameters to be learned.

Hierarchical Self Attention Document Embedding This model embeds a document by applying the attention mechanism at both word and sentence levels (Al-Sabahi et al., 2018; Yang et al., 2016).

Sentence embeddings are obtained by encoding word-level tokens of a sentence using BiLSTM and then aggregating hidden layers using an attention mechanism. Formally, considering a sentence s_i with m words, the sentence encoding h_{s_i} is obtained as a concatenation of all m hidden states of word-level tokens ($h_{s_i} = [h_1, h_2, ..., h_m]$) where $h_{s_i} \in \mathbb{R}^{m \times 2d}$ and d is the embedding dimension for each word. The attention weights are:

$$a_{\text{word}} = softmax\left(W_{\text{attn}} \times h_{s_i}^T\right) \qquad (2)$$

where $W_{\text{attn}} \in \mathbb{R}^{k \times 2d}$ is the model matrix to be learned. Then $a_{\text{word}} \in \mathbb{R}^{k \times m}$ and the embedding for sentence s_i is:

$$E_{s_i} = \underset{k}{average}\left(a_{word} \times h_{s_i}\right) \qquad (3)$$

where $E_{s_i} \in \mathbb{R}^{1 \times 2d}$ and k is the attention dimension which is set to 100 in our experiments.

Document embeddings (E_D) are generated using sentence embeddings (E_{s_i}) built in the previous step. A similar attention layer is applied on top of sentence embeddings to build the document embedding. The sentence level attention works as the weights to emphasize important sentences in document embedding.

4.3 Sentence Ranking

The rank of a sentence depends on its position in the paper, salience, and novelty with respect to the previously selected sentences, calculated below:

$$\begin{aligned} pos &= position \times W_{pos} \\ content &= E_{s_i} \times W_{content} \\ salience &= E_D \times W_{salience} \times E_{s_i}^T \\ novelty &= summary_i \times W_{novelty} \times E_{s_i}^T \\ p(y_i = 1) &= \sigma(pos + content + novelty + \\ & \quad salience) \end{aligned} \tag{4}$$

where $W_{pos} \in \mathbb{R}^{2d \times 1}$,where $W_{content} \in \mathbb{R}^{2d \times 1}$ $W_{salience} \in \mathbb{R}^{2d \times 2d}$, and $W_{novelty} \in \mathbb{R}^{2d \times 2d}$ are parameters to be learned. The $position$ is the position of the sentence in the document specified by a Embedding lookup function, σ is the sigmoid activation function, and pos is its positional embedding. The $salience$ estimates the importance of a sentence. The $novelty$ represents the novelty of a sentence with respect to the current summery. The summary embedding is the weighted sum of the previous sentences added to summary until sentence i:

$$summary_i = \sum_{j=0}^{i-1} p(y_i = 1) \times E_{s_i} \tag{5}$$

The higher chance of adding the sentence to the summary gives it a bigger portion in the summary embedding. Figure 2 shows the architecture for predicting the score for the third sentence in a document.

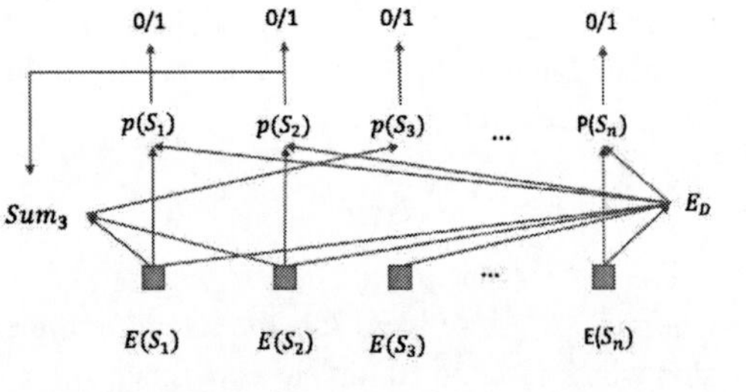

Figure 2: Score prediction for sentence 3 depends on document embedding (E_D), sentence embedding, the embedding of the summary built until step 3 (Sum_3), and position of the sentence which is 3. The summary is the weighted sum of the embeddings of the first and second sentences.

With windowed labeling, the positive labels are sparse. To deal with the imbalanced positive labels, the following weighted cross-entropy loss is adopted. The setting of $w_1 = -85$ and $w_2 = -2$ results in the highest ROUGE score.

$$\begin{aligned} -\sum_{i=0}^{n} w_1 y_i \times \log\left(p(y_i = 1)\right) \\ +w_2(1 - y_i) \times \log\left(1 - p(y_i = 1)\right) \end{aligned} \tag{6}$$

4.4 Sentence Selection

To select the sentences for the slide we tried 1) the greedy approach that sequentially adds sentences with highest scores until the maximum limit is hit and 2) the ILP method that selects the sentences by optimizing the following function using IBM CPLEX Optimizer [2].

$$\begin{aligned} \max \sum_{i \in N_s} l_i x_i \times p(y_i = 1) \\ \sum_i l_i x_i < maxLen, \quad \forall i,\ x_i \in \{0, 1\} \end{aligned} \tag{7}$$

where $p(y_i = 1)$ is the score of the sentence predicted by the model, x_i is a binary variable showing whether sentence i is selected for the summary or not, l_i is the length of sentence i and penalizes short sentences, and $maxLen$ is the maximum length of the summary.

4.5 Slide Generation

A typical presentation slide includes a limited number of bullet points as the first-level, which are usually phrases or shortened sentences. Some slides may contain second-level bullet points for further breakdowns. Table 2 shows that less than 8% of the content of the presentations in the ground truth corpus is covered in third-level bullets. We generate slides containing up to 2 bullet levels. Table 2 also shows that a slide title on average contains 4 words and either Level 1 or Level 2 bullets contains on average 8 words. Each slide consists of on average 36 words in 5 bullets and each level-1 bullet includes 2 second-level bullets.

Sentences selected are treated as the second-level bullets. The first-level bullets are the noun phrases extracted from the sentences. Noun phrases are removed if they contain more than 10 words or just 1 word. Noun phrases with a document frequency greater than 10 are excluded (e.g. "the model"). The section, which the first sentence of a slide is in, is found and its heading is used as the slide title.

[2]https://www.ibm.com/products/ilog-cplex-optimization-studio

Table 1: ROUGE scores for different models. Oracle and TextRank are unsupervised and do not need training. T_{tr} standards for training time in hours based on Nvidia GTX 2080 Ti GPU. SRNN stands for SummaRuNNer.

Models	ROUGE-1	ROUGE-2	ROUGE-L	T_{tr}
Oracle (window=10)	57.12	16.53	27.62	-
Sefid et al. (Sefid et al., 2019)	36.33	8.73	17.02	-
TextRank (Barrios et al., 2016)	38.87	9.28	19.75	-
SRNN+ILP	45.12	11.65	22.96	18
SRNN+greedy	45.04	11.67	23.03	18
Attn+windowed SRNN+ILP	47.49	11.67	22.89	38
Attn+windowed SRNN+greedy	47.56	11.68	23.30	38
windowed SRNN+ILP	**48.29**	12.00	**23.80**	18
windowed SRNN+greedy	48.28	**12.02**	22.14	18

Table 2: Bullet points statistics.

Bullet-Point	Fraction	Avg Word Count
Title	-	3.7
Level 1	56.5%	7.38
Level 2	35.5%	7.22
Level 3	7.9%	6.7

Table 3: ROUGE scores for oracle summaries generated with different window sizes.

Window Size	R-1	R-2	R-L
3	42.95	11.13	21.59
5	44.34	11.43	22.35
7	44.88	11.64	22.47
10	**45.93**	**12.00**	**22.75**
15	45.52	11.84	22.68

The heading is truncated to the first 5 tokens. We limit a maximum of 4 sentences per slide. If a topic has more than 4 related sentences, the slide is split into two distinct ones.

5 Experiments and Results

We estimated the parameters of our model on PS5K. We split the dataset into training, validation, and testing set, each consisting of 4500, 250, and 250 pairs, respectively. We experimented with different window sizes and found that a window size of $w = 10$ gives the best ROUGE-1 recall (Table 3) and is adapted for our model.

The Stanford CoreNLP (Manning et al., 2014) is used to tokenize and lemmatize sentences to the constituent tokens and to extract noun phrases. GloVe (Pennington et al., 2014) 50-dimensional vectors are used to initialize the word embeddings. With the AdaDelta optimizer and a learning rate of 0.1, we trained for 50 epochs. The sentences are truncated or padded to have 50 tokens (only 8% sentences consist of more than 50 tokens). Similarly, we adopt a fixed document size of 500 sentences (only 3.5% of documents in our dataset have more than 500 sentences). We used the standard ROUGE score (Lin, 2004) to evaluate the summaries. The ROUGE scores for summaries are tabulated in Table 1. The summary size can not exceed 20% of the size of the input document in words. TextRank (Mihalcea and Tarau, 2004) is a graph based summarizer that applies the Google PageRank (Page et al., 1999) algorithm to rank the sentences. Sefid et al. (Sefid et al., 2019) rank the sentences by combining surface features, semantic and contextual embeddings. The windowed SummaRuNNer+ILP model outperforms the base SummaRuNNer by at least 3 points in ROUGE-1 recall. Adding attention layer to the model does not improve the ROUGE score while it increases the training time considerably as there are more parameters to be trained.

6 Conclusion

We create and make available PS5K, which is a large slide-paper dataset consisting of 5,000 scientific articles and corresponding manually made slides. This dataset can be used for scientific document summarization and slide generation. We used state of the art extractive summarization methods to summarize scientific articles. Our results show that distributing the positive labels across all sections of a scientific paper, in contrast to summarization methods for news articles, considerably improves performance.

References

Kamal Al-Sabahi, Zhang Zuping, and Mohammed Nadher. 2018. A hierarchical structured self-attentive model for extractive document summarization (hssas). *IEEE Access*, 6:24205–24212.

Federico Barrios, Federico López, Luis Argerich, and Rosa Wachenchauzer. 2016. Variations of the similarity function of textrank for automated summarization. *CoRR*, abs/1602.03606.

Brandon Beamer and Roxana Girju. 2009. Investigating automatic alignment methods for slide generation from academic papers. In *Proceedings of the Thirteenth Conference on Computational Natural Language Learning*, pages 111–119. Association for Computational Linguistics.

Tessai Hayama, Hidetsugu Nanba, and Susumu Kunifuji. 2005. Alignment between a technical paper and presentation sheets using a hidden markov model. In *Proceedings of the 2005 International Conference on Active Media Technology, 2005.(AMT 2005).*, pages 102–106. IEEE.

Sepp Hochreiter and Jürgen Schmidhuber. 1997. Long short-term memory. *Neural computation*, 9(8):1735–1780.

Yue Hu and Xiaojun Wan. 2014. Ppsgen: Learning-based presentation slides generation for academic papers. *IEEE transactions on knowledge and data engineering*, 27(4):1085–1097.

Min-Yen Kan. 2007. Slideseer: A digital library of aligned document and presentation pairs. In *Proceedings of the 7th ACM/IEEE-CS joint conference on Digital libraries*, pages 81–90. ACM.

Guy Lev, Michal Shmueli-Scheuer, Jonathan Herzig, Achiya Jerbi, and David Konopnicki. 2019. Talksumm: A dataset and scalable annotation method for scientific paper summarization based on conference talks. *arXiv preprint arXiv:1906.01351*.

Chin-Yew Lin. 2004. Rouge: A package for automatic evaluation of summaries. *Text Summarization Branches Out*.

Patrice Lopez. 2009. Grobid: Combining automatic bibliographic data recognition and term extraction for scholarship publications. In *Proceedings of the 13th European Conference on Research and Advanced Technology for Digital Libraries*, ECDL'09, pages 473–474.

Christopher D. Manning, Mihai Surdeanu, John Bauer, Jenny Finkel, Steven J. Bethard, and David McClosky. 2014. The Stanford CoreNLP natural language processing toolkit. In *Association for Computational Linguistics (ACL) System Demonstrations*, pages 55–60.

Rada Mihalcea and Paul Tarau. 2004. Textrank: Bringing order into text. In *Proceedings of the 2004 conference on empirical methods in natural language processing*, pages 404–411.

Ramesh Nallapati, Feifei Zhai, and Bowen Zhou. 2017. Summarunner: A recurrent neural network based sequence model for extractive summarization of documents. In *Thirty-First AAAI Conference on Artificial Intelligence*.

Ramesh Nallapati, Bowen Zhou, Caglar Gulcehre, Bing Xiang, et al. 2016. Abstractive text summarization using sequence-to-sequence rnns and beyond. *The SIGNLL Conference on Computational Natural Language Learning (CoNLL), 2016*.

Lawrence Page, Sergey Brin, Rajeev Motwani, and Terry Winograd. 1999. The pagerank citation ranking: Bringing order to the web. Technical report, Stanford InfoLab.

Jeffrey Pennington, Richard Socher, and Christopher Manning. 2014. Glove: Global vectors for word representation. In *Proceedings of the 2014 conference on empirical methods in natural language processing (EMNLP)*, pages 1532–1543.

Athar Sefid, Jian Wu, Prasenjit Mitra, and C Lee Giles. 2019. Automatic slide generation for scientific papers.

Sida Wang, Xiaojun Wan, and Shikang Du. 2017. Phrase-based presentation slides generation for academic papers. In *AAAI*.

Wen Xiao and Giuseppe Carenini. 2019. Extractive summarization of long documents by combining global and local context. In *Proceedings of the 2019 Conference on Empirical Methods in Natural Language Processing and the 9th International Joint Conference on Natural Language Processing, EMNLP-IJCNLP 2019, Hong Kong, China, November 3-7, 2019*, pages 3009–3019. Association for Computational Linguistics.

Zichao Yang, Diyi Yang, Chris Dyer, Xiaodong He, Alex Smola, and Eduard Hovy. 2016. Hierarchical attention networks for document classification. In *Proceedings of the 2016 conference of the North American chapter of the association for computational linguistics: human language technologies*, pages 1480–1489.

Michihiro Yasunaga, Jungo Kasai, Rui Zhang, Alexander R Fabbri, Irene Li, Dan Friedman, and Dragomir R Radev. 2019. Scisummnet: A large annotated corpus and content-impact models for scientific paper summarization with citation networks. In *Proceedings of the AAAI Conference on Artificial Intelligence*, volume 33, pages 7386–7393.

LongSumm 2021: Session based automatic summarization model for scientific document

Senci Ying, Yanzhao Zheng, Wuhe Zou
NetEase, China
{yingsenci, zhengyanzhao, zouwuhe}@corp.netease.com

Abstract

Most summarization task focuses on generating relatively short summaries. Such a length constraint might not be appropriate when summarizing scientific work. The LongSumm task needs participants generate long summary for scientific document. This task usual can be solved by language model. But an important problem is that model like BERT is limit to memory, and can not deal with a long input like a document. Also generate a long output is hard. In this paper, we propose a session based automatic summarization model (SBAS) which using a session and ensemble mechanism to generate long summary. And our model achieves the best performance in the LongSumm task.

1 Introduction

Most of the document summarization tasks focus on generate a short summary that keeps the core idea of the original document. For long scientific papers, a short abstract is not long enough to cover all the salient information. Researchers often summarize scientific articles by writing a blog, which requires specialized knowledge and a deep understanding of the scientific domain. The LongSumm, a shared task of SDP 2021(https://sdproc.org/2021/sharedtasks.html), opts to leverage blog posts created by researchers that summarize scientific articles and extractive summaries based on video talks from associated conferences(Lev et al., 2019) to address the problem mentioned above.

Most of the previous methods divide the document according to section, and use the extraction or abstraction model to predict the summary for each part respectively, and combine the results as the final summary of the document. Section based method may drop some important information among the sections. Generally, only uses one type of model for prediction can not make good use of the advantages of different models. Combined with the later models and solutions, we propose an ensemble method based on session like figure1.

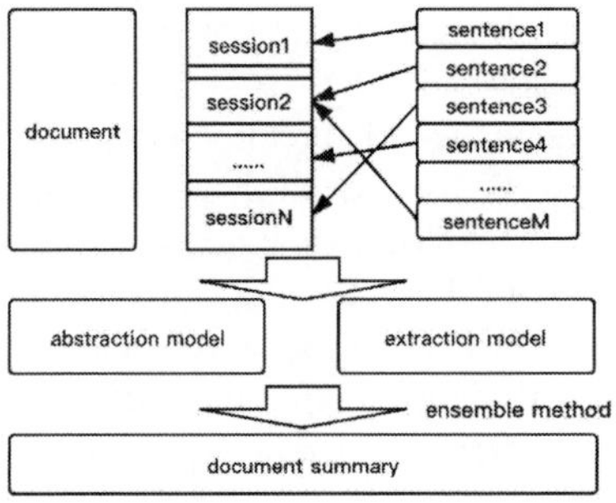

Figure 1: SBAS: a session based automatic summarization model

We split the task into four steps: session generation, extraction, abstraction, and merging the results at the end. First, we split an document into several sessions with a certain size, and use a rouge metric to match the ground truth (sentences from given document's summary). Then, we train two different types of model. One is the abstraction-based model. Specifically, we use the BIGBIRD(Zaheer et al., 2020), a sparse attention mechanism that reduces this quadratic dependency to linear, and PEGASUS(Zhang et al., 2020), a pretrained model specially designed for summarization. The other one is based on extraction method. We test the performance of TextRank(Mihalcea and Tarau, 2004; Xu et al., 2019), DGCNN(Dilate Gated Convolutional Neural Network)(Su, 2018) and BERTSUMM(Liu, 2019). In the end, for each type of model, we generate the summary from the one which has the best performance, and use an ensemble method to merge the summaries together. The result show that our method is effective and beats the state-of-art models in this task.

Proceedings of the Second Workshop on Scholarly Document Processing, pages 97–102
June 10, 2021. ©2021 Association for Computational Linguistics

2 Related Work

The common automatic summarization is mainly divided into the extraction-based summarization and the abstraction-based summarization. The extraction-based model extracts several sentences and words from the original article by the semantic analysis and sentence importance analysis to form the abstract of the article. Typical models include TextRank(Mihalcea and Tarau, 2004; Xu et al., 2019) algorithm which based on sentence importance and the extraction method based on pre-training model(Liu, 2019). The abstracts obtained by the extraction model can better reflect the focus of the article, but because the extracted sentences are scattered in different parts of the article, the coherence of the abstracts is a problem to be challenged. The abstraction-based models are based on the structure of seq2seq, and the pre-training model is used to achieve better generation effect like BART(Lewis et al., 2019), T5(Raffel et al., 2019). Recently, PEGASUS(Zhang et al., 2020), a pre-training model released by Google, specially designed the pre-training mode for the summarization task, and achieved the state-of-art performance on all 12 downstream datasets.

This task focuses on the the solution of the long summary. The input and ouput text of the traditional model is limited due to the memory and time-consuming. However, this task requires the model to summarize scientific papers and generate very long summaries. To solve this problem, most of the solutions in the the previous are based on sections(Li et al., 2020; Roy et al., 2020). They divide scientific papers into sections, generate abstracts for each seciton, and finally combine them to get the final results. Resently, Google's new model BIGBIRD(Zaheer et al., 2020) , using sparse attention mechanism to enable the model fit long text, is suitable for this task scenario.

3 Method

The pre-training model plays a significant role in the field of automatic summarization, but due to its huge amount of parameters, most of the models can only be used for short text tasks. For long articles, there are two common ways to do. One is to directly truncate the long articles, the other is to predict the articles according to the section. This paper proposes a text segmentation method based on session, and use an ensemble method with the extraction model and the abstraction model to generate the final summary.

3.1 Session Generation

Limited by the computational power, many methods chose to truncate long articles directly, which makes the model unable to perceive the content of the following articles, and the generated summary can only reflect part of the input text. Others divide the article into sections, but this also raise some problems. The length and content of section are different between different articles. The division based on section may not reflect the relationship between text and abstract well. This paper proposes a segmentation method based on session, which divides the article into different sessions according to the selected size, predicts the summary for each session, and selects the most appropriate window size in this task by adjusting the size of the session.

The specific data processing steps are as follows: (1) First, select the appropriate session size(2048 words) and a buffer(128 words), which is used to keep the last text of the previous session as the context of the current session. (2) For generating models. The real summary is divided into sentences, and the corresponding summary sentence is assigned to each session according to the rouge metric. In order to make the model predict long summaries as much as possible, a greedy matching rule is used to allocate the summary sentences to each session. we first drop the sentences with the threshold 0.7, which denotes the rouge score between the session and summary sentences. Then we pick the sentences according to the scores until meets the length we set, default 256 words.

Although this may cause different sessions to predict the same summary, we think that duplicate sentences can be detected through the later data processing, and it is more important for the training model to generate long sentences . (3) For the extraction model, we only need to match different sessions with their corresponding summary sentences.

3.2 Abstraction-based Model

The training data contains around 700 abstractive summaries that come from different domains of CS including ML, NLP, AI, vision, storage, etc. And the abstractive summaries are blog posts created by NLP and ML researchers. The traditional generation model is mainly based on the classical transformers structure. In order to solve the problem of long text input , we use the sparse attention structure BIGBIRD(Zaheer et al., 2020), which is proposed by Google recently, and makes fine-tuning on its two open source pre-training models:

(1) Roberta(Liu et al., 2019): a bert model with the dynamic masking and drops the next predict loss

(2) PEGASUS(Zhang et al., 2020): a transformer model while using gap sentences generation to pre-training.

The models used in this paper are both pre-trained on arXiv datasets, so they have strong ability to generate abstracts.

3.3 Extraction-based Model

The extractive data have 1705 extractive summaries which are based on video talks from associated conferences(Lev et al., 2019). We have tried tree different extraction models to select important sentence from the documents.

(1) TextRank(Mihalcea and Tarau, 2004): We simply use the TextRank algorithm to pick out some most important sentences from the documents and limited the number of sentences extracted.

(2) DGCNN-Extraction(Su, 2018): DGCNN is an 1D-CNN Network structure combines two new convolution structure: dilated convolution(Gehring et al., 2017) and gated convolution(Dauphin et al., 2017).

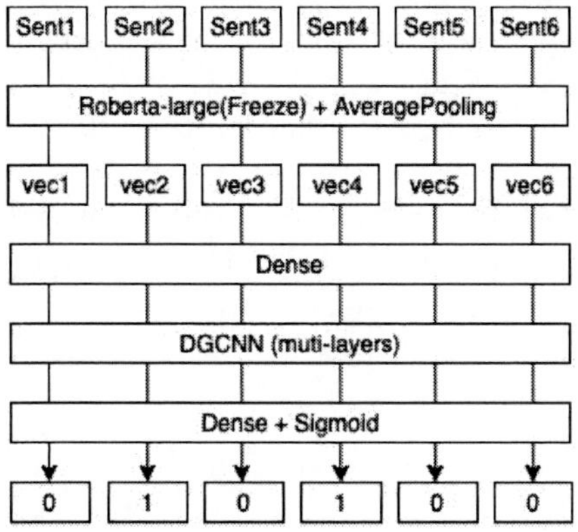

Figure 2: DGCNN-Extraction model structure

The advantage of DGCNN-Extraction model is that it can process the information of every sentence in the text at same time, and identify the important sentence by context. The way we train the model is as follows:

1. We use NLTK to break the original paper into multiple sentences, and label each sentence according to the golden extractive summarize.

2. Transform each sentence by Roberta-Large pre-trained model(Liu et al., 2019), and get the output of last hidden layers as the feature representation, then convert the feature matrix to a fixed-size vector by average-pooling.

3. TRAINING: Feed the obtained sentence vectors into the DGCNN-Extraction model (Figure 2) and binary classify each sentence.

4. INFERENCE: Take the sigmoid-output of the model as the importance score for each sentence, according to which we extract the corresponding sentences from the paper as the extractive summary and the total length of the summary is limited.

(3) BERTSUMM(Liu, 2019): BERTSUMM is a Bert-based model designed for the extractive summarization task. Different from DGCNN-Extraction model, because of the limit of the input length of Bert, we have to divide each paper into sections, then treat each section as a independent sample. As the result, we get 17720 sections in total. Follow the practice in BERTSUMM paper, we insert a [CLS] token before each sentence and a [SEP] token after each sentence and the [CLS] is used as a symbol to aggregate features from one sentence. In each sections we label the [CLS] token of sentences in ground-truth as 1 and others as 0. We split the data into training data and validation data and train the model on the training data. It's a pity that the F1-score of the result of validation data only peaked at 0.35. We think it is because this approach abandon the the information between the sections and the assumption of sections independence is not valid.

According to the performance of this three models on the validation set, we choose DGCNN-Extraction model as the baseline of the extraction model.

3.4 Ensemble Method

Abstraction model and extraction model have their own advantages and disadvantages. The advantage of abstraction model is that it can produce different expression from the original text, and can better summarize the original text, also the generated summary will be more fluent than the extracted summary. However, the disadvantage of this model is that the generated content can not be controlled, and it can not guarantee that the model can predict all the key points of the original text. The extraction model can capture most of the important information directly from the score of the original sentence. Therefore, this paper considers an ensemble method to reorganize the abstracts predicted by the abstraction model and the extraction model so as to further improve the accuracy of the abstracts. The specific implementation method is as follows:

1. self drop: since there are overlapping texts between sessions, the results predicted by the model may have repeated text. This paper first divides the predicted summary into sentences, and judges the sentence similarity according to the rouge metric. The sentences whose similarity are greater than a certain threshold(rough1-f + rough2-f > 0.8) will be determined as repeated sentences, and the longest one (we think that the long sentence carries more information) is selected as the most representative sentence, the rest are dropped.

2. sentence reorder: reorder the abstracted and extracted sentences according to the session. For each session we will predict summaries by both abstracted and extracted model. And we ordered them look like this : $sess_1$: $abs_{11}, .., abs_{1n_1}, ext_{11}, .., ext_{1m_1}; sess_2$: $abs_{21}, .., abs_{2n_2}, ext_{21}, .., ext_{2m_2}; ..; sess_m$. Because the abstraction model predicts the sentence that is usually a summary sentence, we put it before the extracted sentence in the same session.

3. recall: we will filter the combined summaries again and recall the most useful sentence for the final result. To do this, we used TextRank algorithm and dropped the sentences which scores are under 0.9.

After these steps, the predictions from the different models are well cleaned and merged. The most important sentences are selected from the candidate summaries to form the final result. The experiment shows that the comparison of single model and ensemble method has a significant effect.

4 Experiment

We extract the text from the PDF of paper by using Science Parse(`https://github.com/allenai/science-parse`). There is a lot of dirty text in the data, which will make the model hard to converge during training. So we clean the text as follows: (1) replace the URL link in the text with [url](2) remove special characters from the text and keep only some common symbols. (3) merge the broken words and remove some words that is not in the word list.

We spilt the text of each paper into sessions,and the best session size by testing should be 1024 words. The buffer size is 128 which we think is enought to keep the context. Each sentence of ground truth is set as the target summary of one of the sessions according to the location of the most similar sentence in the original paper. We use the NLTK to count words of the session. As for pretrained model, all input session are truncated to a maximum of 1024 words, and their target summary are truncated to a maximum of 128 words. Based on the test results, the best generation model is built as follows: The model is fine-tuned on the pegasus-arxiv pre-trained model released by Google which has about 570 million parameters for 20 epochs with a learning rate of 2e-5. The batch size is 8 and the model is trained on four v100(32G) GPUs for about 20 hours. As for building DGCNN-Extraction model, all input papers are truncated to a maximum of 400 sentences(1024d) and 7 DGCNN-layers (with 1,2,4,8,16,1,1 dilation rate) are added to the model. Then we compile the model with Adam optimizer(learning rate = 0.001). The model is trained for 20 epochs on training set and the batch size is set to 32. DGCNN is a lightweight model that only takes 30 minutes to train.

Follow the method mentioned above, we ensemble the summaries obtained from the best generation model and extraction model.

5 Result

We test three different models on the test set: (1)$SBAS_{extract}$: the model only include the DGCNN-extraction model for summary. (2)$SBAS_{abstract}$: the one using the PEGASUS as a base abstractive model to generate the summary. (3)$SBAS_{ensemble}$: the ensemble model of the $SBAS_{extract}$ and the $SBAS_{abstract}$. We compare the final test scores of all metrics with other teams on the leaderboard in Table 1.

The result show that both $SBAS_{abstract}$ and $SBAS_{extract}$ model are competitive. As for the result of $SBAS_{abstract}$, its recall-score is much

Method	$rouge1_f$	$rouge1_r$	$rouge2_f$	$rouge2_r$	$rougeL_f$	$rougeL_r$
$BART$	0.1921	0.1122	0.0533	0.0310	0.1062	0.0620
$Sroberta$	0.4621	0.4377	0.1280	0.1212	0.1701	0.1610
$Sharingan$	0.5031	0.5164	0.1706	0.1744	0.2114	0.2162
$Summaformers$	0.4938	0.4390	0.1686	0.2498	0.2138	0.1898
$CNLP-NITS$	0.5096	0.5234	0.1538	0.1581	0.1951	0.2008
MTP	0.4858	0.4919	0.1330	0.1348	0.1697	0.1714
$SBAS_{abstract}$	0.5080	0.4755	0.1740	0.1634	0.2156	0.2016
$SBAS_{extract}$	0.5275	0.5415	0.1711	0.1747	0.2209	0.2262
$SBAS_{ensemble}$	**0.5507**	**0.5660**	**0.1945**	**0.1998**	**0.2295**	**0.2357**

Table 1: Result for Long Scientific Document Summarization 2021

lower than F1-score, this might be caused by the summary generated by $SBAS_{abstract}$ is shorter than the ground truth. We limit the length of summary extracted by $SBAS_{extract}$ to 900 words, and get an excellent result compared with other teams. The result of $SBAS_{ensemble}$ is far superior to the others models, we believe this is because our ensemble method not only remove the redundant sentences in the combined summary, but also make the output of $SBAS_{extract}$ well supplement for the result of $SBAS_{abstract}$.

We extract some of the abstract for manual evaluation, and find that the abstract generated by our method can generate sentences with high readability and cover a lot of important information of the paper, but sentence to sentence is not coherent, the fluency of the abstract is insufficient. And we will try to improve the fluency of the summary in future work.

6 Conclusion

Pre-train models such as Bert and GPT have obvious effects in all NLP fields, but they can't deal with long text due to their huge amount of parameters and computation. In this paper, we propose an ensemble model based on session for the LongSumm task. In our method, the document is firstly segmented according to the session, and some context semantics are reserved. Then, the labels corresponding to each session are matched by a specific algorithm to generate a new dataset. The extraction and abstraction models are trained on the new dataset, and the final summary is obtained by merging the results of different models through the ensemble method. The method proposed in this paper considers the context of the text as much as possible while limiting the memory growth, so that the summary predicted by the model is more coherent. And the method of merging two different types of summary models is proposed for the first time. The prediction results of different models are dropped and combined for the second time, so as to make the results closer to the real summary.

Our model has achieved the best performance in all metrics of this task, but there for improvement. The current approach is to compress the input and output to make the task adapt to the model, but the best design idea is to make the model fit the task. One of the biggest problems is how to reduce the resource consumption of the transformers structure model. BIGBIRD model proposed by Google alleviates this problem through sparse attention mechanism, but after our test, because of the decoding part of the model still uses full attention, BigBird does not solve the problem of long text output, and it is difficult to directly generate a complete long summary from scientific documents in this task. Therefore, future research can focus on how to decode longer text, so that the language model can adapt to more NLP scenarios.

References

Yann N Dauphin, Angela Fan, Michael Auli, and David Grangier. 2017. Language modeling with gated convolutional networks. In *International conference on machine learning*, pages 933–941. PMLR.

Jonas Gehring, Michael Auli, David Grangier, Denis Yarats, and Yann N Dauphin. 2017. Convolutional sequence to sequence learning. In *International Conference on Machine Learning*, pages 1243–1252. PMLR.

Guy Lev, Michal Shmueli-Scheuer, Jonathan Herzig, Achiya Jerbi, and David Konopnicki. 2019. Talksumm: A dataset and scalable annotation method for scientific paper summarization based on conference talks. *arXiv preprint arXiv:1906.01351*.

Mike Lewis, Yinhan Liu, Naman Goyal, Marjan Ghazvininejad, Abdelrahman Mohamed, Omer Levy, Ves Stoyanov, and Luke Zettlemoyer. 2019. Bart: Denoising sequence-to-sequence pre-training for natural language generation, translation, and comprehension. *arXiv preprint arXiv:1910.13461*.

Lei Li, Yang Xie, Wei Liu, Yinan Liu, Yafei Jiang, Siya Qi, and Xingyuan Li. 2020. Cist@ cl-scisumm 2020, longsumm 2020: Automatic scientific document summarization. In *Proceedings of the First Workshop on Scholarly Document Processing*, pages 225–234.

Yang Liu. 2019. Fine-tune bert for extractive summarization. *arXiv preprint arXiv:1903.10318*.

Yinhan Liu, Myle Ott, Naman Goyal, Jingfei Du, Mandar Joshi, Danqi Chen, Omer Levy, Mike Lewis, Luke Zettlemoyer, and Veselin Stoyanov. 2019. Roberta: A robustly optimized bert pretraining approach. *arXiv preprint arXiv:1907.11692*.

Rada Mihalcea and Paul Tarau. 2004. Textrank: Bringing order into text. In *Proceedings of the 2004 conference on empirical methods in natural language processing*, pages 404–411.

Colin Raffel, Noam Shazeer, Adam Roberts, Katherine Lee, Sharan Narang, Michael Matena, Yanqi Zhou, Wei Li, and Peter J Liu. 2019. Exploring the limits of transfer learning with a unified text-to-text transformer. *arXiv preprint arXiv:1910.10683*.

Sayar Ghosh Roy, Nikhil Pinnaparaju, Risubh Jain, Manish Gupta, and Vasudeva Varma. 2020. Scientific document summarization for laysumm'20 and longsumm'20.

Jianlin Su. 2018. Dgcnn: a reading comprehension model based on cnn.

Jiacheng Xu, Zhe Gan, Yu Cheng, and Jingjing Liu. 2019. Discourse-aware neural extractive text summarization. *arXiv preprint arXiv:1910.14142*.

Manzil Zaheer, Guru Guruganesh, Avinava Dubey, Joshua Ainslie, Chris Alberti, Santiago Ontanon, Philip Pham, Anirudh Ravula, Qifan Wang, Li Yang, et al. 2020. Big bird: Transformers for longer sequences. *arXiv preprint arXiv:2007.14062*.

Jingqing Zhang, Yao Zhao, Mohammad Saleh, and Peter Liu. 2020. Pegasus: Pre-training with extracted gap-sentences for abstractive summarization. In *International Conference on Machine Learning*, pages 11328–11339. PMLR.

CNLP-NITS @ LongSumm 2021: TextRank Variant for Generating Long Summaries

Darsh Kaushik, Abdullah Faiz Ur Rahman Khilji, Utkarsh Sinha, Partha Pakray
Department of Computer Science and Engineering
National Institute of Technology Silchar
Assam, India
{darsh_ug, abdullah_ug, utkarsh_ug, partha}@cse.nits.ac.in

Abstract

The huge influx of published papers in the field of machine learning makes the task of summarization of scholarly documents vital, not just to eliminate the redundancy but also to provide a complete and satisfying crux of the content. We participated in LongSumm 2021: The 2nd Shared Task on Generating Long Summaries for scientific documents, where the task is to generate long summaries for scientific papers provided by the organizers. This paper discusses our extractive summarization approach to solve the task. We used TextRank algorithm with the BM25 score as a similarity function. Even after being a graph-based ranking algorithm that does not require any learning, TextRank produced pretty decent results with minimal compute power and time. We attained 3rd rank according to ROUGE-1 scores (0.5131 for F-measure and 0.5271 for recall) and performed decently as shown by the ROUGE-2 scores.

1 Introduction

Text summarization or summarizing large pieces of texts into comparatively smaller number of words is a challenging machine learning (ML) task that has gained significant traction in recent years. The applications are immense and diverse, from condensing and comparing legal contractual documents to summarizing medical and clinical texts. Often the two approaches (Maybury, 1999) adopted for solving this task are:

- Extractive summarization:
  Here those unmodified segments of the original text are extracted and concatenated which play the most significant role in expressing the salient sentiment of the entire text. This technique is mostly used for generating comparatively longer summaries.
- Abstractive summarization:
  Here an abstract semantic representation of the original content is formed by the model which helps generate novel words/phrases for the summary by text generation and paraphrasing methods. This technique is often useful for generating concise summaries.

Recently, the task of summarizing scholarly documents has grasped the attention of researchers due to the vast quantity of papers published everyday, especially in the field of machine learning. This makes it challenging for researchers and professionals to keep-up with the latest developments in the field. Thus, the task of summarizing scientific papers aims not just to avoid redundancy in text and generate shorter summaries but also to cover all the salient information present in the document which often demands longer summaries. This would aid researchers to grasp the contents of the paper beyond abstract-level information without reading the entire paper.

Prior work on summarization of scientific documents is mostly targeted towards generation of short summaries but as mentioned before, in order to encompass all the important ideas longer summaries are required. LongSumm 2021[1] shared task, on the other hand, aims to encourage the researchers to focus on generating longer-form summaries for scientific papers.

As mentioned before, extractive summarization methods are better accustomed for generating longer-form summaries than abstractive summarization methods, in this paper we try to summarize scientific documents using the extractive summarization technique of TextRank (Mihalcea and Tarau, 2004) algorithm. It is a graph-based ranking algorithm to rank the sentences in a document according to their importance in conveying the

[1] https://sdproc.org/2021/sharedtasks.html

Proceedings of the Second Workshop on Scholarly Document Processing, pages 103–109
June 10, 2021. ©2021 Association for Computational Linguistics

information of the document. Different 'similarity' functions can be used while creating the graph which leads to varied results (Barrios et al., 2016), therefore we chose BM25 as the similarity function.

2 Related Works

Upon scrutinizing various approaches of document summarization, we have found some of the concurrent works in the field. One of these is (Christensen et al., 2013). This work describes extractive summarization as a joint process of selection and ordering. It uses graph as its elemental part, which is used to approximate the discourse relativeness using co-reference, deverbal nouns, etc. Similar works are shown by (Li et al., 2011), (Goldstein et al., 2000) and (Barzilay et al., 1999). Other works use the Google TextRank algorithm (Mihalcea and Tarau, 2004) to bring out the order in the text extraction. One of the works (Mallick et al., 2019) uses the modified TextRank plus graph infrastructure to extract contextual information. It uses the sentence as nodes in the graph and inverse cosine similarity[2] to form the weights of the edges of the graph. This graph is passed as an input to the TextRank algorithm which generates the required summary. Similar approach is followed by (Ashari and Riasetiawan, 2017) which uses the power of TextRank and semantic networks to form extractive summaries which bear the semantic relations.

Some of the works like (Nallapati et al., 2017), (Al-Sabahi et al., 2018) use capabilities of neural networks to semantically extract the information from the description and present it in human readable form. One of the works (Nallapati et al., 2016) uses a joint framework of classification and selection on the textural data to form summaries. Classifier architecture makes a decision as to whether a particular sentence in sequence (as selected by selector) will be the part of the membership of the summary or not, whereas the selector framework randomly selects the sentences from the description and places it in the summary.

Apart from these, varied approaches were adopted by the participants of the previous edition of the shared task, LongSumm 2020, as mentioned in (Chandrasekaran et al., 2020). For instance, a divide and conquer approach, DANCER, was used in (Gidiotis et al., 2020) to summarize key sections of the paper separately and combine them through a PEGASUS based transformer to generate the final summary. Another team (Ghosh Roy et al., 2020) used a neural extractive summarizer to summarize each section separately. A different team utilized the BERT summarizer as shown in (Sotudeh Gharebagh et al., 2020). The main idea was based on multi-task learning heuristic in which two tasks are optimized, namely the binary classification task of sentence selection and the section prediction of input sentences. They also suggested an abstractive summarizer based on the BART transformer that runs after the extractive summarizer. Other methods were Convolutional Neural Network (CNN) in (Reddy et al., 2020), Graph Convolutional Network (GCN) and Graph Attention Network (GAN) in (Li et al., 2020), and unsupervised clustering in (Mishra et al., 2020) and (Ju et al., 2020).

3 Dataset

3.1 Description

The LongSumm dataset is distinctive in the sense that it consists of scientific documents which have scientific jargon targeted for a niche audience, unlike other summarization corpuses like news articles for the general public. Due to the same reason, it is difficult to find domain-specific scientific documents with their longer-form summaries covering all their important details in a concise manner.

The organizers of LongSumm 2021 provided corpus for this task includes a training set that consists of 1705 extractive summaries, and 531 abstractive summaries of NLP and Machine Learning scientific papers. The extractive summaries are based on video talks (Chandrasekaran et al., 2020) from associated conferences while the abstractive summaries are blog posts created by NLP and ML researchers.

We used Textrank (Mihalcea and Tarau, 2004) which is a graph-based ranking model for ranking sentences in a document for extractive summarization. Therefore, only extractive summaries were used as validation data. The extractive summaries

[2] https://link.springer.com/chapter/10.1007/978-3-642-41278-3_74

are based on the TalkSumm (Lev et al., 2019) dataset. The dataset contains 1,705 automatically generated noisy extractive summaries of scientific papers from the NLP and Machine Learning domain based on video talks from associated conferences (like ACL, NAACL, ICML). URL links to the papers and their summaries and could be found in the Github repository[3] devoted to this shared task. Each summary provides the top-30 sentences, which are on average around 990 words.

Another list of 22papers [4] was provided as test data (blind). The summaries generated for these papers were used for evaluation. ROUGE-1, ROUGE-2 and ROUGE-L scores were used to evaluate the performance of the system.

3.2 Preprocessing

After retrieving the text from the papers (links to which were provided by the organizers) the sections before 'Introduction' (like Authors, Abstract etc.) and after 'Conclusion/Results' (like References, Acknowledgements etc.) were removed as the text in these sections do not add much valuable sentiments to the summary as compared to the left over sections of the paper. Further citation indexing, hyperlinks, newline and redundant white-space characters were eliminated.

4 System Description

Our approach essentially was to use the TextRank algorithm (Mihalcea and Tarau, 2004) to rank the sentences corresponding to their relevance to the whole text and use the most significant (highest ranked) sentences as the summary.

4.1 TextRank

TextRank is a graph-based ranking algorithm which is proven to be quite impactful for keyword and sentence extraction from natural language texts.

According to (Mihalcea and Tarau, 2004) for sentence extraction, a graph is constructed for the given document in which each vertex represents an entire sentence. Now the semantic links amongst the vertices are identified by the "similarity" between the sentences, where "similarity" is measured as a function of their content overlap. The formal expression for determining the similarity of two sentences, $S_a = w_1^a, w_2^a, ..., w_{N_a}^a$ with N_a words, and $S_b = w_1^b, w_2^b, ..., w_{N_b}^b$ with N_b words as defined in (Mihalcea and Tarau, 2004):

$$Sim(S_a, S_b) = \frac{|\{w_k | w_k \in S_a \& w_k \in S_b\}|}{log(|S_a|) + log(|S_b|)}$$

The text in the document can thus be represented as a weighted on which the ranking algorithm is run to sort the vertices (each representing a sentence in the text) in reversed order of the obtained score, from which we include the 30 most significant sentences are selected and present them in the same order as they appear in the document.

4.2 Gensim TextRank Summarizer

Variants of the similarity function can be chosen to obtain improved results, an analysis of which is shown in (Barrios et al., 2016). The different similarity functions including LCS (Longest Common Substring), cosine similarity, BM25 (Robertson et al., 1994), BM25+ (Lv and Zhai, 2011) and original TextRank similarity function were evaluated using ROUGE-1, ROUGE-2 and ROUGE-SU4 as metrics in (Barrios et al., 2016) and the best results were obtained using BM25 and BM25+.

The Summarizer module of the Gensim project [5] uses BM25-TextRank algorithm for summarization, therefore we proceeded with this implementation of TextRank to prepare the summaries. BM25 is a variation of the TF-IDF model using a probabilistic model. Given two sentences R, S, BM25 is defined as:

$$BM25(R, S) = \sum_{i=1}^{n} IDF(s_i) \cdot \frac{TF(s_i, R) \cdot (k+1)}{TF(s_i, R) + k \cdot (1 - b + b \cdot \frac{|R|}{L_{avg}})}$$

where k and b are parameters, and L_{avg} is the average length of the sentences in the document. TF is the term-frequency and IDF is the correction formula given as:

$$IDF(s_i) = \begin{cases} log(\frac{N - n(s_i) + 0.5}{n(s_i) + 0.5}) & \text{if } n(s_i) > N/2 \\ \epsilon \cdot avgIDF & \text{if } n(s_i) \leq N/2 \end{cases}$$

[3]https://github.com/guyfe/LongSumm/tree/master/extractive_summaries

[4]https://github.com/guyfe/LongSummtest-data-blind

[5]https://github.com/summanlp/gensim

where ϵ takes a value between 0.5 and 0.3 and avgIDF is the average IDF for all terms.

5 Result and Analysis

5.1 Result

The participating systems were evaluated by ROUGE(Lin, 2004) scores, specifically using ROUGE-1, ROUGE-2 and ROUGE-L metrics. Our team's name was CNLP-NITS and the result of our system on blind test data of 22 papers using TextRank with BM25 similarity is given in Table 1.

Metric	F-measure	Recall
ROUGE-1	0.5131	0.5271
ROUGE-2	0.161	0.1656
ROUGE-L	0.1916	0.1971

Table 1: ROUGE scores for blind test data

As 22 papers was not a large dataset, we also applied TextRank on the given dataset of extractive summaries (1700 of them) to get statistically sound ROUGE scores for analysis, and the scores obtained are shown Table 2.

Metric	F-measure	Recall
ROUGE-1	0.59389	0.5960
ROUGE-2	0.3349	0.3362
ROUGE-L	0.3393	0.3405

Table 2: ROUGE scores for training dataset of extractive summaries

5.2 Analysis

Individual ROUGE scores for each paper in the training set was calculated for finding the average scores.

The predicted and reference summary for the paper [6] with one of the best ROUGE scores (as given in Table 3) are as shown,

Metric	F-measure	Recall
ROUGE-1	0.88	0.88
ROUGE-2	0.8164	0.8164
ROUGE-L	0.8217	0.8217

Table 3: ROUGE scores for predicted summary of the paper[6] with one of the best performances

[6]https://www.aclweb.org/anthology/P17-1098.pdf

Predicted summary (best performance):

> "Over the past few years neural models based on the encode-attend-decode (Bahdanau et al., 2014) paradigm have shown great success in various natural language generation (NLG) tasks such as machine translation (Bahdanau et al., 2014), abstractive summarization ((Rush et al., 2015),(Nallapati et al., 2016)) dialog (Li et al., 2016), etc. One such NLG problem which has not received enough attention in the past is query based abstractive text summarization where the aim is to generate the summary of a document in the context of a query. Thus given a document on "the super bowl", the query "How was the half-time show?", would result in a summary that would not cover the actual game itself. Note that there has been some work on query based extractive summarization in the past where the aim is to simply extract the most salient sentence(s) from a document and treat these as a summary. Since, we were interested in abstractive (as opposed to extractive) summarization we created a new dataset based on debatepedia. This dataset contains triplets of the form (query, document, summary)...."[7]

Reference summary (best performance):

> "Over the past few years neural models based on the encode-attend-decode (Bahdanau et al., 2014) paradigm have shown great success in various natural language generation (NLG) tasks such as machine translation (Bahdanau et al., 2014), abstractive summarization ((Rush et al., 2015),(Nallapati et al., 2016)) dialog (Li et al., 2016), etc. One such NLG problem which has not received enough attention in the past is query based abstractive text summarization where the aim is to generate the summary of a document in the context of a query. In general, abstractive summarization, aims to cover all the salient points of a document in a compact and coherent fashion. On the other hand, query focused summarization highlights those points that are relevant in the context of the query. Thus given a document on the super bowl, the query How was the half-time show?, would result in a summary that would not cover the actual game itself. Note that there has been some work on query based extractive summarization in the past where the aim is to simply extract the most salient sentence(s) from a document and treat these as a summary...."[8]

The predicted and reference summary for the paper[11] with one of the worst ROUGE scores (as given in Table 4) are as shown,

[7]Complete summary at https://bit.ly/3914zEy
[8]Complete summary at https://bit.ly/3c5elHQ

Metric	F-measure	Recall
ROUGE-1	0.305	0.305
ROUGE-2	0.0301	0.0301
ROUGE-L	0.1217	0.1217

Table 4: ROUGE scores for predicted summary of the paper[11] with one of the worst performances

Predicted summary (worst performance):

"Although state-of-the-art sensors can detect various natural disasters in advance (e.g., Mexico City's alarm system can timely sense earthquakes originating in the southern states) [1], the devastating consequences of these events in urban areas are usually severe. As an example, in the 2010 earthquake in Haiti, the use of instant messages sent by civilians from different locations facilitated the reporting of trapped individuals, the provision of medical assistance, and the delivery of basic needs, such as food, water, and shelter [5]. Personal mobile devices can be linked to Online Social Networks (OSNs) and enable synchronization among applications, e.g., Twitter, Facebook, and Instagram, which allows users to post and update their activities in real time [7,8]. A tweet providing the location (spatial information) of a collapsed building, along with a timestamp (temporal information), one day after the 2017 earthquake in Mexico City. Recently, Twitter has been the center of attention in different research fields related to Marketing, Social Sciences, Natural Language Processing (NLP), Opinion Mining, and Predictive analysis [17]...."[9]

Reference summary (worst performance):

"Second, dividing a corpus into separate time bins may lead to training sets that are too small to train a word embedding model. Hence, one runs the risk of overfitting to few data whenever the required temporal resolution is fine-grained, as we show in the experimental section. We show the ten words whose meaning changed most drastically in terms of cosine distance over the last 150 years. We thereby automatically discover words such as computer or radio whose meaning changed due to technological advances, but also words like peer and notably whose semantic shift is less obvious. Their approach uses a non-Bayesian treatment of the latent embedding trajectories, which makes the approach less robust to noise when the data per time step is small. trained end-to-end and scales to massive data by means of approximate Bayesian inference. For each pair of words i, j in the vocabulary, the model assigns probabilities that word i appears in the context of word j. ..."[10]

[9]Complete summary at https://bit.ly/3cWCmjo

[10]Complete summary at https://bit.ly/3f2XO9i

6 Conclusion and Future Work

In this paper we targeted our efforts towards TextRank algorithm in order to generate long extractive summaries of given scientific research papers. Our approach TextRank when used with BM25 similarity function, even after not being a learning algorithm, was able to achieve appreciable ROUGE-1 scores while remaining competitive in ROUGE-2 scores. As TextRank is a graph-based ranking algorithm that ranks the sentences independently for each document, it requires no training, thus being compute and time efficient.

Although we approached the task using an algorithm which does not require training and were still able to produce substantial results, there is definitely a scope for leveraging training data to gather a general semantic structure from a collection of documents as a whole instead of working on each document independently using neural network based learning algorithms. This will definitely be our prime focus for future work in extractive text summarization. Nonetheless, through our participation in LongSumm 2021 we tried to optimise TextRank algorithm and put it to test against other learning-based approaches of other teams and were able to pull off significant results with comparatively low machine and time requirements.

Acknowledgements

We would like to thank Department of Computer Science and Engineering and Center for Natural Language Processing (CNLP) at National Institute of Technology Silchar for providing the requisite support and infrastructure to execute this work. The work presented here falls under the Research Project Grant No. IFC/4130/DST-CNRS/2018-19/IT25 (DST-CNRS targeted program). The authors would also like to thank LongSumm 2021 shared task organizers for organizing this event.

References

Kamal Al-Sabahi, Zhang Zuping, and Mohammed Nadher. 2018. A hierarchical structured self-attentive model for extractive document summarization (hssas). *IEEE Access*, 6:24205–24212.

Ahmad Ashari and Mardhani Riasetiawan. 2017. Document summarization using textrank and semantic network. *International Journal Intelligent Systems and Applications*, pages 26–33.

[11]https://www.mdpi.com/1424-8220/19/7/1746

Federico Barrios, Federico López, Luis Argerich, and Rosa Wachenchauzer. 2016. Variations of the similarity function of textrank for automated summarization.

Regina Barzilay, Kathleen McKeown, and Michael Elhadad. 1999. Information fusion in the context of multi-document summarization. In *Proceedings of the 37th annual meeting of the Association for Computational Linguistics*, pages 550–557.

Muthu Kumar Chandrasekaran, Guy Feigenblat, Eduard Hovy, Abhilasha Ravichander, Michal Shmueli-Scheuer, and Anita de Waard. 2020. Overview and insights from the shared tasks at scholarly document processing 2020: CL-SciSumm, LaySumm and LongSumm. In *Proceedings of the First Workshop on Scholarly Document Processing*, pages 214–224, Online. Association for Computational Linguistics.

Janara Christensen, Stephen Soderland, Oren Etzioni, et al. 2013. Towards coherent multi-document summarization. In *Proceedings of the 2013 conference of the North American chapter of the association for computational linguistics: Human language technologies*, pages 1163–1173.

Sayar Ghosh Roy, Nikhil Pinnaparaju, Risubh Jain, Manish Gupta, and Vasudeva Varma. 2020. Summaformers @ LaySumm 20, LongSumm 20. In *Proceedings of the First Workshop on Scholarly Document Processing*, pages 336–343, Online. Association for Computational Linguistics.

Alexios Gidiotis, Stefanos Stefanidis, and Grigorios Tsoumakas. 2020. AUTH @ CLSciSumm 20, LaySumm 20, LongSumm 20. In *Proceedings of the First Workshop on Scholarly Document Processing*, pages 251–260, Online. Association for Computational Linguistics.

Jade Goldstein, Vibhu O Mittal, Jaime G Carbonell, and Mark Kantrowitz. 2000. Multi-document summarization by sentence extraction. In *NAACL-ANLP 2000 Workshop: Automatic Summarization*.

Jiaxin Ju, Ming Liu, Longxiang Gao, and Shirui Pan. 2020. Monash-summ@LongSumm 20 SciSummPip: An unsupervised scientific paper summarization pipeline. In *Proceedings of the First Workshop on Scholarly Document Processing*, pages 318–327, Online. Association for Computational Linguistics.

Guy Lev, Michal Shmueli-Scheuer, Jonathan Herzig, Achiya Jerbi, and David Konopnicki. 2019. Talksumm: A dataset and scalable annotation method for scientific paper summarization based on conference talks.

Lei Li, Yang Xie, Wei Liu, Yinan Liu, Yafei Jiang, Siya Qi, and Xingyuan Li. 2020. CIST@CL-SciSumm 2020, LongSumm 2020: Automatic scientific document summarization. In *Proceedings of the First Workshop on Scholarly Document Processing*, pages 225–234, Online. Association for Computational Linguistics.

Peng Li, Yinglin Wang, Wei Gao, and Jing Jiang. 2011. Generating aspect-oriented multi-document summarization with event-aspect model. Association for Computational Linguistics.

Chin-Yew Lin. 2004. ROUGE: A package for automatic evaluation of summaries. In *Text Summarization Branches Out*, pages 74–81, Barcelona, Spain. Association for Computational Linguistics.

Yuanhua Lv and ChengXiang Zhai. 2011. Lower-bounding term frequency normalization. In *Proceedings of the 20th ACM International Conference on Information and Knowledge Management*, CIKM '11, page 7–16, New York, NY, USA. Association for Computing Machinery.

Chirantana Mallick, Ajit Kumar Das, Madhurima Dutta, Asit Kumar Das, and Apurba Sarkar. 2019. Graph-based text summarization using modified textrank. In *Soft computing in data analytics*, pages 137–146. Springer.

Mani Maybury. 1999. *Advances in automatic text summarization*. MIT press.

Rada Mihalcea and Paul Tarau. 2004. TextRank: Bringing order into text. In *Proceedings of the 2004 Conference on Empirical Methods in Natural Language Processing*, pages 404–411, Barcelona, Spain. Association for Computational Linguistics.

Santosh Kumar Mishra, Harshavardhan Kundarapu, Naveen Saini, Sriparna Saha, and Pushpak Bhattacharyya. 2020. IITP-AI-NLP-ML@ CL-SciSumm 2020, CL-LaySumm 2020, LongSumm 2020. In *Proceedings of the First Workshop on Scholarly Document Processing*, pages 270–276, Online. Association for Computational Linguistics.

Ramesh Nallapati, Feifei Zhai, and Bowen Zhou. 2017. Summarunner: A recurrent neural network based sequence model for extractive summarization of documents. In *Proceedings of the AAAI Conference on Artificial Intelligence*, volume 31.

Ramesh Nallapati, Bowen Zhou, and Mingbo Ma. 2016. Classify or select: Neural architectures for extractive document summarization. *arXiv preprint arXiv:1611.04244*.

Saichethan Reddy, Naveen Saini, Sriparna Saha, and Pushpak Bhattacharyya. 2020. IIITBH-IITP@CL-SciSumm20, CL-LaySumm20, LongSumm20. In *Proceedings of the First Workshop on Scholarly Document Processing*, pages 242–250, Online. Association for Computational Linguistics.

S. Robertson, S. Walker, Susan Jones, M. Hancock-Beaulieu, and Mike Gatford. 1994. Okapi at trec-3. In *TREC*.

Sajad Sotudeh Gharebagh, Arman Cohan, and Nazli Goharian. 2020. GUIR @ LongSumm 2020: Learning to generate long summaries from scientific documents. In *Proceedings of the First Workshop on Scholarly Document Processing*, pages 356–361, Online. Association for Computational Linguistics.

Unsupervised document summarization using pre-trained sentence embeddings and graph centrality

Juan Ramirez-Orta* and Evangelos Milios
Department of Computer Science
Dalhousie University

Abstract

This paper describes our submission for the LongSumm task in SDP 2021. We propose a method for incorporating sentence embeddings produced by deep language models into extractive summarization techniques based on graph centrality in an unsupervised manner. The proposed method is simple, fast, can summarize any document of any size and can satisfy any length constraints for the summaries produced. The method offers competitive performance to more sophisticated supervised methods and can serve as a proxy for abstractive summarization techniques.

1 Introduction

Automatic text summarization is a very old and important task in Natural Language Processing (NLP) that has received continued attention since the creation of the field in the late 50's (Luhn, 1958), mainly because of the ever-increasing size of collections of text. The objective of the task is, given a document, to produce a shorter text with maximum information content, fluency and coherence. The summarization task can be classified into extractive and abstractive. Extractive summarization means that the summary is composed exclusively of passages present in the original document and abstractive summarization means that there can be words in the summary that did not appear in the original document.

Since the creation of the first neural language models (Bengio et al., 2003), vector representations of text that encode meaning (called embeddings) have played a significant role in NLP. They allow the application of statistical and geometrical methods to words, sentences and documents ((Pennington et al., 2014), (Mikolov et al., 2013), (Reimers and Gurevych, 2019)), leading to state-of-the-art performance on several NLP tasks like Information Retrieval, Question Answering or Paraphrase Identification. Among these neural language models, very deep pre-trained neural language models, like BERT (Devlin et al., 2018), T5 (Raffel et al., 2020), and GPT-3 (Brown et al., 2020) have shown impressive performance in tasks like language modelling and text generation or benchmarks like GLUE (Wang et al., 2018).

An important variation of extractive summarization that goes back as far as the late 90's (Salton et al., 1994, 1997) utilizes graphs, where the nodes represent text units and the links represent some measure of semantic similarity. These early graph-based summarization techniques involved creating a graph where the nodes were the sentences or paragraphs of a document and two nodes were connected if the corresponding text units had a similar vocabulary. After creating the document graph, the system created a summary by starting at the first paragraph and following random walks defined by different algorithms that tried to cover as much of the graph as possible.

A more evolved approach was the creation of *lexical centrality* (Erkan and Radev, 2004) (Mihalcea and Tarau, 2004) (Wolf and Gibson, 2004), which is a measure of the importance of a passage in a text where the sentences of the document are connected by the similarity of their vocabularies.

The current state of the art in automatic summarization with graphs is mainly based on algorithms like PageRank (Brin and Page, 1998) enhanced with statistical information of the terms in the document (like in (Ramesh et al., 2014)) or Graph Neural Networks (Kipf and Welling, 2016) on top of deep language models (like in (Xu et al., 2019)).

Only two systems from the previous Scholarly Document Processing workshop held in 2020 are based on graphs: CIST-BUPT and Monash-Summ.

In CIST-BUPT (Li et al., 2020), they used Recurrent Neural Networks to create sentence embeddings that can be used to build a graph which

*Please send correspondence to juan.ramirez.orta@dal.ca

Proceedings of the Second Workshop on Scholarly Document Processing, pages 110–115
June 10, 2021.

is then fed into a Graph Convolutional Network (Kipf and Welling, 2016) and a Graph Attention Network (Veličković et al., 2018) to create extractive summaries. To generate abstractive summaries, they used the gap-sentence method of (Zhang et al., 2019) to fine-tune T5 (Raffel et al., 2020).

In Monash-Summ (Ju et al., 2020), they propose an unsupervised approach that leverages linguistic knowledge to construct a sentence graph like in SummPip (Zhao et al., 2020). The graph nodes, which represent sentences, are further clustered to control the summary length, while the final abstractive summary is created from the key phrases and discourse from each cluster.

This work focuses on extractive summarization using graphs leveraging sentence embeddings produced by pre-trained language models. The essential idea is that, while the sentence embeddings produced by SBERT (Reimers and Gurevych, 2019) are not well suited for clustering algorithms like Hierarchical Clustering or DBSCAN (Ester et al., 1996), they produce excellent results in Paraphrase Identification or Semantic Textual Similarity when compared with Cosine Similarity, which implies that they can be used along with graph centrality methods. The text summarization method proposed in this paper has the following contributions:

- Is unsupervised and can be used as a proxy for more advanced summarization methods.
- Can easily scale to arbitrarily large amounts of text.
- Is fast and easy to implement.
- Can fit any length requirements for the production of summaries.

2 Methodology

In this section, we describe how the system works. The system is composed of three main steps: first, we use SBERT to produce sentence embeddings for every sentence in the document to summarize; next, we form a graph by comparing all the pairs of sentence embeddings obtained and finally, we rank the sentences by their degree centrality in this graph. Fig. 1 gives an overview of the whole method.

2.1 Sentence tokenization

The first step of our pipeline is to split the input text into a list of sentences. This step is critical because

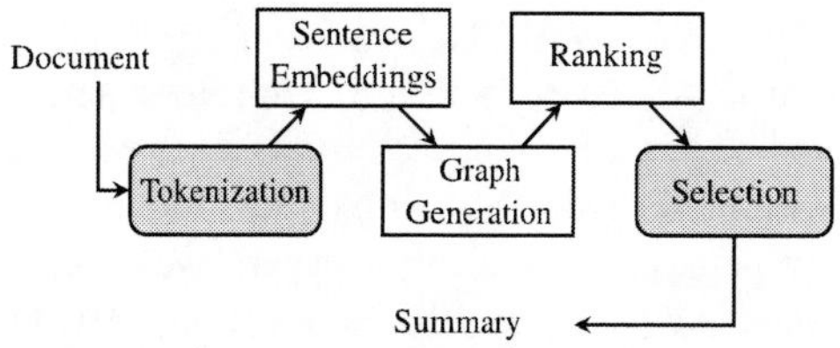

Figure 1: The complete pipeline of the proposed method. In the first step, we split the input text into sentences by using a regular expression handcrafted specifically for scientific documents. In the second step, we compute the sentence embeddings of the parsed sentences using SBERT. In the third step, we create a graph by comparing all the pairs of sentence embeddings obtained using cosine similarity. In the fourth step, we rank the sentences by the degree centrality in the generated graph. In the fifth and final step, we only keep a certain number of sentences or words to adjust to the length requirements of the summary.

if the sentences are too long, the final summary will have a lot of meaningless content (therefore losing precision). However, if the sentences are too short, there is a risk of not having enough context to produce an accurate sentence embedding for them or extracting meaningless sequences, like data in tables or numbers that lie in the middle of the text. We found that the function `sent_tokenize()` from the NLTK package (Bird et al., 2009) often failed because of the numbers in the tables and the abbreviations, like "et al.", which are very common in scientific literature. Because of this, we used a regular expression handcrafted specifically to split the text found in scientific documents.

2.2 Computing sentence embeddings

After extracting the sentences, the next step is to produce the sentence embedding of each sentence using SBERT (Reimers and Gurevych, 2019), which is a Transformer-based (Vaswani et al., 2017) model built on top of BERT (Devlin et al., 2018) that takes as input sentences and produces sentence embeddings that can be compared with cosine similarity, which is given by the following formula:

$$sim(x, y) = \frac{x \cdot y}{|x||y|}.$$

As shown in (Reimers and Gurevych, 2019), these sentence embeddings are superior in quality than taking the CLS token of BERT or averaging the sentence embeddings of the words in the sentence produced by BERT, GloVe (Pennington et al., 2014), or Word2Vec (Mikolov et al., 2013).

SBERT, like BERT, was pre-trained on a general large text collection to learn good sentence embeddings, but it has to be fine-tuned on a more specific data set according to the task. Since we are working with scientific papers, we picked the "base" version of RoBERTa (Liu et al., 2019) that was fine-tuned in the MSMARCO data set (Bajaj et al., 2016) for the Information Retrieval task.

2.3 Generation of the sentence graph

After the sentence embeddings have been produced, the next step is to produce a weighted complete graph with a node for each sentence in the text. Its edges are weighted according to the cosine similarities of the corresponding sentence embeddings. An example graph is depicted in Fig. 2.

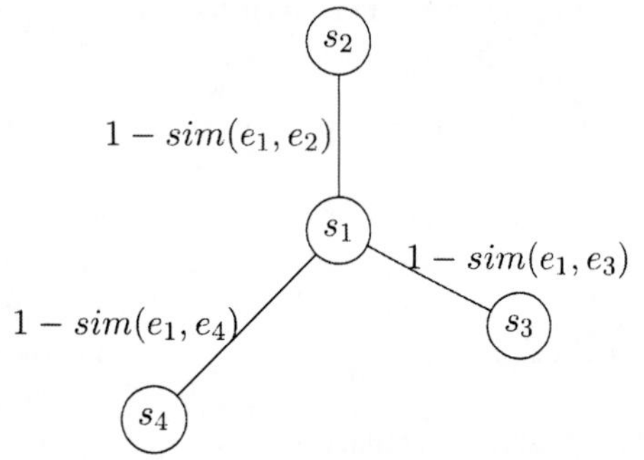

Figure 2: The process of graph generation and ranking of the sentences. Every node in the generated complete graph represents a sentence in the document and the weight of each edge is given by the similarity between the nodes it conects. The importance of the sentence in the document is modelled as $rank(s_i) = \sum_{j=1}^{n} 1 - sim(\dot{e}_i, e_j)$, where e_i and e_j are the corresponding SBERT sentence embeddings of s_i and s_j.

To build this graph, the first step is to gather all the pairwise cosine similarities in a matrix. Let $D = (s_1, s_2, ..., s_n)$ be a document. Using SBERT, we produce a sequence of vectors $(e_1, e_2, ..., e_n)$, where e_i is the sentence embedding of s_i. Then, we can compute the matrix A, where $A[i, j] = 1 - sim(e_i, e_j)$.

We make the following observations:

- The diagonal of A is composed exclusively of zeros, because $A[i, i] = 1 - sim(e_i, e_i) = 0$.
- The matrix A is symmetric, because $A[i, j] = 1 - sim(e_i, e_j) = 1 - sim(e_j, e_i) = A[j, i]$.
- All the entries in A are non-negative, because $-1 \leq sim(e_i, e_j) \leq 1$.

These observations imply that the matrix A can be interpreted as the adjacency matrix of a weighted complete graph $G = (V, E)$ where $V = \{s_1, s_2, ..., s_n\}$, $E = \{(s_1, s_2)|s_1, s_2 \in V\}$ and the edges are weighted by the following function: $w(s_1, s_2) = 1 - sim(e_1, e_2)$.

2.4 Ranking by centrality

The forth step is to assign a score for each sentence that allows us to sort them by their importance in the document. As a consequence, we define the importance rank for each sentence as follows:

$$rank(s_i) = \sum_{j=1}^{n} A[i, j] = \sum_{j=1}^{n} 1 - sim(e_i, e_j), \tag{1}$$

where e_i and e_j are the corresponding SBERT sentence embedding for s_i and s_j.

To motivate this definition, we observe that adding the entries of the matrix A columnwise gives naturally a ranking of the nodes of G that is a natural generalization of the degree centrality. However, in our ranking, the most "central" sentences (sentences that are similar to many other sentences in the document) have lower scores than the ones that are less "central."

To further support this definition, we observe that if G were an undirected, unweighted simple graph $G = (V, E)$ (that is, the entries of A are either 0 or 1, A is symmetric and only has zeros in its diagonal), then we would have that

$$\sum_{j=1}^{n} A[i, j] = \#\{v \in V | (v_i, v) \in E\}, \tag{2}$$

which is the definition of the degree of node v_i and is clearly a (somewhat crude) measure of the importance of the node in the graph.

It is important to note that in scientific papers, which have around 300 sentences, the proposed method takes around 1 second for the whole process. This result implies that there is no obstacle for applying this method to longer documents since producing the sentence embeddings with the SBERT implementation is very efficient, and the only thing that we are doing is compare all the pairs of sentence embeddings, which can be done with highly efficient linear algebra libraries.

2.5 Summary selection

The final step in the method is to select the sentences that are going to form the summary. To do this, we can take only the bottom n-percentile in reverse (as opposed to the top n-percentile, since in our method, a lower rank means that the sentence is more important in the document) or concatenate the ranked sentences in reverse (so that the sentences with the lowest ranks -that is, the most important ones- come first) and take the first k words to satisfy a word-length constraint for the summaries.

3 Experimental setup

3.1 Data set

Since our method is for unsupervised extractive summarization, we only used the extractive summaries in the TalkSumm data set (Lev et al., 2019) to estimate the appropriate threshold value for the sentence selection phase. As suggested in the task, we used science-parse (AllenAI, 2019) to extract the text of the scientific articles and split it into sections. Given that the objective of the task is to produce long summaries for the documents, we discarded the title and abstract and then took as input for the algorithm the remaining text as a single block.

3.2 Evaluation

As is customary in summarization tasks, we used ROUGE (Lin, 2004) in its variations ROUGE-1, ROUGE-2 and ROUGE-L.

3.3 Percentile threshold in the selection phase

We tried with $p = \{1, 1.5, 2, 2.5, 5, 10, 15\}$ as the value of the bottom percentage of sentences to keep for the final summary and truncated the output to satisfy the 600 word limit for the task when the summary was longer. It is important to note that the freedom of this parameter allows the system to produce summaries of arbitrary length, depending on the task at hand.

4 Results

Overall, we observed that the 600-word constraint of the task prevented our method from performing better, but we also observed that the best summaries produced by our method are too long (around 1,000 words or more). Table 1 displays the performance of the method variations that we submitted to the task.

Bottom %	R-1 F	R-1 R	R-2 F	R-2 R	R-L F	R-L R
1.0	0.24	0.15	0.06	0.03	0.11	0.07
1.5	0.29	0.21	0.08	0.05	0.13	0.09
2.0	0.33	0.25	0.08	0.06	0.14	0.10
2.5	0.37	0.29	0.09	0.07	0.15	0.11
5.0	0.44	0.39	0.12	0.10	0.16	0.14
10.0	0.46	0.43	0.12	0.12	0.17	0.16
15.0	0.46	0.43	0.12	0.12	0.17	0.16

Table 1: performance of the different variations of the proposed method submitted to the task. In this setting, the ranked sentences were sorted in reverse and concatenated to form a preliminary output, which was truncated at 600 words to comply with the task's requirements. The "Bottom %" column displays the percentile used in the sentence selection phase of the method. R-N F stands for the F-measure in ROUGE-N, while R-N R stands for the Recall in ROUGE-N.

5 Conclusion and Future Work

The method introduced in this work displays competitive performance with more sophisticated methods and can be useful when there is not enough labelled data to train a deep neural summarization system while being fast, simple and efficient. Overall, we observed that the precision component of ROUGE for the proposed method has much room for improvement, as having sentences as the minimal text units prevents it from filtering out the less important phrases. Another important future direction is to reduce the redundancy of the summaries, as it is common to have several versions of the same important sentence scattered across the document, so all these versions of the sentence appear in the final summary.

References

AllenAI. 2019. Science parse. GitHub repository, `https://github.com/allenai/science-parse`. Visited on April 23, 2021.

Payal Bajaj, Daniel Campos, Nick Craswell, Li Deng, Jianfeng Gao, Xiaodong Liu, Rangan Majumder, Andrew McNamara, Bhaskar Mitra, Tri Nguyen, Mir Rosenberg, Xia Song, Alina Stoica, Saurabh Tiwary, and Tong Wang. 2016. MS MARCO: A Human Generated MAchine Reading COmprehension Dataset. *arXiv preprint arXiv:1611.09268*.

Yoshua Bengio, Réjean Ducharme, Pascal Vincent, and Christian Janvin. 2003. A neural probabilistic language model. *J. Mach. Learn. Res.*, 3(null):1137–1155.

Steven Bird, Ewan Klein, and Edward Loper. 2009. *Natural Language Processing with Python*. O'Reilly Media.

Sergey Brin and Lawrence Page. 1998. The anatomy of a large-scale hypertextual web search engine. In *COMPUTER NETWORKS AND ISDN SYSTEMS*, pages 107–117.

Tom Brown, Benjamin Mann, Nick Ryder, Melanie Subbiah, Jared D Kaplan, Prafulla Dhariwal, Arvind Neelakantan, Pranav Shyam, Girish Sastry, Amanda Askell, Sandhini Agarwal, Ariel Herbert-Voss, Gretchen Krueger, Tom Henighan, Rewon Child, Aditya Ramesh, Daniel Ziegler, Jeffrey Wu, Clemens Winter, Chris Hesse, Mark Chen, Eric Sigler, Mateusz Litwin, Scott Gray, Benjamin Chess, Jack Clark, Christopher Berner, Sam McCandlish, Alec Radford, Ilya Sutskever, and Dario Amodei. 2020. Language models are few-shot learners. In *Advances in Neural Information Processing Systems*, volume 33, pages 1877–1901. Curran Associates, Inc.

Jacob Devlin, Ming-Wei Chang, Kenton Lee, and Kristina Toutanova. 2018. Bert: Pre-training of deep bidirectional transformers for language understanding. *arXiv preprint arXiv:1810.04805*.

Günes Erkan and Dragomir R. Radev. 2004. Lexrank: Graph-based lexical centrality as salience in text summarization. *J. Artif. Int. Res.*, 22(1):457–479.

Martin Ester, Hans-Peter Kriegel, Jörg Sander, and Xiaowei Xu. 1996. A density-based algorithm for discovering clusters in large spatial databases with noise. In *Proceedings of the Second International Conference on Knowledge Discovery and Data Mining*, KDD'96, page 226–231. AAAI Press.

Jiaxin Ju, Ming Liu, Longxiang Gao, and Shirui Pan. 2020. Monash-summ@LongSumm 20 SciSummPip: An unsupervised scientific paper summarization pipeline. In *Proceedings of the First Workshop on Scholarly Document Processing*, pages 318–327, Online. Association for Computational Linguistics.

Thomas N Kipf and Max Welling. 2016. Semi-supervised classification with graph convolutional networks. *arXiv preprint arXiv:1609.02907*.

Guy Lev, Michal Shmueli-Scheuer, Jonathan Herzig, Achiya Jerbi, and David Konopnicki. 2019. Talk-Summ: A dataset and scalable annotation method for scientific paper summarization based on conference talks. In *Proceedings of the 57th Annual Meeting of the Association for Computational Linguistics*, pages 2125–2131, Florence, Italy. Association for Computational Linguistics.

Lei Li, Yang Xie, Wei Liu, Yinan Liu, Yafei Jiang, Siya Qi, and Xingyuan Li. 2020. CIST@CL-SciSumm 2020, LongSumm 2020: Automatic scientific document summarization. In *Proceedings of the First Workshop on Scholarly Document Processing*, pages 225–234, Online. Association for Computational Linguistics.

Chin-Yew Lin. 2004. ROUGE: A package for automatic evaluation of summaries. In *Text Summarization Branches Out*, pages 74–81, Barcelona, Spain. Association for Computational Linguistics.

Yinhan Liu, Myle Ott, Naman Goyal, Jingfei Du, Mandar Joshi, Danqi Chen, Omer Levy, Mike Lewis, Luke Zettlemoyer, and Veselin Stoyanov. 2019. Roberta: A robustly optimized bert pretraining approach. *arXiv preprint arXiv:1907.11692*.

H. P. Luhn. 1958. The automatic creation of literature abstracts. *IBM Journal of Research and Development*, 2(2):159–165.

Rada Mihalcea and Paul Tarau. 2004. TextRank: Bringing order into text. In *Proceedings of the 2004 Conference on Empirical Methods in Natural Language Processing*, pages 404–411, Barcelona, Spain. Association for Computational Linguistics.

Tomas Mikolov, Ilya Sutskever, Kai Chen, Greg S Corrado, and Jeff Dean. 2013. Distributed representations of words and phrases and their compositionality. In *Advances in Neural Information Processing Systems*, volume 26. Curran Associates, Inc.

Jeffrey Pennington, Richard Socher, and Christopher D. Manning. 2014. Glove: Global vectors for word representation. In *Empirical Methods in Natural Language Processing (EMNLP)*, pages 1532–1543.

Colin Raffel, Noam Shazeer, Adam Roberts, Katherine Lee, Sharan Narang, Michael Matena, Yanqi Zhou, Wei Li, and Peter J. Liu. 2020. Exploring the limits of transfer learning with a unified text-to-text transformer. *Journal of Machine Learning Research*, 21(140):1–67.

Animesh Ramesh, K. Srinivasa, and Pramod .N. 2014. Sentencerank — a graph based approach to summarize text. In *5th International Conference on the Applications of Digital Information and Web Technologies, ICADIWT 2014*, pages 177–182.

Nils Reimers and Iryna Gurevych. 2019. Sentence-bert: Sentence embeddings using siamese bert-networks. In *Proceedings of the 2019 Conference on Empirical Methods in Natural Language Processing*. Association for Computational Linguistics.

Gerard Salton, James Allan, Chris Buckley, and Amit Singhal. 1994. Automatic analysis, theme generation, and summarization of machine-readable texts. *Science*, 264(5164):1421–1426.

Gerard Salton, Amit Singhal, Mandar Mitra, and Chris Buckley. 1997. Automatic text structuring and summarization. *Information Processing & Management*, 33(2):193–207. Methods and Tools for the Automatic Construction of Hypertext.

Ashish Vaswani, Noam Shazeer, Niki Parmar, Jakob Uszkoreit, Llion Jones, Aidan N Gomez, Ł ukasz Kaiser, and Illia Polosukhin. 2017. Attention is all you need. In *Advances in Neural Information Processing Systems*, volume 30. Curran Associates, Inc.

Petar Veličković, Guillem Cucurull, Arantxa Casanova, Adriana Romero, Pietro Liò, and Yoshua Bengio. 2018. Graph Attention Networks. *International*

Conference on Learning Representations. Accepted as poster.

Alex Wang, Amanpreet Singh, Julian Michael, Felix Hill, Omer Levy, and Samuel Bowman. 2018. GLUE: A multi-task benchmark and analysis platform for natural language understanding. In *Proceedings of the 2018 EMNLP Workshop BlackboxNLP: Analyzing and Interpreting Neural Networks for NLP*, pages 353–355, Brussels, Belgium. Association for Computational Linguistics.

Florian Wolf and Edward Gibson. 2004. Paragraph-, word-, and coherence-based approaches to sentence ranking: A comparison of algorithm and human performance. In *Proceedings of the 42nd Annual Meeting of the Association for Computational Linguistics (ACL-04)*, pages 383–390, Barcelona, Spain.

Jiacheng Xu, Zhe Gan, Yu Cheng, and Jingjing Liu. 2019. Discourse-aware neural extractive model for text summarization. *CoRR*, abs/1910.14142.

Jingqing Zhang, Yao Zhao, Mohammad Saleh, and Peter J. Liu. 2019. Pegasus: Pre-training with extracted gap-sentences for abstractive summarization. *arXiv preprint arXiv:1912.08777*.

Jinming Zhao, Ming Liu, Longxiang Gao, Yuan Jin, Lan Du, He Zhao, He Zhang, and Gholamreza Haffari. 2020. Summpip: Unsupervised multi-document summarization with sentence graph compression. In *Proceedings of the 43rd International ACM SIGIR Conference on Research and Development in Information Retrieval*, SIGIR '20, page 1949–1952, New York, NY, USA. Association for Computing Machinery.

QMUL-SDS at SCIVER:
Step-by-Step Binary Classification for Scientific Claim Verification

Xia Zeng
Queen Mary University of London
x.zeng@qmul.ac.uk

Arkaitz Zubiaga
Queen Mary University of London
a.zubiaga@qmul.ac.uk

Abstract

Scientific claim verification is a unique challenge that is attracting increasing interest. The SCIVER shared task offers a benchmark scenario to test and compare claim verification approaches by participating teams and consists in three steps: relevant abstract selection, rationale selection and label prediction. In this paper, we present team QMUL-SDS's participation in the shared task. We propose an approach that performs scientific claim verification by doing binary classifications step-by-step. We trained a BioBERT-large classifier to select abstracts based on pairwise relevance assessments for each <claim, title of the abstract> and continued to train it to select rationales out of each retrieved abstract based on <claim, sentence>. We then propose a two-step setting for label prediction, i.e. first predicting "NOT_ENOUGH_INFO" or "ENOUGH_INFO", then label those marked as "ENOUGH_INFO" as either "SUPPORT" or "CONTRADICT". Compared to the baseline system, we achieve substantial improvements on the dev set. As a result, our team is the No. 4 team on the leaderboard.

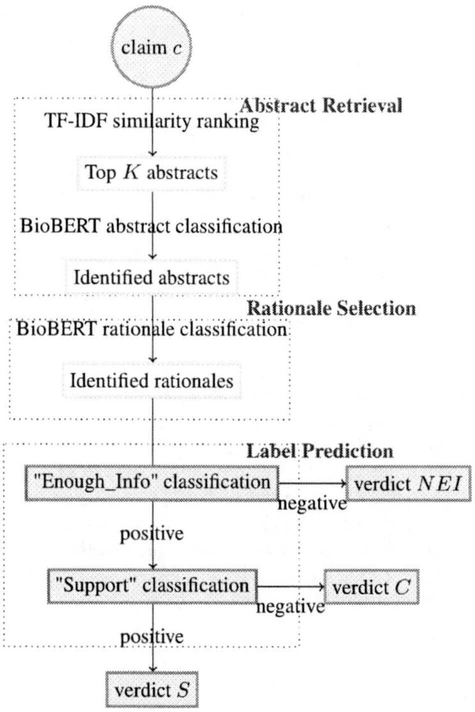

Figure 1: Overview of our step-by-step binary classification system. NEI stands for "NOT_ENOUGH_INFO", C stands for "CONTRADICT" and S stands for "SUPPORT". Given claim c, our system first retrieves top K TF-IDF similarity abstracts out of the corpus, then uses a BioBERT binary classifier to further identify desired abstracts on top of that. With retrieved abstracts, our system then uses another BioBERT binary classifier to select rationales. We finally do label prediction in a two-step fashion, i.e. first make verdicts on "ENOUGH_INFO" or not and, if positive, then make verdicts on "SUPPORT" or not.

1 Introduction

As online content continues to grow at an unprecedented rate, the spread of false information online increases the potential of misleading people and causing harm. Where the volume of information shared online is difficult to be managed by human fact-checkers, this leads to an increasing demand on automated fact-checking, which is formulated by researchers as 'the assignment of a truth value to a claim made in a particular context'(Vlachos and Riedel, 2014).

Though a body of research focuses on conducting fact-checking in the politics domain, scientific claim verification has also gained increasing interest in the context of the ongoing COVID-19 pandemic. The SCIVER shared task provides a valuable benchmark to build and evaluate systems performing scientific claim verification. Given a scientific claim and a corpus of over 5000 abstracts, the task consists in (i) identifying abstracts relevant to the claim, (ii) delving into the abstracts to select

Proceedings of the Second Workshop on Scholarly Document Processing, pages 116–123
June 10, 2021. ©2021 Association for Computational Linguistics

evidence sentences relevant to the claim, and (iii) subsequently predicting claim veracity.

This paper presents and analyses team QMUL-SDS's participation in the SCIVER shared task. In particular, we explore creative approaches of solving the challenge with limited resources. Figure 1 provides an overview of our system. While many other systems make use of external datasets, e.g. FEVER (Thorne et al., 2018), our system focuses on efficient use of the SCIFACT dataset (Wadden et al., 2020). Furthermore, in the interest of keeping the efficiency of our system, we limit our model choices to the size of RoBERTa-large (Liu et al., 2019), ruling out for example GPT-3 (Brown et al., 2020) and T5 (Raffel et al., 2020), which were used in other participating systems. More specifically, our system mainly uses RoBERTa (Liu et al., 2019) and BioBERT (Lee et al., 2020). The latter is pre-trained on biomedical text and therefore is very close to our target domain. With improved pipeline design, our system shows competitive performance with limited computing resources, achieving the 6th position in the task and ranked 4th when distinct teams are considered. [1]

2 Related Work

Several approaches have been proposed to perform scientific claim verification in the three-step settings proposed in SCIVER.

Upon publication of the SCIFACT dataset (Wadden et al., 2020), the authors introduced VERISCI as a baseline system. It is a pipeline with three modules: abstract retrieval, rationale selection and label prediction. The abstract retrieval module returns the top K highest-ranked abstracts determined by the TF-IDF similarity between each abstract and the claim at hand. The rationale selection module trains a RoBERTa-large model to compute relevance scores with a sigmoid function and then selects sentences whose relevance scores are higher than the threshold T. The label prediction module trains a RoBERTa-large model to do three-way classification regarding sentence-pairs, where the candidate labels are "SUPPORT", "CONTRADICT" and "NOT_ENOUGH_INFO". Empirically the system set the K value to 3 and the T value to 0.5. Due to its inspiring design, reasonable performance and good efficiency, in this paper we take VERISCI system as our baseline.

After the publication of the SCIFACT dataset, several approaches have been published, some of which chose to participate in the SCIVER shared task. We next discuss the top 3 ranked entries. The VERT5ERINI system (Pradeep et al., 2020) ranked 1st on the leaderboard. This system first retrieves a shortlist of top 20 abstracts by using the BM25 ranking score (Robertson et al., 1994), which is then fed into a T5 model to rerank and retrieve the top 3 abstracts; it then trains a T5 model to calculate relevance scores for each sentence, on which a threshold of 0.999 is applied to select rationales; it finally trains a T5 model to do three-way classification for predicting labels. This system has demonstrated the performance advantages of using T5, a model that is substantially bigger than other language models.

The ParagraphJoint system (Li et al., 2021) ranked 2nd on the leaderboard. It first uses BioSentVec (Chen et al., 2019) to retrieve the top K abstracts and then jointly trains a RoBERTa-large model to do rationale selection and label prediction in a multi-task learning setting. The system is first trained on the FEVER dataset and then trained on SCIFACT dataset. Its application of multi-task learning techniques proved to be very successful and inspires further research in this direction.

The team who ranked 3rd on the leaderboard, Law & Econ (Stammbach and Ash), fine-tuned their e-FEVER system on SCIFACT dataset, which requires usage of GPT-3 and training on FEVER dataset. Despite the big difference on model sizes, our system achieves close performance to the e-FEVER system on the leaderboard.

3 Approach

Following the convention of automated fact-checking systems (Thorne et al., 2018) and the VERISCI baseline system, we explore novel ways of tackling the challenge by handling the three subtasks: abstract retrieval, rationale selection and label prediction.

3.1 Abstract Retrieval

Abstract retrieval is the task of retrieving relevant abstracts that can support the prediction of a claim's veracity. Inspired by the baseline system, which retrieves the top K ($K = 3$) abstracts with the highest TF-IDF similarity to the claim, initially we attempted a similar method with a state-of-the-art similarity metric, i.e., BERTscore (Zhang et al.,

[1]Code is available here.

2020). It computes token similarity using BERT-based contextual embeddings. However, the results we achieved were not satisfactory[2] and was ruled out in subsequent experiments.

Instead of completely relying on available metrics, we investigated performing abstract retrieval in a supervised manner. In contrast to previous work (Pradeep et al., 2020) which performed reranking, we formulate it as a binary classification problem. We first empirically limit the corpus to the top 30 abstracts with highest TF-IDF similarity to the claim. We fine-tuned a BioBERT model (Lee et al., 2020) with a linear classification head, which we name as the BioBERT classifier thereafter, to do binary classification on the top 30 TF-IDF abstracts, i.e. predicting whether the abstract at hand is correctly identified for the claim at hand given the pairwise input <claim c, title t of the abstract>. Due to the input length limits of BERT models, we only use the title of the abstract at this stage, assuming that the title represents a good summary of the abstract.

3.2 Rationale Selection

Rationale Selection is the task of selecting rationale sentences out of the retrieved abstracts. To avoid manually tuning the threshold on various settings like the baseline system, we address the problem as a binary classification task in a very similar manner to the last step. We continued training the BioBERT classifier inherited from the abstract retrieval step to do rationale selection, i.e. making binary predictions on whether the sentence at hand is correctly identified for the claim at hand given sentence pair <claim c, sentence s>. As our classifier model only outputs binary predictions with its linear head on individual sentence pair cases, there is no need to apply various ranking thresholds. Aiming to achieve better overall pipeline performance, our models are trained on abstracts retrieved in the first step, rather than oracle abstracts.

3.3 Label Prediction

Label prediction is the task of predicting the veracity label given the target claim and rationale sentences selected in the preceding step of the pipeline. A good selection of relevant abstracts and rationales therefore is vital in the capacity of the veracity label prediction system.

The baseline system we initially implemented trained a RoBERTa-large model to do three-way classification into one of "NOT_ENOUGH_INFO", "SUPPORT" and "CONTRADICT". We observed that, while the model was in general fairly accurate, it performed poorly in predicting the "CONTRADICT" class due to the scarcity of training data pertaining to this class. However, it is known that claims belonging to the "CONTRADICT" class are particularly difficult to collect, and that automated fact-checking datasets tend to create them synthetically by manually mutating naturally occurring claims originally pertaining to the "SUPPORT" class (Thorne et al., 2018; Wadden et al., 2020; Sathe et al., 2020). With the aim of improving model performance on this class without using extra data, we try to decrease wrong predictions accumulated by wrong predictions on the other labels. For instance, the model may predict a claim to be "NOT_ENOUGH_INFO" while it should be "CONTRADICT", which makes it a false positive for the "NOT_ENOUGH_INFO" class and a true negative for the "CONTRADICT" class. If the model has better performance on the "NOT_ENOUGH_INFO" predictions, it would in turn help the performance on the "CONTRADICT" class.

Hence, we explore label prediction within a two-step setting. First, we merge claims from the "SUPPORT" and "CONTRADICT" classes as "ENOUGH_INFO". With this altered dataset, we train a RoBERTa-large model as a neutral detector to do binary classification into "ENOUGH_INFO" or "NOT_ENOUGH_INFO". Second, we merge data from "NOT_ENOUGH_INFO" and "CONTRADICT" to be "NOT_SUPPORT" and train another RoBERTa-large model as a support detector to do binary classification on "SUPPORT" or "NOT_SUPPORT". Finally, when doing predictions, we first use the neutral detector to predict "ENOUGH_INFO" or "NOT_ENOUGH_INFO" and only if the first prediction is "ENOUGH_INFO" we use the support detector to predict "SUPPORT" or "NOT_SUPPORT". We take "NOT_SUPPORT" instances as equivalent to "CONTRADICT" instances in the three-way classification.

4 Results

We perform various experiments on the SCIFACT dataset to identify the best models and techniques to be submitted to the task. Unless explicitly specified, models are trained on the SCIFACT's train set

[2]See detailed results in appendix A

and evaluated on the SCIFACT's dev set.

4.1 Abstract Retrieval

We limit the candidate abstracts to the top 30 with the highest TF-IDF similarity scores, as this setting achieves a high recall of 91.39%. With our binary classification method, we experimented with BioBERT models that are pre-trained on close domain texts (Lee et al., 2020). To explore the potentials of adapting pre-trained language models to the current settings, we also conducted task adaptive pre-training (Gururangan et al., 2020) on the SCIFACT corpus with BioBERT-base for 50 epochs with batch size 1, which leads to a final perplexity of 2.68. This parameter choice is made primarily based on our limited time and computational resources for the SCIVER shared task participation. Further extensive exploration may lead to interesting results. This model is denoted as BioBERT-base*.

Table 1 reports performance of the baseline, BioBERT-base, BioBERT-base* and BioBERT-large models on abstract retrieval. The baseline directly retrieves the top 3 abstracts with highest TF-IDF similarity, which is also the method used in the VERISCI system (Wadden et al., 2020). We also report abstract level pipeline performance with baseline rationale selector and baseline label predictor to demonstrate its substantial impact on pipeline performance.

Our method achieves noticeable improvements over the baseline by largely decreasing the false positive rate. More specifically, BioBERT-base has the highest precision score, BioBERT-base* has highest F1 score and BioBERT-large has the highest recall score. With increased model size, BioBERT-large has gained significant improvements on recall but suffers with a precision drop compared to BioBERT-base and BioBERT-base*, which may suggest model underfitting. Overall our approach leads to an approximate 10% increase over the baseline approach on abstract level downstream performance.

Abstract Retrieval			
Method	P	R	F1
Baseline	16.22	69.86	26.33
BioBERT-base	**83.23**	64.11	72.43
BioBERT-base*	81.61	67.94	**74.15**
BioBERT-large	62.75	**74.16**	67.98
Downstream Performance			
Abstract Level Label Only			
Method	P	R	F1
Baseline	56.42	48.33	52.06
BioBERT-base	84.30	48.80	61.82
BioBERT-base*	**84.92**	51.20	**63.88**
BioBERT-large	79.71	**52.63**	63.40
Abstract Level Label + Rationale			
Method	P	R	F1
Baseline	54.19	46.41	50.00
BioBERT-base	81.82	47.37	60.00
BioBERT-base*	**82.54**	49.76	**62.09**
BioBERT-large	76.81	**50.72**	61.10

Table 1: Comparison of abstract retrieval methods on the dev set of SCIFACT.

4.2 Rationale Selection

In order to improve the overall design of the system, we trained our rationale selection models with abstracts retrieved by our abstract retrieval module rather than oracle abstracts. We use abstracts retrieved by BioBERT-large due to its highest recall score. In this step, we experiment with our binary classification approach to identify rationale sentences from retrieved abstracts for the claim at hand. Given a sentence-pair <claim c, sentence s>, the model, which was trained to do abstract selection in last step, is now trained to predict whether the sentence at hand is correctly identified for the claim at hand.

Table 2 reports results of the baseline, BioBERT-base, BioBERT-base* and BioBERT-large models on rationale selection. We also present sentence level pipeline performance with oracle cited abstracts [3] and baseline label predictor.

Our method leads to an increase in precision score, a small decrease in recall score and a small increase in F1 score. Interestingly, the three BioBERT variants don't show clear performance differences, despite substantial differences in model sizes. A small improvement on downstream sentence-level performance is achieved overall.

4.3 Label Prediction

For label prediction, we use the two-step approach that leverages RoBERTa-large as described in §3.3. This approach is denoted as TWO-STEP thereafter. Table 3 reports performance results for the label prediction task with oracle cited abstracts and ora-

[3]It includes abstracts that are of "SUPPORT", "CONTRADICT" and "NOT_ENOUGH_INFO" relations to the claims' veracity. It is also referred as oracle abstracts with NOT_ENOUGH_INFO (NEI) setting in SCIFACT dataset paper.

Sentence Selection			
Method	P	R	F1
Baseline	64.99	**70.49**	67.63
BioBERT-base	**77.97**	62.84	**69.59**
BioBERT-base*	74.38	65.03	69.39
BioBERT-large	77.08	63.39	69.57

Downstream Performance			
Sentence Level Selection Only			
Method	P	R	F1
Baseline	74.48	**59.02**	65.85
BioBERT-base	**83.81**	56.56	67.54
BioBERT-base*	80.84	57.65	67.30
BioBERT-large	80.75	58.47	**67.83**
Sentence Level Selection + Label			
Method	P	R	F1
Baseline	66.90	53.01	59.15
BioBERT-base	**74.90**	50.55	60.36
BioBERT-base*	72.41	51.64	60.29
BioBERT-large	72.08	**52.19**	**60.54**

Table 2: Comparison of rationale selection methods on the dev set of SCIFACT.

cle rationales. The baseline is the RoBERTa-large three-way classifier used on VERISCI. Our TWO-STEP method leads to a 4% increase in accuracy, macro-F1 and weighted-F1 over the baseline. We further present confusion matrices for each system for analysis, where C stands for "CONTRADICT", N stands for "NOT_ENOUGH_INFO" and S stands for "SUPPORT". As the confusion matrix shows, our method successfully improves the overall predictions on the "CONTRADICT" class without leveraging extra data.

Furthermore, Table 4 reports results on the abstract-level label prediction with various settings of upstream modules. Interestingly, both methods show noticeably decreased performance when given an evidence of lower quality. From the oracle evidence to the evidence retrieved by our system, the baseline module's F1 performance dropped by 19.70% and the TWO-STEP module dropped by 20.26% in absolute values; from the oracle evidence to the evidence retrieved by the baseline system, the baseline module's F1 score dropped by 30.14% and the TWO-STEP module dropped by 37.26% in absolute values.

Despite that, our TWO-STEP method always outperforms the baseline method when given improved evidence. Its F1 score is 2.02% - 2.58% higher than the baseline on improved evidence retrieval settings. When given oracle cited abstracts and oracle rationales, our method achieves 84.78% F1 score.

Label Prediction Performance			
Method	Accuracy	Macro-F1	Weighted-F1
Baseline	81.93	80.19	81.85
TWO-STEP	**85.98**	**84.69**	**85.84**

Confusion Matrix of Baseline			
	C	N	S
C	47	17	7
N	6	104	2
S	8	18	112

Confusion Matrix of TWO-STEP			
	C	N	S
C	53	7	11
N	2	107	3
S	12	10	116

Table 3: Comparison of label prediction methods with oracle cited abstracts and oracle rationales.

Oracle Abstract + Oracle Rationale			
Method	P	R	F1
Baseline	**90.75**	75.12	82.20
TWO-STEP	88.54	**81.33**	**84.78**
OurSystem Abstract + OurSystem Rationale			
Method	P	R	F1
Baseline	**76.92**	52.63	62.50
TWO-STEP	73.62	**57.42**	**64.52**
Baseline Abstract + Baseline Rationale			
Method	P	R	F1
Baseline	**56.42**	48.32	**52.06**
TWO-STEP	43.31	**52.63**	47.52

Table 4: Comparison of label prediction methods with various upstream modules.

4.4 Full Pipeline

Table 5 reports full pipeline performance on the SCIFACT dev set. The baseline is the VERISCI system. We compare pipeline systems with different evidence retrieval models, i.e., BioBERT-base, BioBERT-base* and BioBERT-large, combined with the two-step label predictor using RoBERTa-large.

Overall our system achieves substantial improvements over the baseline. Across the evaluation metrics, our precision scores are 15.75%-23.37% higher than the baseline system, recall scores are 3.82%-14.21% higher and F1 scores are 10.11%-16.08% higher than the baseline in terms of absolute values. Interestingly, BioBERT-base obtains the highest precision score, BioBERT-base* the highest recall score and BioBERT-large the highest

Label Only			
System	P	R	F1
Baseline	56.42	48.33	52.06
BioBERT-base + TWO-STEP	**79.56**	52.15	63.00
BioBERT-base* + TWO-STEP	78.91	55.50	**65.17**
BioBERT-large + TWO-STEP	73.62	**57.42**	64.52
Label+Rationale			
System	P	R	F1
Baseline	54.19	46.41	50.00
BioBERT-base + TWO-STEP	**75.91**	49.76	60.11
BioBERT-base* + TWO-STEP	73.47	51.67	60.67
BioBERT-large + TWO-STEP	69.94	**54.55**	**61.29**
Selection Only			
System	P	R	F1
Baseline	54.27	43.44	48.25
BioBERT-base + TWO-STEP	**77.64**	52.19	62.42
BioBERT-base* + TWO-STEP	72.00	54.10	61.78
BioBERT-large + TWO-STEP	72.76	**57.65**	**64.33**
Selection+Label			
System	P	R	F1
Baseline	48.46	38.80	43.10
BioBERT-base + TWO-STEP	**68.29**	45.90	54.90
BioBERT-base* + TWO-STEP	64.00	48.09	54.92
BioBERT-large + TWO-STEP	64.83	**51.37**	**57.32**

Table 5: Comparison of full pipeline performance on the dev set of SCIFACT.

Label Only			
System	P	R	F1
Baseline	47.51	47.30	47.40
OURSYSTEM	**74.32**	**49.55**	**59.46**
Label+Rationale			
System	P	R	F1
Baseline	46.61	46.40	46.50
OURSYSTEM	**72.97**	**48.65**	**58.38**
Selection Only			
System	P	R	F1
Baseline	44.99	47.30	46.11
OURSYSTEM	**81.58**	**58.65**	**68.24**
Selection+Label			
System	P	R	F1
Baseline	38.56	40.54	39.53
OURSYSTEM	**66.17**	**47.57**	**55.35**

Table 6: Full pipeline performance on SCIFACT's test set. OURSYSTEMuses BioBERT-large for abstract retrieval and rationale selection with two-step label prediction, all trained on trained set and dev set.

F1 for most of metrics.

Table 6 compares full pipeline performance on SCIFACT test set with models trained on the combination of SCIFACT train set and dev set. We used BioBERT-large evidence selector and two-step label predictor as our system due to its overall best performance. This submission ranked No. 6 on the leaderboard.

5 Discussion and Future Work

Our intuitive step-by-step binary classification system achieves substantial improvements over the baseline without demanding additional data or extra large models.

An improved evidence retrieval module has made the main contributions to the performance boost. Our system makes an effort to improve the abstract retrieval module after applying a scalable traditional information retrieval weighting scheme, TF-IDF. Instead of handling it as a re-ranking task and manually selecting thresholds (Pradeep et al., 2020), we formulate it as a binary classification task, which makes better use of the available training data and decreases the false positive rate effectively. When applying a similar approach to rationale selection, our model, which is only trained on the SCIFACT dataset, still achieves improvements over the baseline model, which makes use of the FEVER dataset first. Furthermore, our model is less dependent on parameters than other systems, which is ideal in practical settings where one would like to apply the model on new datasets without having to find the best parameters for the dataset at hand.

In addition, our TWO-STEP label prediction module also makes positive contributions to overall improvements. The difference on the label prediction performance is very noticeable on different upstream settings. Unsurprisingly, both methods have the best performance with F1 scores higher than 80% on the oracle setting, which is the closest to their training data. Interestingly, this performance fluctuation leads to the following observation: a label prediction module that has better performance on the oracle evidence doesn't necessarily have better performance when given the incorrect evidence. Regarding our TWO-STEP label prediction method, it shows that our neutral detector is not robust enough on the pipeline setting. One possible solution is to train it on evidence retrieved by previous modules rather than on the oracle evidence so that it learns to optimise for the pipeline setting.

Nevertheless, this problem is inevitable for a pipeline system that has multiple machine learning modules, as errors in each of the modules will accumulate throughout the pipeline. A better system design is desired such that it tackles the challenge in a more systematic way. A promising approach is to train a model to learn three subtasks in a multitask learning manner so that it may optimise for better overall performance.

6 Conclusions

In this paper, we proposed a novel step-by-step binary classification approach for the SCIVER shared task. Our submission achieved an F1 score of 55.35% on the test set, ranking 6th among all the submissions and 4th among all the teams. We show that (1) concerning evidence retrieval, a classification based approach is better than a ranking based approach with manual thresholds; (2) two-step binary label prediction has better performance than three-way label prediction with limited training data; (3) a more systematic design of automated fact-checking system is desired.

Acknowledgements

This work was supported by the Engineering and Physical Sciences Research Council (grant EP/V048597/1). Xia Zeng is funded by China Scholarship Council (CSC). This research utilised Queen Mary's Apocrita HPC facility, supported by QMUL Research-IT. http://doi.org/10.5281/zenodo.438045

References

Tom B. Brown, Benjamin Mann, Nick Ryder, Melanie Subbiah, Jared Kaplan, Prafulla Dhariwal, Arvind Neelakantan, Pranav Shyam, Girish Sastry, Amanda Askell, Sandhini Agarwal, Ariel Herbert-Voss, Gretchen Krueger, Tom Henighan, Rewon Child, Aditya Ramesh, Daniel M. Ziegler, Jeffrey Wu, Clemens Winter, Christopher Hesse, Mark Chen, Eric Sigler, Mateusz Litwin, Scott Gray, Benjamin Chess, Jack Clark, Christopher Berner, Sam McCandlish, Alec Radford, Ilya Sutskever, and Dario Amodei. 2020. Language Models are Few-Shot Learners. *arXiv:2005.14165 [cs]*. ArXiv: 2005.14165.

Qingyu Chen, Yifan Peng, and Zhiyong Lu. 2019. BioSentVec: creating sentence embeddings for biomedical texts. *2019 IEEE International Conference on Healthcare Informatics (ICHI)*, pages 1–5. ArXiv: 1810.09302.

Suchin Gururangan, Ana Marasović, Swabha Swayamdipta, Kyle Lo, Iz Beltagy, Doug Downey, and Noah A. Smith. 2020. Don't Stop Pretraining: Adapt Language Models to Domains and Tasks. *arXiv:2004.10964 [cs]*. ArXiv: 2004.10964.

Jinhyuk Lee, Wonjin Yoon, Sungdong Kim, Donghyeon Kim, Sunkyu Kim, Chan Ho So, and Jaewoo Kang. 2020. BioBERT: a pre-trained biomedical language representation model for biomedical text mining. *Bioinformatics*, 36(4):1234–1240. Publisher: Oxford Academic.

Xiangci Li, Gully Burns, and Nanyun Peng. 2021. A Paragraph-level Multi-task Learning Model for Scientific Fact-Verification. *arXiv:2012.14500 [cs]*. ArXiv: 2012.14500.

Yinhan Liu, Myle Ott, Naman Goyal, Jingfei Du, Mandar Joshi, Danqi Chen, Omer Levy, Mike Lewis, Luke Zettlemoyer, and Veselin Stoyanov. 2019. RoBERTa: A Robustly Optimized BERT Pretraining Approach. *arXiv:1907.11692 [cs]*. ArXiv: 1907.11692.

Ronak Pradeep, Xueguang Ma, Rodrigo Nogueira, and Jimmy Lin. 2020. Scientific Claim Verification with VERT5ERINI. *arXiv:2010.11930 [cs]*. ArXiv: 2010.11930.

Colin Raffel, Noam Shazeer, Adam Roberts, Katherine Lee, Sharan Narang, Michael Matena, Yanqi Zhou, Wei Li, and Peter J. Liu. 2020. Exploring the Limits of Transfer Learning with a Unified Text-to-Text Transformer. *arXiv:1910.10683 [cs, stat]*. ArXiv: 1910.10683 version: 3.

Stephen E. Robertson, Steve Walker, Susan Jones, Micheline Hancock-Beaulieu, and Mike Gatford. 1994. Okapi at TREC-3. In *Proceedings of the third text REtrieval conference*, volume 500-225 of *NIST special publication*, pages 109–126. National Institute of Standards and Technology (NIST).

Aalok Sathe, Salar Ather, Tuan Manh Le, Nathan Perry, and Joonsuk Park. 2020. Automated Fact-Checking of Claims from Wikipedia. In *Proceedings of the 12th Language Resources and Evaluation Conference*, pages 6874–6882, Marseille, France. European Language Resources Association.

Dominik Stammbach and Elliott Ash. e-FEVER: Explanations and Summaries for Automated Fact Checking. page 12.

James Thorne, Andreas Vlachos, Christos Christodoulopoulos, and Arpit Mittal. 2018. FEVER: a large-scale dataset for Fact Extraction and VERification. *arXiv:1803.05355 [cs]*. ArXiv: 1803.05355.

Andreas Vlachos and Sebastian Riedel. 2014. Fact Checking: Task definition and dataset construction. In *Proceedings of the ACL 2014 Workshop on Language Technologies and Computational Social Science*, pages 18–22, Baltimore, MD, USA. Association for Computational Linguistics.

David Wadden, Shanchuan Lin, Kyle Lo, Lucy Lu Wang, Madeleine van Zuylen, Arman Cohan, and Hannaneh Hajishirzi. 2020. Fact or Fiction: Verifying Scientific Claims. *arXiv:2004.14974 [cs]*. ArXiv: 2004.14974.

Tianyi Zhang, Varsha Kishore, Felix Wu, Kilian Q. Weinberger, and Yoav Artzi. 2020. BERTScore: Evaluating Text Generation with BERT. *arXiv:1904.09675 [cs]*. ArXiv: 1904.09675.

A Appendix

Table 7 reports performance of using BERTscore as a metric to do abstract retrieval. We chose DistilBERT as the BERT model for global ranking for efficiency reasons, which was ran on a simgle GPU for approximately 36 hours and it turned out to be worse than TF-IDF.

We then tried various relevant BERT variants to do reranking out of the top 30 abstracts with the highest TF-IDF similarity. In general, with reasonable large models that are trained on relevant tasks, results are better than TOP 3 TF-IDF. However, the improvements remain trivial and it is not comparable to our classification approach.

TOP K Global Ranking with DistilBERT			
Method	P	R	F1
TF-IDF TOP 1	60.11	54.07	56.93
BERTscore TOP 1	51.06	45.93	48.36
TF-IDF TOP 3	25.89	69.86	37.78
BERTscore TOP 3	23.58	63.64	34.41
TF-IDF TOP 30	03.39	91.39	06.54
BERTscore TOP 30	03.26	88.04	06.29
TOP 3 BERTscore Reranking under TOP 30 TF-IDF			
Model	P	R	F1
BERT-tiny	23.94	64.59	34.93
SciBERT	25.89	69.86	37.78
BioBERT-base	28.37	76.56	41.40
BioBERT-large	26.60	71.77	38.81
RoBERTa-large rationale selector	20.39	55.02	29.75
RoBERTa-large label predictor	25.89	69.86	37.78

Table 7: BERTscore abstract retrieval performance on the dev set of SCIFACT.

Author Index

Association for Computational Linguistics
209 N. Eighth Street
Stroudsburg, Pennsylvania 18360

ISBN 978-1-7138-3027-6

9 781713 830276

CURRAN ASSOCIATES INC. proceedings.com